John
Chrysostom
and the Jews

The Transformation of the Classical Heritage

Peter Brown, General Editor

John Chrysostom and the Jews

RHETORIC AND REALITY IN THE LATE 4TH CENTURY

Robert L. Wilken

University of California Press

BERKELEY   LOS ANGELES

LONDON

University of California Press
Berkeley and Los Angeles, California

University of California Press, Ltd.
London, England

© 1983 by
The Regents of the University of California

Printed in the United States of America

1   2   3   4   5   6   7   8   9

#8388423

Library of Congress Cataloging in Publication Data

Wilken, Robert Louis, 1936–
  John Chrysostom and the Jews.

  (The Transformation of the classical
heritage; 4)
  Bibliography: p.
  1. Chrysostom, John, Saint, d. 407.
2. Antioch (Turkey)—Religion.
3. Christianity and other religions—Judaism.
4. Judaism—Relations—Christianity.
5. Apologetics—Early church, ca. 30–600.
I. Title.   II. Series.
BR65.C46W54   261.2′6′09394   82-4935
ISBN 0-520-04757-5   AACR2

To
Elsa
Naomi
Sophie
Adrienne

with love and devotion

Contents

· Contents ·

Preface

I have long been interested in John Chrysostom's relation to the Jews, but it was as a member of the working group on the social history of early Christianity under the auspices of the Society of Biblical Literature that I first gave serious attention to his writings on judaizing Christians and Jews in ancient Antioch. I am grateful to the members of this group for their interest and criticism at an early stage of my research. I wish also to thank friends and colleagues who read all or part of the manuscript in various stages of preparation: Robert Grant, Ann and Stanley Hauerwas, David Ladouceur, Jean Laporte, David Levenson, C. Thomas McCollough, Wayne Meeks, Richard J. Neuhaus, William Schoedel, Alan Segal, and John Yoder. I am appreciative, too, of the assistance of Doris Kretschmer and Mary Lamprech of the University of California Press; Peter Dreyer, who edited the manuscript for publication; David Hunter who prepared the index; and Peter Brown, editor of the series, the Transformation of the Classical Heritage.

Robert L. Wilken

Notes and Abbreviations

As far as possible, all references are given in the body of the text. Footnotes are used to provide further information. Most of the ancient Christian authors I have cited can be found in the major collections of patristic sources:

Patrologia Graeca (*PG*) and *Patrologia Latina* (*PL*) of J. P. Migne, *Patrologiae cursus completus*, Paris, 1844–

Corpus Scriptorum Ecclesiasticorum Latinorum (*CSEL*), Vienna, 1866 ff.

Corpus Scriptorum Christianorum Orientalium, (*CSCO*), Louvain, 1903 ff.

Corpus Christianorum (*CC*), Turnhout and Paris, 1953 ff.

Die Griechische Christlichen Schriftsteller (*GCS*), Leipzig, 1897 ff.

Sources chrétiennes (*SC*), Paris, 1941 ff.

Many of the classical writings referred to are available in the bilingual editions of the Loeb Classical Library.

Abbreviations of ancient works are taken from the standard lexica:

A Patristic Greek Lexicon (*PGL*), edited by G. W. H. Lampe, Oxford, 1961.

Dictionnaire latin-français des auteurs chrétiens, edited by Albert Blaise and Henri Chirat, Turnhout, 1954.

A Greek-English Lexicon, compiled by Henry George Liddell and Robert Scott, revised by Henry Stuart Jones with the assistance of Roderick McKenzie, Oxford, 1968.

A *Latin Dictionary*, edited by Charlton T. Lewis and Charles
Short, Oxford, 1975.

References to the works of John Chrysostom are from *Patrologia Graeca*, even when modern critical editions exist, since this is the
one edition most readily available. More recent editions have been
consulted and are listed in the bibliography. The form of citation
employed is as follows, using the abbreviations of *PGL*: *Oppug.*
1.2;47. 322 = *Adversus oppugnatores vitae monasticae*, book 1,
chapter 2; *PG*, vol. 47, column 322. When a work is cited frequently,
for example the *Homiliae adversus Iudaeos*, the volume number of
PG is omitted: *Jud.* 8.1; 928 = *Adversus Iudaeos*, Homily 8, section
1; PG 48, column 928.

Chrysostom's commentaries and biblical homilies are cited as
follows:

Hom. 8.5 *in Col.* 3.2; 62. 357–58 = Homily 8, section 5 on
chapter 3, verse 2 of the Book of Colossians, in *PG*, vol. 62,
cols. 357–58.

Commentaries of other ecclesiastical authors are normally cited by
reference to the chapter and verse on which the author is commenting:
Jerome *Comm. in Isa.* 12:5 = Jerome, *Commentary on Isaiah*, chapter 12, verse 5.

In cases where a commentary is divided into homilies and the verses
of the biblical book do not provide easy reference, I have cited as follows: Origen *Hom.* 15.2 *Jerem.* = Homily 15, section 2 on the Book
of Jeremiah.

In citing the letters of Julian, I have first given the number of
the letter in the Bidez-Cumont edition, followed by the number of
Wright's edition in brackets: *Ep.* 204 [25] Bidez.

Other abbreviations:

M. = *Mishnah*, e.g., *M. Ta'anith*
b. = Babylonian Talmud, e.g., *b. Sanhedrin* 24a
p. = Palestinian Talmud, e.g., *p. Sotah* 7.1; 21b
CIJ = *Corpus inscriptionum Judaicarum*
CT = *Codex Theodosianus*
PGM = *Papyri Graecae magicae*

References to modern works are given in parentheses in the text,
with full citation in the bibliography:

Downey 1961, p. 24 = Glanville Downey, *A History of Antioch in Syria from Seleucus to the Arab Conquests* (Princeton, 1961), p. 24.

Alon 1970, 2:313–14 = G. Alon, *Studies in the History of Israel* (Tel Aviv, 1970), vol. 2, pp. 313–14.

Introduction

John Chrysostom's writings on the Jews have been called "the most horrible and violent denunciations of Judaism to be found in the writings of a Christian theologian" (Parkes 1969, p. 153). This judgment is based on a series of sermons preached in the city of Antioch, where John was a presbyter, at the end of the fourth century. These sermons, eight in all and delivered over the course of two years, were directed at Christians in his congregation who were participating in Jewish festivals and taking part in other Jewish observances. Among early Christian writings dealing with Judaism, John's sermons are among the most significant: they are not only a compendium of many of the themes that emerged in the Christian polemic against Judaism, but have also had an enormous influence on later Christian attitudes toward the Jews.

As important as the sermons on the Judaizers are, and as often as they have been cited by Christian as well as Jewish scholars (seldom on the basis of acquaintance with the text itself) to illustrate Christian attitudes toward the Jews, the sermons themselves are almost unknown, except to specialists in the field. A French translation, based on a Latin translation of the Greek text, was published in the mid-nineteenth century, but the first modern translations in English did not appear until a few years ago. Several important articles and essays have appeared over the last forty or fifty years, as well as two dissertations, one of which was a translation of the homilies into English (Simon, 1936; Ritter; Visser; Meeks and Wilken; Grissom; Maxwell). It is time now for a thorough study of the homilies in the context of late antiquity. My purpose, however, is not so much to analyze John Chrysostom's ideas about the Jews as to use his homilies as a window on the fourth century through which to view the relations between Jews and Christians in the later Roman Empire.

A good part of the book is devoted to constructing the world John Chrysostom inhabited, the impact on his thinking of the society in which he lived, and the interaction of the various groups in Antioch: Christian parties, judaizing Christians, Jews, and the exponents of traditional Hellenism ("pagans"). I have been much less interested in the background of John's ideas, his relation to other Christian writers, his place in the development of theological conceptions about the Jews, or the exegetical basis of his thinking. These are important fields of investigation, but much of what John says in these areas is commonplace, and is known from other studies of patristic attitudes toward the Jews. What has interested me is John's "foreground"—the people, the religious practices, the ideas that he met as a presbyter in ancient Antioch, his perception of himself and Christianity in his time, and the impact of his social and religious world on his response to the Judaizers and Jews.

For these reasons, I have cast a rather wide net over much material usually ignored in considering the interaction between Jews and Christians in the ancient world. To some readers, it may appear that I have ranged too widely, especially in devoting sustained attention to the continuing role of Hellenism ("paganism") in the later fourth century. However, I am convinced that to understand John's response to the Jews in Antioch an understanding of this larger context, which included the traditional religion and culture of the Greek cities of the Roman Empire, is essential. Only by viewing the conflict between Jews and Christians within this context is it possible to interpret John's sermons on the Judaizers and his statements on the Jews with any evenhandedness. Too much of the later unhappy history of Jewish-Christian relations has been projected onto the early Church and onto John Chrysostom.

That the Jews remained a vital social and religious force in the later Roman Empire is central to the argument of this book and to the interpretation of Jewish-Christian relations in the ancient world. During John Chrysostom's life, the Jews were a lively presence in the cities of the eastern Mediterranean. In almost all studies of this period in Christian history, except for the seminal work of Marcel Simon (1964), they have been ignored, and historians are hard put to explain why Christians remained so hostile and antagonistic to them after Christianity became a dominant force in the Roman world. Judaism, it will be argued, continued to be a rival to Christianity throughout the fourth century and "judaizing Christians" were a source of embarrassment and concern to Christian leaders, especially in Syria and Palestine.

The conflict between Jews and Christians must be set within the political and cultural milieu of the Roman Empire in the later fourth century. Hellenism was still very much alive in cities such as Antioch, not only in the writings of intellectuals, but in the schools and other social institutions, the mores of the citizens, the art that adorned people's homes and the architecture that graced the streets, and the values that shaped people's ideas and attitudes. Even though the emperor was a Christian, the culture was still informed by traditional pagan values, and Christians had no reason to suppose that a Christian emperor was to be a permanent feature of the Roman Empire. Christianity could not exert its will on pagans, Jews, or others who disagreed with Christian principles. The Christian Church had to contend with rivals and to defend itself against informed and skillful critics. It cannot be overemphasized that the fourth century was not medieval Europe and that the cultural and social traditions of the cities of the Roman world were not only independent of Christianity, but often innocent of Christian influence.

John Chrysostom was a contemporary of the emperor Julian. In any account of Christianity in the later fourth century, the figure of Julian must play a major role. Neglected in most histories of Christianity, he has begun to achieve a long-deserved place of importance due to the work of historians of Rome and classical scholars (Browning; Bowersock), and, in one case, of a Jewish scholar (Lewy). For the early fourth century, Constantine was the key figure in shaping Christian perceptions, as one can see in the writings of his contemporary Eusebius of Caesarea, but any assessment of the later period cannot overlook the series of emperors who intervened, several of whom were Arian supporters but chief of whom was Julian, who in his short reign of nineteen months (361–63 C.E.) made a deep and lasting impression on Christians.

This book, then, hopes to be more than a study of John Chrysostom and the Jews of Antioch. Though my focus is on the homilies on the Judaizers, I have addressed a number of larger questions about fourth-century Christianity in its relation to Judaism and Hellenism. In this way, I hope to provide a perspective from which to interpret not only the situation in Antioch, but the interaction between Christianity and Judaism in the Roman world.

Greek From Ancient Times

Antioch is proud of its magnificent buildings,
fine streets, the lovely countryside around it,
its teeming population; proud too
of its glorious kings, its artists and sages,
its very rich yet prudent merchants.
But far more than all this,
Antioch is proud to be a city
Greek from ancient times, related to Argos
through Ione, founded by Argive colonists
in honor of Inachos' daughter.

C. P. Cavafy

· I ·

John Chrysostom
and Christianity in Antioch

Antioch, a large Greek-speaking
city in northern Syria founded by the Seleucids in 300 B.C.E., stood on
a narrow strip of land twenty miles from the Mediterranean, wedged
between the Orontes River and a chain of mountains running parallel
to the coast. On its journey to the sea, the Orontes flows northward
along the eastern edge of the mountains, only to swing around Mt.
Silpius, the last of the chain, before flowing southward along the western side. As the river rushes past the mountain, in places only two
miles from its foot, it forms a long rectangle bordered on one side by
the steep walls of Mt. Silpius, rising 500 meters above sea level, and
on the other, by the bank of the Orontes. Antioch was set in the
southernmost end of this rectangle where the mountain and river
almost meet.

   To the north and east of the city lay a large and fertile plain offering
level and arable land, always at a premium in the mountainous and
rocky terrain surrounding the Mediterranean. South of the city, where
the river deserts the mountains to head towards the sea, the plain
gradually ascends to the site of the famous suburb of Daphne high on
a plateau overlooking the Orontes valley. Daphne's springs, only five
miles from the city and situated high enough for the water to flow nat-

urally downward, provided abundant water for the city's needs. With its many public baths, its fountains, its grand private homes, its numerous markets, Antioch required two aqueducts to serve the opulent life of its citizens, who in the words of one ancient historian "thought only of festivals, of good living, and of continuous theaters and circus plays" (Procopius *Pers.* 1.17.37).

For centuries Antioch had charmed visitors with its magnificence and delighted inhabitants with its comforts. In the latter years of the fourth century, the years that John Chrysostom lived in Antioch, the city had reached the acme of splendor, rivaled by only one or two other cities in the Roman Empire. She seemed without peer, "the fair crown of the east" (Ammianus *Hist.* 22.9.14), and her famous citizens, brilliant culture, and handsome buildings exhibited the highest accomplishments of Greek civilization. Antioch's central colonnaded street was the most famous of all ancient streets. One wealthy citizen decorated a room of his home with a large mosaic floor in which he celebrated the magnificence of the city by displaying some of its public buildings and scenes from its life (Levi 1947, 1:323–45). Another citizen, Libanius, the most famous rhetor of the fourth century, pictured the city's grandeur in one of his orations:

> I think that there can be found none of those [cities] which
> now exist which possess such size with such a fair situation.
> Beginning from the east it stretches straight to the west, extend-
> ing a double line of stoas. These are divided from each other by
> a street, open to the sky, which is paved over the whole of its
> width between the stoas. . . . Side streets begin from the stoas,
> some running to the north through the completely level area;
> the others, which run to the south toward the first slopes of the
> mountain, rise gently, extending the inhabited area to such a
> distance that it preserves harmony with the scheme of the re-
> mainder of the city but is not, by being raised too high, cut off
> from it. [*Or.* 11, 196–98]

Captured as much by his own rhetoric as by the city's magnificence, Libanius, in the style of late antique rhetoric, exaggerates. Yet most would have agreed. Late Roman Antioch was a grand and splendid city.[1]

In the years that John Chrysostom lived there, Antioch was the resi-

1. For the history of ancient Antioch, see Downey, 1961, and Schultze, 1930; for the fourth-century city, see Liebeschuetz, 1972, and Petit, 1956. Reports of the archaeological investigations conducted in the 1930s can be found in *Antioch-on-the-Orontes*, 1934–72.

dence of the Roman governor of Syria and the *comes orientis*, the ranking imperial official in the east. The chief military officer of the eastern provinces, the *magister militum per orientem*, made his headquarters in Antioch. Peripatetic emperors of the later empire often resided at Antioch for months at a time, conducting official business there, enjoying the intellectual chatter of the salons of the wealthy, relaxing at the springs of Daphne. While preparing for his campaign against Persia, the emperor Julian stayed in Antioch for nine months, long enough for the citizens to learn to dislike his long hair, unkempt beard, and shaggy breast, and for Julian, a grumpy moralist, to disdain their love of horseracing (Julian *Mis.* 340a).

Ancient Antioch covered most of the level land between the river and the mountain for a distance of over two miles, and houses had been built up the mountain side. Even today the extent of the ancient city impresses the visitor, though few actual remains can be seen. Antioch has been inhabited continuously since ancient times. Estimates of the population of ancient cities are always conjectural, but ancient Antioch had at least 150,000 inhabitants, and perhaps as many as 300,000, which by the standards of the day was a large city. In making comparisons between cities, Jews used the phrase "as large a city as Antioch." It was said that if a woman's husband were crucified in the city where she lived she should leave it, "unless it is as large as Antioch" (*Semahoth* 2.11). In size, it compared favorably to Alexandria and Carthage (*Sifre Numbers* 131; Horowitz, p. 170).

When Antioch was founded in 300 B.C.E., it was considered second to Seleucia Pieria, which was built directly on the Mediterranean coast. But Seleucia, in spite of its privileged location, was quickly outclassed by its neighbor and was later to be known chiefly as the port of Antioch. Antioch's proximity to the large plain to the north and east, its prominence astride the north-south route from Phoenicia to Asia Minor, its accessibility to the roads leading into the Tigris-Euphrates valley, and its good harbor at Seleucia destined it for a singular role in the eastern Mediterranean. "Our city," wrote John Chrysostom, is the "head and mother of the cities which lie to the east" (*Stat.* 3.1; 49.47).

Like all ancient cities, Antioch was closely dependent on the surrounding land for life and sustenance (Libanius *Or.* 50.34−35). It embraced a large area beyond its walls, and served as the economic and administrative center for the territory extending northeast to Aleppo and south approximately twenty-five miles, an area of 2,500 square miles. Men came from all over this area to do business, use the courts, meet with government officials residing in the city, study, shop, and play. On market days and festivals, Syriac-speaking peasants, "at variance with us in language but one in faith," said John, crowded the city (*Stat.* 19.1; 49.188). At one time, Antioch may have included a native Syrian quarter, but by the fourth century the city was thoroughly Greek, not only in language, but also in education, in civic organization, in art and architecture, in its tastes and prejudices. It was a Greek island in a Semitic sea, but it did not stand alone. To the east lay Beroea (Aleppo) and Chalcis; to the south, Apamea; and on the coast, Laodicea—cities whose citizens shared common ties nurtured by commerce and education, religion and family. Parts of the mosaic floor of a Jewish synagogue in Apamea were contributed by a wealthy Antiochene Jewish family.

Within the city of Antioch, life was closely stratified along class and economic lines. At the top of the social hierarchy stood the older wealthy families whose ancestors had lived in the city for generations. "The majority of the upper class owed their status to the inherited landed wealth of their families. Some were self-made men. These too would consolidate their position by investing in land. The upper class of Antioch was a landowning aristocracy. Its characteristic economic activities were landowning, corn-selling [wheat] and money-lending. But the corn-selling and money-lending arose out of landowning. None of these men could justly be described as a banker or a corn-merchant" (Liebeschuetz 1972, p. 48). Through inherited wealth, through the respect and prestige of a family name, men from this class dominated the political, economic and cultural life of the city. The city council was drawn almost entirely from this class. Conservative in outlook, chary of the new, these men, whose fathers and grandfathers had served on the city council, maintained and guarded the city's Hellenic traditions, transmitting them to their children.

In the social stratification of Antioch, the upper class included a large number of professional men, lawyers, teachers of rhetoric, high-ranking civil servants, and the higher clergy. Some of these men were the sons of the older aristocratic families, some were the children of men who had become wealthy in their own lifetimes. With changes in the administrative organization of the Roman Empire in the fourth century, the demand for skilled professionals increased. The *comes orientis*, for example, had a staff of six hundred in Antioch. Often these men earned handsome salaries, allowing them to invest in land and to fill places on the city council. They shared with the older families a common educational background based on their rhetorical education and a common set of social and cultural values drawn from Greek literature. Wealthy Christians and Jews could be found in this class as well.

John Chrysostom

John, later to be called "golden mouth" (Chrysostom) was born in Antioch in 349 C.E. into a good, though undistinguished, family belonging to the educated upper classes.[2] From his birth until he was made bishop of Constantinople in 398 he lived in Antioch, except for a brief period spent outside the city under the tutelage of an old monk. Although the family did not possess great wealth, John's father, Secundus, held a good position in the service of the ranking military officer in the Eastern Empire, the *magister militum per Orientem*. Secundus died when John was a boy, but like others in a similar position, he had accumulated enough resources to hand on an inheritance to his family. Using the money earned from the family's property, John's mother, Anthusa, undertook the responsibility of overseeing John's education.

From an early age, the boy's exceptional gifts were evident, and his parents hoped he would someday have a career in law or in the imperial service, possibly in the *sacra scrinia*, a branch of the government charged with the task of drafting official edicts (Jones, 1953). Such an appointment, high in prestige, could be a stepping stone to a more distinguished position in the imperial service. It would also advance the family's reputation and standing within the city.

By the time John was twelve years old, he had completed his elementary education and begun his rhetorical studies. As a result of his mother's ambitions for her son, as well as her connections in the city, John was able to study with a man as renowned as Libanius (Chrysostom *Ad viduam* 1.2; 48.601). From Libanius John acquired the skills for a career in rhetoric, as well as a love of the Greek language and literature. In his early writings, especially, John self-consciously models his language on Libanius, borrowing phrases and expressions from him (Fabricius: 120), and drawing on classical texts to illustrate and support his religious views (Dumortier 1953). As natives of Antioch, both Libanius and John had a great love for the city, but this love gradually came to divide them. For Antioch was, on the one hand, the embodiment of Greek culture and civility and, on the other, a leading city in the Christian world. As John grew older and became more deeply committed to Christianity, a tension developed between his love for the city and its culture, as symbolized by Greek language and literature, and his new loyalty to the Christian tradition, symbolized by the unlettered monks living in the mountains around Antioch. Eventually

2. The date of John's birth is disputed. I have adopted Carter's date. For discussion see Carter, 1962, and Dumortier, 1951.

he was led to attack his old teacher Libanius (*Pan. Bab.* 2.18–20; 50.560–65). That John, a student of the great pagan rhetor Libanius, would become such an eloquent spokesman for Christianity delighted Christians as much as it dismayed his fellow rhetors. According to one Christian writer, the historian Sozomen, Libanius was supposed to have said on his deathbed that John would have been his successor "if the Christians had not taken him from us" (Sozomen *Hist. eccl.* 8.2).

When John completed his studies under Libanius (ca. 367), it was expected that he would pursue a career in law. John himself says that as a young man he "frequented the lawcourts and delighted in the pleasure of the theater" (*Sac.* 1.4; 47.624). Most people assumed, when they heard him speak, that a man with such gifts of "eloquence and persuasion" (Socrates *Hist. eccl.* 6.3) would become a lawyer. John chose instead to be baptized and to become active in the Church in Antioch. The ancient sources present John's baptism as a radical break with his former life, a turning away from the world (Palladius *Dial.* 5.18). The truth is somewhat more complex.

Without attempting to belittle the spiritual significance of John's decision to join the catechumenate and eventually to be baptized, it must be recalled that, by the end of the fourth century, the Church offered career opportunities for the educated and well born equal to careers in law, the teaching of rhetoric, or the civil service. Most of the bishops in this period came from the upper classes, particularly from the curial families who dominated the social, political and economic life of the cities of the empire. Flavian, later to become the bishop of Antioch who ordained John, came from one of the wealthiest families in the city. Basil the Great and Gregory of Nyssa, bishops in Cappadocia in eastern Asia Minor, came from old and distinguished families, as did other bishops from the area (Kopecek 1973).

These ecclesiastical leaders had a background and education similar to the men who belonged to the "secular" professions. Without a literary and classical education, a man could not function as a member of the higher clergy, much less as bishop in a city such as Antioch. On occasion, people in the cities complained of bishops who still had the trace of an accent (because their native language was not Greek). The only ecclesiastical offices open to members of the lower classes were those of reader, acolyte, exorcist, and similar positions below the level of presbyter. Members of certain occupations, for example, bakers, were explicitly excluded from holding any office within the Church.

Joining the clergy also offered financial benefits. In the large cities, the clergy were often better paid than other professionals. A career in the higher clergy "offered social and financial advantages which, if negligible to a senator, were attractive to a man of the middle class"

(Jones 1964a, p. 924). In one city, for example, the bishop received six times the salary of a public doctor; in Carthage a bishop received a salary five times that of a professor of rhetoric. Often a bishop's salary would equal that of a provincial governor. Even presbyters and deacons were well paid in large cities, discouraging priests in the cities from accepting bishoprics in smaller towns: the rise in status from priest to bishop did not compensate for the loss in pay. On the other hand, the lower clergy often had to supplement their income with a trade. And, even if members of the lower clergy had the ambition and intelligence to move up the Church hierarchy, they were prevented from doing so by lack of education.

In casting his lot with the Church, John turned his back on neither his social class nor his education. His family and friends all belonged to the world from which the higher clergy were drawn. A young widow to whom he wrote on the death of her husband had to worry about running a large household with slaves and to oversee the family business (*Ad viduam* 1.1; 48.599–600). The families John alludes to in his early writings are all wealthy, reputable, powerful. They own comfortable homes in the city and farms in the countryside; as parents they want their sons to have servants, horses, beautiful clothes (*Oppug.* 3.7; 47.360). In choosing to join the Church, John was selecting a socially acceptable career with as much, if not greater, potential for success as law or the civil service. Indeed, the Church offered an opportunity to rise much higher than his father (if John became bishop), and in an ecclesiastical career his rhetorical education would find ample opportunity for expression in preaching and writing.

In describing John's decision to join the Church in terms of the career it offered, I am not speaking of John's motivation. Speculation on his motives is fruitless. I wish only to call attention to the social approval and personal satisfaction that would accompany a Church career among the better classes of Antioch. No doubt John was more religious than most of his contemporaries. As his years in the desert indicate, conventional piety within the Church did not satisfy his spiritual needs. But in deciding to be baptized and to study the Christian Scriptures, John made a career choice that was, if not conventional, at least not unusual, and one that had its own rewards.

John was baptized in 368 C.E. and immediately began the study of the Scriptures under Bishop Meletius. In the fourth century, the Church had no seminaries or theological schools. It was assumed that a young man who wished to become a deacon or presbyter would already have received the traditional rhetorical education. He was then placed under the supervision of the bishop or a learned presbyter for intensive study of the Scriptures. This period of study, which often lasted several years, introduced the student to the books of the Church, acquainted him with the unique style and vocabulary of the Bible, taught him the traditional interpretation of the text, and required that he memorize parts of the Bible by heart. After three years of study, John was ordained as lector, one of the minor offices leading eventually to the diaconate and presbyterate.

Under the influence of friends who had taken up the monastic life, John decided to spend some time as a monk before assuming his role as lector. The monastic movement, which had begun several generations earlier in Egypt, had spread throughout the Christian world, particularly the East, including Syria (Brown; Canivet, pp. 147–205). Within a few decades, the reputation of the Syrian monks rivaled that of the Egyptians. Jerome, a westerner, came to Syria, not Egypt, to learn the monastic life, and many others flocked to the caves of the Syrian desert to find God and to marvel at the bizarre practices of these uncultured, but holy, men. Fiercely independent, unlettered Syrian monks exerted a strong influence on the piety of ordinary Christians in the villages and cities. One of John's earliest books, *Against Those Who Oppose the Monastic Life*,[3] is an essay written to persuade wealthy parents to allow their sons to become monks in the desert.

On festivals the monks sometimes came into the city, but it was more common for people from the city and villages to go into the countryside to the deserted forts, caves, and tops of hills where the holy men lived. There they did not find the tidy and trim buildings of a modern monastery, with its ordered routine of prayer and work. Instead they found wizened and emaciated men, living in dens and caves, eating roots and plants, or simply bread and a few greens (Theodoret *Hist. relig.* 8.3), sometimes bound by chains (ibid. 21.8), dressed in sackcloth, staring back with eyes hollow from want of sleep (Chrysostom *Subintro.* 5.47.501). Unlearned and anti-social, these recluses nevertheless attracted many followers (Theodoret *Hist. relig.* 2.2). No matter how egregious their behavior, they offered a compelling ideal for clergy and laity alike. The monastic life was rapidly becoming the ideal for all Christians. Pagans found the monks offensive, outrageous in dress and behavior, and anti-intellectual, a "black-robed tribe that eats more than elephants" (Libanius *Or.* 30.8). But no one could stop the flow of men into the desert.

For John the decision to leave the city was difficult. Even after listening to the entreaties of his friends, he hesitated, fearful of leaving behind familiar comforts. "When I recently decided, having left the city, to go to the huts of the monks, I zealously inquired and investi-

---

3. Text in *Patrologia Graeca* 46. 319–86.

gated how one obtained the necessities of life, and whether one was able to eat fresh bread every day, whether someone would compel me to use the same oil for my lamp as for my food, whether someone would force on me the distressing fare of vegetables and drive me to severe work, such as being forced to dig the ground, carry wood, draw water and other similar tasks" (*Compunct.* 1.6; 47.403).

A greater obstacle, however, stood in his way—his mother. She had lost her husband through death, and now she could see herself losing her only son to the monks. Pleading with John, she begged him "not to inflict on me a second bereavement and raise again my sleeping grief" (*Sac.* 1.5; 47.625). John relented. For a time he attempted to live a monastic life in the city. Antioch proved too distracting, however, and when his mother died several years later, he immediately fled to the desert. The opposition of John's mother was characteristic of parents from the upper classes. As John observes, Christian parents resisted their sons becoming monks because the decision deprived them of grandchildren, and prohibited the perpetuation of the family name and the handing on of family property. A generation later, Theodoret, son of a wealthy Antiochene family, also met opposition from his parents when he wished to become a monk, and only after their death left the city to join the monks (Canivet, p. 55).

After his mother's death, John went into the desert to spend several years with an old Syrian monk, practicing the disciplines of mortification of the body and solitude of the soul. He ate little, slept on the bare ground, rose often for prayer. His extreme devotion to the ascetic ideal seems permanently to have affected his health (Socrates *Hist. eccl.* 6.4). His enemies also thought it affected his personality. In Constantinople they called him "hard, passionate, morose, arrogant" (Sozomen *Hist. eccl.* 8.9). No doubt his practice of eating alone and abstaining from wine contributed to this portrait (Palladius *Dial.* 12). Whatever the physical or psychological consequences of his extreme austerity, he came back to the city convinced that the ascetic ideal was the goal of the Christian life (*Oppug.* 1.7–8; 47.328–29).

In 381 John was ordained deacon by Meletius, bishop of Antioch. The same year, Meletius went to Constantinople to preside over a great council meeting there, but he was never to return, dying before the council was ended. He was succeeded by Flavian, an old man at the time of his consecration, yet one who was to rule as bishop of Antioch for another twenty years. Because of his own age as well as John's extraordinary oratorical gifts, Flavian immediately entrusted him with a large share of the responsibility for teaching in the city's churches. In 386 John was ordained to the presbyterate and from that time until summoned to Constantinople in 398 to become patriarch he was one of the principal preachers in the city, though only a priest, not a bishop.

Flavian, a native of Antioch, came from a very wealthy and distinguished family. On his father's death, he had inherited a large estate, which provided him with a handsome income throughout his life. As bishop he continued to live in the family mansion, but according to his friends, he lived simply, even ascetically, and used his money to help the sick and poor. John became an avid supporter of the new bishop. In a sermon preached at his own ordination to the presbyterate in 386, John praised Flavian for his "self-control, his mastery of his stomach, his contempt of delicacies, his despising of a sumptuous table, though raised in a wealthy home. One would not be astonished if one raised in poverty practiced such a simple and austere life. . . . But one who is the master of riches can not easily remove himself from such opportunities" (*Ordin.* 3; 48.696). To modern taste, this sermon, delivered in Flavian's presence, appears obsequious. Even the nineteenth-century *Dictionary of Christian Biography* calls it a "labored eulogium," which "good taste would have reserved for another occasion" (Venables, p. 530). But in the world of the fourth century, where excess and exaggeration were the marks of skillful preaching, such rhetorical exuberance was commonplace. More to the point, however, the comments about wealth and life style illustrate the social background shared by Flavian and John. It is not surprising that John became Flavian's protégé, and, though still relatively young and inexperienced, was thrust to the forefront of the religious controversies in Antioch.

Christianity in Antioch

In the years when John was growing up in Antioch, several Christian groups competed for the loyalty of Christians living in the city.[4] For over a generation, the Arians had dominated Antioch's ecclesiastical life. Even after John was ordained in 386, the Arian party, now bereft of its bishop, claimed the allegiance of some Christians. One of John's first undertakings as presbyter was to preach a series of sermons attacking the Arians in the city.

Throughout the fourth century, Antioch spawned leaders for the Arian party in the empire. Aetius, the founder of the neo-Arian party (second- and third-generation Arians who led the opposition to the

---

4. Devreesse, pp. 17–38; see also Cavallera. For the history of Arianism in this period, see Kopecek, 1979, pp. 361–543.

Nicene Creed), was a native of Antioch. He had been ordained to the diaconate by Leontius, bishop of Antioch. Eudoxius, later bishop of Constantinople, was bishop of Antioch from 357 to 360. More important than either of these men was Euzoius, consecrated bishop of Antioch in 361, who ruled the Christian congregations in the city, at times as the official bishop recognized by the imperial authorities, until 376 C.E. On the other hand, Meletius, the man who baptized John, was head only of one of two Nicene groups in the city during these years and was himself banished by the emperor Constantius and later by the emperor Valens, both Arian sympathizers.

The controversy generated by the Council of Nicaea in 325 C.E. dominated the churches of the east for several generations. To later generations of Christians, the council seemed to have settled the perplexing issue of the relation of Christ to God the Father (in the famous term, "of one substance," *homoousios*). To many living at the time, however, Nicaea represented a dangerous innovation. By introducing non-biblical terminology into the creed, and by making the Son equal to God the Father, the council seemed to compromise the primitive Christian belief that God the Father is one, the sole source and origin of all that exists.

Boasting resourceful leaders, popular support in certain key cities, among which was Antioch, and for a time the allegiance of the emperors, the Arians were estimable opponents. In 371 Basil, bishop of Caesarea, lamented, "Almost the whole East . . . is being shaken by a mighty storm and flood, since the heresy, sown long ago by Arius, the enemy of truth . . . at last prevails, because the champions of orthodox teaching in every diocese have been banished from their churches through slander and insult and the administration of affairs has been surrendered to men who are making prisoners of the souls of those more pure in faith" (*Ep.* 70). In the struggle for control of the major episcopal sees, Antioch, because of its central location, its hegemony over the churches of northern Syria, and its symbolic importance as a Christian city, became a center of the struggle. "What could be more vital to the churches of the world than the church of Antioch?" wrote Basil (*Ep.* 66). During the reign of Constantius (d. 361), the Arians had gained control of the churches in the city. Nevertheless, a group of Christians in Antioch did remain faithful to the Nicene cause, and it was this group Basil hoped to aid. Under bishop Meletius, the Nicene Christians in Antioch had separated themselves from the Arians to "hold their assemblies apart" (Socrates *Hist. eccl.* 2.44). Unfortunately, the Nicenes were themselves divided. Meletius had been ordained by an Arian, and some members of the Nicene party in the city spurned his leadership. They formed yet another group and consecrated a man named Paulinus as bishop. By the middle of the 360s, then, there were three Christian groups in Antioch: the Arian party, the Nicene party under Meletius, and the Nicene party under Paulinus. The Arian bishop, Euzoius was, however, the official bishop of the city.

Contemporary sources, often written to defend one Christian party against another, attribute the divisions to theological ideas or, in some cases, to the ambition of leaders and the zeal of their followers. But here and there documents from the period hint that there may have been more to the conflict. When describing the rise and fall of the bishops of the various groups, contemporary writers also mention disputes about the possession of the church buildings. At this time there were at least two major church buildings in Antioch, the "great church," built under Constantine, and the "old church," dating from an earlier period, as well as a number of *martyria*, i.e., shrines or chapels dedicated to local Antiochene martyrs. By the time John was ordained in 386, another church, the church of St. Babylas (an Antiochene martyr under the emperor Decius [ca. 250 C.E.]), had been built outside the city in the field to the west of the river (Eltester).

The church buildings were symbols of authority as well the setting for the liturgy and preaching. Some of the church buildings were also sources of revenue drawn from endowments. These endowments were frequently drawn from land, usually farms, whose income provided the churches with revenue for salaries, maintenance, and grain, as well as money to care for the sick, widows, and orphans. A church in Rome, for example, received an endowment of more than fourteen thousand *solidi* a year, or more than 200 pounds of gold, from lands in Italy, Africa, Crete, and Gaul. The clergy, who had possession of the churches, received the revenue from the endowments, and also had control of the distribution of grain and other privileges. Nicene clergy, for example, saw to it that grain was distributed to Nicene supporters, not to Arians (Grant 1977, pp. 144–45, 152). Julian, the pagan emperor, realized the importance of the endowments. In Edessa he transferred such money from the church to soldiers and confiscated its property, reminding the Christians that they were to seek first the kingdom of God (*Ep.* 115 [40] Bidez).

Shifts in power among the competing Christian parties often centered on the possession of the churches. When Eudoxius became bishop of Antioch in 347, he took possession of the "church of Antioch" and proclaimed his heresy "openly" (Sozomen *Hist. eccl.* 4.13). After Julian's death, when Jovian became emperor, the Meletians (followers of Meletius, the head of the other, or Nicene, party) seized the "old church" (*Chronicon paschale* 296; PG 92.741). The historian

Socrates says that when Euzoius, the Arian bishop, "had possession of the churches," Paulinus, the head of the second Nicene group, "only retained a small church within the city from which Euzoius had not ejected him on account of his personal respect for him. But Meletius assembled his adherents outside the gates of the city" (Socrates *Hist. eccl.* 3.9; cf. Rufinus *Hist. eccl.* 10.31).

Religious disputes in Antioch and other cities, as illustrated by the conflict over control of church buildings, were neither simply controversies among a few intellectuals nor exclusively disputes about religious ideas (Gregory). Frequently they turned on the competing loyalties of the populace and were symbolized by possession of buildings and by rituals, such as the proper form of the doxology. One point of dispute between Christians and Jews was a synagogue that had been dedicated to the Maccabean martyrs.

Religious leaders promoted a partisan spirit and called for unswerving allegiance among their followers. John's followers were so devoted to him that they formed a clique that would follow him around the city to hear his sermons (Van de Paverd, p. 13). When they were not able to follow him, the next time John preached to them he expressed his fondness of their support. "I was gone from you for one day and sad and so distressed was I during the time that it was as though I had been separated from you for a whole year" (*Hom. in Gal.* 2.11; 51.371).

To grow up in the Christian Church in Antioch during the late fourth century was to know a divided community, with competing parties seldom presenting a united front to outsiders. John's bishop Flavian was only one bishop among several. Besides Flavian, there were another Nicene bishop and an Arian bishop. And for a brief period after 375 C.E., there was also a fourth bishop, the head of another party founded by Apollinaris, a vigorous opponent of the Arians but the author of a new view of Christ. Under his leadership, Vitalis was ordained bishop of Antioch (Theodoret *Hist. eccl.* 5.4). By his personality, his exemplary life, and the appeal of his religious ideas, Vitalis attracted a large number of followers (Devreesse, pp. 31–35).

Antioch was not an isolated case; Christians were divided into competing parties in other cities as well. In 380 Theodosius I had issued the edict *Cunctos Populos*, declaring that all people subject to the authority of the Roman emperor confessed belief in the "one deity of the Father, the Son, and the Holy Spirit, in equal majesty and in a Holy Trinity" (*CT* 16.1.2). Those who did not assent to this confession were refused the name of "churches" for their conventicles and were forbidden to occupy and use church buildings in the empire. The decree was directed against the Arians, but since many Arians considered themselves Trinitarian Christians, though not according to the Nicene standard, the law specified which bishops in the empire would serve as arbitrators of the norm by which orthodoxy would be judged. In one decree, Theodosius mentions the bishops of Rome and Alexandria; in a second decree, in 381, he mentions Laodicea, Tarsus, Iconium, Caesarea, and others. The absence of Antioch from this list is pointed; it reflects the unresolved dispute between rival claimants to the see (Jones 1964a, p. 166).

In the years following the council of Constantinople in 381, the emperor issued a series of laws affirming the right of Nicene bishops to control church buildings. The need for further laws indicates that the Arians still had to be reckoned with and that, in some cities, they were able to control churches even though the law forbad it (CT 16.5.12).

In 386, for example, the year John was ordained presbyter and six years after the issuance of *Cunctos Populos*, the Arian bishop of Milan, Auxentius, was still confident enough of his position to pressure the emperor to grant Arians legal status and the right to occupy churches. The result was the following rescript:

> We bestow the right of assembly upon those persons who believe according to the doctrines which in the time of Constantius were decreed as those that would endure forever when the priests had been called together from all the Roman world and the faith was set forth at the council of *Ariminum* [359 C.E.] by these very persons who are now known to dissent, a faith which was also confirmed by the Council of Constantinople. The right of voluntary assembly shall also be open to those persons for whom we have so ordered. If those persons who suppose that the right of assembly has been granted to them alone [as the Catholic bishop of Milan, Ambrose, had claimed] should attempt to provoke any agitation against the regulation of our Tranquility, they shall know that, as authors of sedition and as disturbers of the peace of the church, they shall also pay the penalty of high treason with their life and blood. Punishment shall no less await those persons who may attempt to supplicate us surreptitiously and secretly, contrary to this our regulation. [CT 16.1.4]

When this rescript was issued, the Nicene party became alarmed. Ambrose envisioned a general expulsion of Nicene clergy from the churches and a return to the situation prior to *Cunctos Populos* (*Eps.* 20–21). No doubt, in an attempt to have the law repealed, Ambrose exaggerated the situation. But the Arians had put him on the defensive, and in other cities the new law strengthened the Arian position.

Whether this law was enforced in Antioch we cannot say, but it was surely known to the Arians there by late spring 386, after the shipping season opened for the summer.

In this same summer, 386, the Arian party was ready to begin pressing its case anew among Christians in Antioch. During the bishop's absence from the city, the Arians challenged the new presbyter to discuss their views. Since winter John had begun to preach regularly in the churches of the city, but his sermons were chiefly expository homilies on the text of the Bible. The Arians wanted a series of sermons on the theological difference between themselves and the Nicene party, i.e., Flavian's group, but they also wished to test the new presbyter, to see how well he could hold his own before the lively throng that would fill the church. John knew that, if he accepted the challenge, the church would be filled with a shouting and jeering crowd, with people who came not for spiritual edification but for amusement, less to be instructed than to behave like "critics at a play or a concert." If John failed, he would leave the pulpit in disgrace, a "victim of countless jeers and complaints" (*Sac.* 5.5; 48.675).

From the sermon on the Arians, it is clear that John is speaking to Arian as well as Nicene Christians and that the division between the groups ran throughout the Christian community in Antioch. Members of the same family took different sides; close friends quarreled with each other. It is even possible that some members of the older generation opposed the ideas of the young presbyter. John says one should keep away from the Arians "even if they are your parents" (*Incomprehens.* 1.7; 48.708). John was in his late thirties, and had been nurtured in the new theological climate of the sixties and seventies, when the Nicene party had begun to gain the support of many of the younger bishops. To the former generation, men and women the age of John's parents, the Nicene position was a new and confusing departure from the faith they had been taught. Basil, bishop in Caesarea, ran into stiff opposition when he introduced a new doxology to conform more closely with Nicene theology (*Spir.* 13). His opponents called him an innovator (Basil *Ep.* 226.3). To many Christians, a modified Arianism seemed closer to the traditional faith than the ideas of the Nicene party.

In response to the challenge, John began to preach a series of homilies in late summer 386, dealing with questions raised by the Arians. Over the next few months, he preached five homilies, usually entitled *On the Incomprehensibility of God* (PG 48.701–812). In these homilies, as well as in other writings dealing with the Arians, John presents his opponents as a group of intellectuals who hold a rationalistic view of God and offer philosophical arguments for their views. But from the homilies it is clear that the Arians in Antioch were not an elitist group of intellectuals, but ordinary Christians who represented a different form of Christian piety and teaching, no less Christian, in their view, than the teaching of John and his followers. Charging that the Nicene Christians had abandoned traditional doctrines (*Incomprehens.* 5.4; 48.740–42; *Hom. 3.2 in Jo.* 1.1; 59.39) (Kopecek 1979, pp. 529–39), they appealed to the Scriptures to support their views. They also appealed to their experience of Christ as validation for their theological views. The Nicene Christians, say the Arians, are not the only ones who know Christ, for we too "have Christ speaking in [us]" and he "is teaching us these things" (*Incomprehens.* 2.5; 48.716).

Eventually John's party would become *the* Christian Church in the city, but in the years when he was being educated as a Christian, the years of his diaconate, and his first years as presbyter, the victory of the Nicene party was imperfect. The division within the Church was profound, aggravated by decades of infighting, and visible to those within as well as without the Church. John's homilies reflect an atmosphere in which he is striving to maintain the unity and cohesion of the followers of Flavian, to prevent attrition, and win the backsliders. His sermons have a defensive tone; he seems besieged by his foes. Outwardly he is brash and self-assured, but his language betrays uncertainty. In one sermon from this period, addressed to Jews (not Arians), he pleads with his followers not to speak about Christians attending the synagogue, for by mentioning the practice it will seem more widespread than it actually is, attracting others (*Jud.* 8.4; 48.933). The fragile ark of the Church seemed threatened by outspoken opponents and fickle followers.

Traditional Hellenism in Antioch

The division among Christians in Antioch shaped John's outlook as a young presbyter. In the years before he was ordained, however, while serving as deacon, he was preoccupied with a number of other concerns engendered by the unique situation of Christianity in Antioch. These were monasticism and Hellenism, seemingly distinct phenomena, but in John's mind two sides of a common problem (Festugière 1959). To understand how they relate to each other and what importance they play in the formation of John's outlook, we must now examine the form that paganism, or traditional Hellenism, took in Antioch during the years when John was living there.

It is often assumed that Christianity had become the dominant reli-

gion within a predominately Christian empire by the end of the fourth
century. As we shall see in the following chapter, this view hardly does
justice to the vitality of Judaism in this period. It is, of course, true,
due to the large number of people who joined the churches, the increasing number of Christians in high political positions, the sophis-
tication of Christian thinkers, the appeal of the new monastic movement, and the impact of the reign of Constantine in the life of the
empire, that Christianity had become the most formidable spiritual
force in the Roman world. Yet it is misleading to say that Christianity
now stood alone, that its rivals were vanquished, or that the new
movement had succeeded in stamping its values on the life of society
or its cultural institutions. A hundred years later, after the council of
Chalcedon, when christological disputes become a major preoccupation of imperial policy, this is more apparent. By the reigns of Zeno
(474–91) and his successor Anastasius (491–518), one has the distinct feeling that the Roman Empire has become a Christian kingdom.
But in the fourth century this was not the case. Paganism was alive in
the public life of the cities and towns as well as in the piety and practices of many individuals. The world was still pluralistic.

The form and extent of traditional paganism during this period
have been much debated in recent years. It has been noted, for example, that a pagan revival took place in the west during the reign of the
orthodox Christian emperor Theodosius I (in the 390s), and this has
been taken as evidence of the continuing vigor of paganism (Bloch,
1963). Yet others have argued that the revival was "short-lived and
ineffective" (Cameron).[5] Similarly, distinguished literary figures in the
east—Libanius and Themistius are two of the better known ones—
were profoundly committed to the values of traditional Hellenism and
went about their work as though Christianity did not exist. Yet one
wonders whether in the writings of these men the traditional symbols
have largely been divested of religious meaning.

It is not my intention to enter fully into a discussion of the persistence of paganism in the later Roman Empire, but it is helpful to
keep this debate in mind in the discussion of the relation between traditional religion and society in Antioch in the later fourth century. For
how one assesses the strength of paganism in this period will depend,
to a large extent, on where one looks. If one draws too heavily on the
writings of cultured literary figures, it is possible to miss the real impact that religious values had on the life of society. If, however, one
looks at the way religion was interwoven with the institutions of the

5. On the pagan revival, see also Bloch, 1945; O'Donnell; and Wytzes.

city, how it was unconsciously built into the very fabric of society, one can see that it was still an integral part of the world men and women inhabited. John Chrysostom surely perceived things in this way.

The impact of paganism on the lives of men and women living in the late fourth century can be seen in the public life of the cities. When Julian visited Antioch, he lamented the presence of many Christians in the city, especially among the lower classes (*Mis.* 357d). What he did not say, however, but is obvious to anyone who looks closely at the architecture, institutions, literary and artistic tastes, and even calendar of the city, is that Antioch, in spite of its large Christian population, still retained the marks of traditional Hellenism. The city had numerous temples and pagan shrines; it celebrated the ancient festivals and games associated with the Greek gods; its shrines were still the objects of pilgrimage. Its educational system was thoroughly Greek.

In the spacious halls and corridors of the homes of the wealthy, in baths and wading pools, in dining rooms and gardens, the fourth-century Antiochene looked at pictures, mosaics, statues, and decorations celebrating the joys and satisfactions of civilized urban life and illustrating and personifying traditional Greek virtues, *apolausis* (enjoyment), *soteria* (security and well being), *mnemosyne* (memory, mother of the muses), *chresis* (use of acquired wealth); inhabitants saw Greek Psyches sailing the boat of Eros, Hermes carrying the newly born Dionysus to the nymphs, winged female figures representing the four seasons; hunting scenes picturing sacrifices to the goddess Artemis, dancing satyrs, the divine couple Oceanus and Tethys (Levi, 1947). As late as the end of the fourth century, the art in the homes of wealthy Antiochenes shows no influence of Christianity.

The most striking mosaic from Antioch, dating from the fifth century, depicts *megalopsychia*, generosity of spirit. Around the central medallion portraying *megalopsychia* as a female figure are six panels picturing hunting scenes, enclosed in an extensive framed border including over fifty individual scenes of buildings, bridges, shopkeepers, innkeepers, a church, men and women walking the streets. The scenes are taken from the city of Antioch and many can be identified by reference to literary sources from the period. The female figure in the center extends her right hand with the palm forward and coins appear to be falling from her hand. This gesture, technically known as *sparsio*, the act of public generosity, was often ascribed to a new ruler who, on ascending the throne, showed his largesse to the citizenry. In this case, the medallion symbolizes the ancient Greek virtue of generosity, described by Aristotle in his *Nicomachean Ethics*, and is complemented by another Greek virtue, *andreia*, courage, which is represented in the hunting scenes (Levi 1947, pp. 323–45).

Other mosaics underscore the tastes and interests of the Antiochenes. There are scenes from the plays of Euripides, such as the *Hippolytus, Medea,* and *Troades,* dealing with passionate and destructive love; scenes from the *Iliad,* for example, the moving account in book one where Briseis is taken from Achilles; material from the lost plays of the Hellenistic dramatist Menander. Several mosaics represent the "evil eye," a terrifying picture of a large open eye attacked by animals and weapons while a dwarf scornfully turns his back. (Levi 1941, pp. 220–32; Weitzmann 1941a, pp. 233–47; *Antioch-on-the-Orontes,* vol. 3, passim). Among the objects discovered at Antioch was a collection of sculpture put together by an ancient art dealer or collector at the beginning of the fifth century. This collection of art testifies to the "survival of classical taste" in the early Christian era and the persistence of pagan values in Antioch (Brinkerhoff, p. 4). There is little difference between the art in the homes of people living in the fourth century and that in those of the first or second centuries. The same motifs persist (Elderkin).

The pervasiveness of paganism was equally visible in the statues that lined the streets, in the decorations on public buildings, in carvings on fountains, bridges, gates, and other public places (Schultze, pp. 229–302). Citizens encountered statues of Artemis, Tyche, Zeus, Athena, Calliope. The rhythm of city life was determined by the traditional pagan calendar with its recurring festivals dedicated to the gods. In May the city celebrated a festival to Artemis; in summer theatrical shows and chariot races were dedicated to Calliope; in late summer a festival to Apollo was held at Daphne. Every third year the city sponsored a festival in honor of Dionysus and Aphrodite (Liebeschuetz 1972, p. 228).

In the course of the fourth century, laws had been passed concerning the observance of Sunday as a day of rest and forbidding the conducting of business on Sundays (*CT* 2.8.1; 2.18.9; 8.8.3; 15.5.2). But the Christian calendar was still in an embryonic stage of development. Sunday had not assumed the religious significance for the society it would have in the fifth and sixth centuries (Rordorf, pp. 162–71). Pagan festivals, on the other hand, were enthusiastically celebrated by pagans and Christians, much to the annoyance of Christian leaders (Pasquato, pp. 251–65). John fulminated against the annual New Year's festival, the Kalends, but Christians were unwilling to give up the traditional practice of exchanging gifts on that day or the pleasures of an all-night drinking party. On the Kalends, the "city [was] decorated like an elegant and rich woman . . . adorned with finery," and each merchant tried to outdo the decorations of his neighbor. The whole city took part in the celebrations, for the citizens believed that if they celebrated New Year's Day as a day of joy the whole year would be filled with joy (Chrysostom *Kal.* 1–2; 48.953–54).

The educational system was still thoroughly pagan. From the first scratching a child made on his wax tablet, he wrote sentences such as "Homer was not a man but a god." At a later stage, when the child began to read the *Iliad*, the schoolmaster asked: "Which gods were favorable to the Trojans?" To which the youngster would reply: "Aphrodite, Apollo, Ares, Artemis, Leto, Scamander" (Marrou 1956, pp. 164–68). As the child grew older, he read Euripides, Hesiod, and Demosthenes and was immersed in the traditional classical values: honor, glory, the benefit of noble birth, courage, urbanity.

There is nothing to distinguish the content of school books from this period from what had been taught six or seven centuries earlier. The same lists of mythological names appear, the same legends, the same moral maxims. Even when a cross was added to the top of a page, or a "Blessed be God" at the beginning of a book, this "was hardly enough to make the general atmosphere of the school Christian" (Marrou, 1956, p. 325). No wonder that Church orders include the injunction: "Have nothing to do with pagan books" (*Didascalia apostolorum* 1.6.1). The backbone of the educational system was the study of the Greek classics, a body of literature that immersed the young boy in the legends and myths of ancient Greece. Though much time was devoted to grammar, vocabulary, style, and the organization of speeches, the themes and examples were taken from the myths and legends of ancient Greece. Parents and teachers alike understood that literature did not simply teach language and style or sharpen a boy's aesthetic sense; it formed his character and outlook on life.

A rhetorical education was necessary for advancement in society and for social intercourse among the upper classes. Bound together not only by intermarriage, property, and friendship, but also by a common cultural tradition transmitted through the educational system, the ties between members of this class were often stronger than the religious differences that might separate them. Rhetoric symbolized the traditional culture and set late Roman society apart from the "barbarians" outside its borders. "If we lose rhetoric," wrote Libanius, "we will be equal to the barbarians" (*Ep.* 369.9). Even though Christians and pagans intermarried frequently during this period, "the solidarity of class and culture was in general stronger than the community of belief" (Petit, pp. 214–16). The primary bearer of the values of the culture was the educational system. Hence a rhetorical education served a dual function; it ensured that the young men could pursue a career, and it instilled in them the mores of the urban culture to which their families belonged.

Christians from the upper classes were hardly distinguishable in lifestyle from their friends who were pagan. Wealthy Christians contributed to the upkeep and decoration of the city (Natali, pp. 57–59). They gave money to construct baths, promenades and other public buildings (*Hom. 48.5 in Gen.* 23.5–6; 54.550). Like other wealthy citizens, they ostentatiously displayed their wealth (*De educandis liberis* 5–6). They refused to have anything to do with members of the lower classes: sandalmakers, dyers (*Hom. 20 in 1 Cor.* 8.1; 61.168), dealers in purple, coppersmiths, tentmakers, tanners (*Hom. 1.4 in Rom.* 16:3; 51.192).

Traditional pagan practices marked the normal conventions of family life. Marriage, if it was to have any legal significance, had to be celebrated according to custom and civil law; if not, the couple would not enjoy the benefits of a legitimate marriage, such as rights to inheritance, property, and so on. In the early third century, Tertullian had complained about the "idolatry" associated with the marriage ceremony (*De Idololatria* 16), and by John's time the situation had not changed significantly. Especially in the domain of marriage, old customs lingered and the Church was slow to claim any prerogatives (Ritzer, pp. 130–42; Schultze, pp. 197–98). John complains that Christian families would not even allow a clergyman to come to their daughter's wedding to say a prayer or offer a blessing (*Hom. 48.6 in Gen.* 23:5–6; 54.443). To the citizens of Antioch, Hellenism did not appear as a "separate" religion, the faith of a particular community; it was woven into the fabric of life.

I do not wish to overstate the importance of paganism in the life of Antioch in the fourth century. Christianity was a powerful new force. Its presence could be felt in the decurions who sat on the city council and the artisans who made and sold their wares in tiny shops throughout the city. The Church owned property; its presbyters were active in the distribution of grain; its bishops wielded influence in the city and beyond. Bishop Flavian, for example, went on an embassy to the emperor Theodosius after the riot of the statues in 387. In the city's economy, the Church was a factor to be reckoned with; it purchased food and wine from local merchants, owned horses. Christians also operated hospitals for the sick, maintained hostels for travelers, cared for the poor and needy (*Hom. 66.3 in Mt.* 20.29; 58.630).

Furthermore, since 379 the emperor had been an orthodox Christian. In 386 Libanius wrote an essay to Theodosius, *On the Temples*, pleading with the emperor to prohibit the lawless destruction of temples by Christian monks. That Libanius should have to entreat a Christian emperor to protect the temples is a sign of the changing status of paganism. Yet the very fact that Libanius addressed his plea to the emperor shows that the law was still on his side, and he could rely on a Christian emperor to be receptive to a plea for the protection of pagan temples. The wanton acts of fanatic monks, not the emperor or public officials, were destroying the traditional religious shrines. In Antioch, however, the temples were unmolested. Libanius mentions, among others, temples to Fortune, Zeus, Athena, Dionysus (*Or.* 30.51).

In his study of municipal life in Antioch in this period, Paul Petit tabulated the religious preferences of persons mentioned in Libanius's correspondence. This data showed that Christians were beginning to hold important positions in the provincial and imperial administrations. From 335 C.E. to 365 C.E., Libanius mentions 31 members of the curial class from Antioch, 15 of whom were pagan and 3 Christian. Among Libanius's students, 67 were pagans and 10 were Christians, out of a total of 143. The religious preferences of the remainder are not known. In the long period from 354 to 392, 7 of the *comites orientis* were pagan and 5 Christian, out of a total of 20. In the same period, 14 of the *consulares* of Syria were pagan, 5 Christian. Out of 17 praetorian prefects, 8 were Christian, 6 pagan (Petit, pp. 200 ff.). Admittedly these figures are highly selective and randomly chosen, but they do indicate the growing presence of Christians in official circles.

Already in 362, when Julian came to Antioch, he met with opposition from Christians on the city council. He complained that Antioch had begun to love Christ instead of Zeus, Apollo, and Calliope, going on to say that the common people prefer "atheism," that is, Christianity (*Mis.* 357d). Julian lamented that in religious questions curials had begun to adopt the beliefs of their wives or governesses or cooks. These statements suggest that Christians were better represented among the lower classes, but were beginning to make significant inroads among the curials. A few curial families had been Christian for generations. The family of Thalassius I is one example. He was praetorian prefect under Constantius and he held land throughout the empire. During the reign of Julian, the family's property was seized and one of its houses was made into a pagan temple. Another example, as we saw earlier in this chapter, was the bishop Flavian, who came from a very wealthy Antiochene family.

In the later fourth century, both paganism and Christianity were present and alive in the city, each in its own form. The more interesting question, however, is the relative importance of paganism and Christianity in the life of the city and the significance of each for the outlook of the inhabitants. In his study of Antioch in this period, Liebeschuetz, drawing on the comments of contemporaries such as John Chrysostom (*Jud.* 1.4; 48.849), says that the city was "effectively Christian" (Liebeschuetz 1972, pp. 239). What Liebeschuetz means by this phrase is not explained, but he seems to mean that a large number of people in the city, perhaps the majority, identified with Christianity. That is, he is speaking primarily about the religious preferences of individuals. His statement needs qualification, I think, not because individual preference is unimportant, but because it is an inadequate index of the place of religion in an ancient city.

In the ancient world, religion was less a matter of individual choice than a social reality created by traditional institutions and patterns of life, with their accompanying social, cultural, and moral values. These values were not "secular" in the modern sense. They were intimately intertwined with religious traditions. Religion grounded and legitimated institutions, determined patterns of behavior, sanctioned established customs. These customs, roles, and institutions, were not, however, perceived as "religious" in the sense that they involved a conscious decision. They were simply the way things were done, and had been done for as long as people could remember. Religion served to unite the past with the present, law with morality, education with politics, the family with society, architecture with mythology, the calendar with religious ritual. "The worship of the gods and the study of letters are kin to each other," wrote Libanius (Or. 62.8).

In a civilization such as ours, formed by the "personal" religion of Christianity, which stresses the internal conversion of the heart and mind, and cherishes authenticity and conscious choice, the religion of the ancients appears superficial, enslaved to trivia and externals, preoccupied with ritual acts rather than belief. It is said that Libanius, a defender of the traditional religion, seldom visited the temples, and even stayed at home reading when Julian came to town and presided over the sacrifice of a bull. Yet he can speak of the gods as the protectors of the city and emphasize that the temples were the first buildings to be constructed in the city (Or. 30.4). For Libanius, as well as for many others, religion consisted in preserving ancient traditions, in the general belief that the gods would watch over the affairs of men and protect the city; in contributing money through public "liturgies," such as funding a chariot race or providing heat for the baths; and in the transmission of the ancient literature and language. Such religion was, of course, deeply conservative, but the conservatism was not simply a cultural conservatism; it rested on religious convictions. "Belief in the city as the essential form of social organization, and in the values of the cults of the city are different aspects of the same attitude of cultural conservatism," Liebeschuetz observes (1972, pp. 12–13). Civic loyalty and devotion to the gods went hand in hand, especially among educated and wealthy citizens.

In this setting, religious values were more concerned with public life than with the private lives of individuals. In his classic study of religion in the ancient city, Fustel de Coulanges argued that modern distinctions between religious and secular simply did not exist in early Greece and Rome. In the ancient cities, "the state and religion were so completely confounded that it was impossible to distinguish the one from the other" (Fustel de Coulanges, pp. 166–67). Religion united the institutions of the city, and its greatest symbolic expression took place in the public realm. Indeed, without religion there could be no city, no society, no state. "In all probability the disappearance of piety toward the gods," wrote Cicero, "will entail the disappearance of loyalty and social union among men as well, and of justice itself, the queen of virtues" (*De natura deorum* 1.4). What de Coulanges recognized in the middle of the nineteenth century has become a commonplace among modern sociologists, who speak of the place of religion in "world maintenance." Religion legitimates the institutions of society, its patterns of life, by relating them to a larger, or an ultimate, reality.

Looked at from this perspective, Antioch was still a pagan city, for those features of its life that transmitted and nurtured the values of its citizens and molded the character of its young people—education, social custom, literature, art and architecture, legends and myths—were still untouched by Christianity. In the fourth century, for example, the Church had no educational system except the catechumenate, whose purpose was solely to instruct people in the creed and the liturgy and to teach them a few simple prayers. The clergy relied on memory, because most catechumens could not read (Cyril of Jerusalem *Cat.* 5.12).

It is a striking feature of the fourth century that the Church had created no schools for the education of the young. Indeed, the idea of Christian schools had not even dawned on Christian leaders. As Marrou observes in his study of education in antiquity, the Christian writings dealing with education—for example, Basil of Caesarea's *Exhortation to Youths as to How They Shall Best Profit by the Writings of Pagan Authors*—were discussions of the traditional classical education and how it was to be appropriated by Christians. They do not address the question of Christian educational principles. The classical education and the Christian Scriptures belong to two different orders; Basil only envisages a "Christian usage of the traditional education" (Marrou 1958, pp. 397–99). Jerome complains that the clergy neglect the gospels and the prophets to read comedies and the amorous poems of the poets (*Ep.* 21.13). And Augustine says that when Christian parents send their children to school to learn to read, they do not tell them "learn to read so you can read the Scriptures," but "learn to read" so that you can "become a man"—which, acknowledges Augustine, means become a prominent person in society (*De disciplina Christiana* 11.12). Chrysostom encouraged parents to tell their children stories from the Bible rather than Greek legends to teach moral values (Chrysostom, *De educandis liberis* 37–53), but parental initiative and will, then as now, were no substitute for a well-established, successful, socially approved system of education. Christian parents simply ignored the advice.

Christian literature was still in its infancy. What books were produced were commentaries on the Bible, polemical and theological treatises, and a few devotional works. In the conventional sense of the term, and in the view of educated Greeks, there was no Christian literature (Marrou 1958, pp. 328–29). Christian art was almost nonexistent, and what Christians had produced borrowed heavily from the styles and motifs already present within the classical tradition. In contrast to the rich tradition of classical themes in the pagan art in Antioch from this period, Christian art is chiefly decorative— geometric designs and ornamental borders, sometimes enclosing inscriptions. Such motifs were commonplace and could be found equally in Jewish synagogues, on the floor of a noble's bathroom, or in the apse of the Christian church. There was little art representing Christian themes. In Antioch the first representations of Christian subjects do not appear until the end of the fifth century (Wietzmann 1941b).

In many other small but significant ways traditional Hellenic customs persisted. John complains that Christians do not name their children after the saints and martyrs, but after fathers, mothers, grandfathers and grandmothers, great-grandfathers and great-grandmothers who did not have Christian names (*De educ. liber.* 47). Some followed other "Hellenic customs," as for example giving a baby the name of the torch that burnt the longest after its birth so that the child would have long life (*De educ. libr.* 48); some hung amulets and bells on the child to bring good luck (*Hom. 12.7 in I Cor.* 4.6; 61.105).

In the domain of family life, the Church had developed no conception of a Christian vocation for people who were married, raised children, owned property, or held civic office. The most compelling ideal of Christian life was the celibate man or woman who had fled the city to live alone in the desert or in a cave on the side of a mountain. "One who wishes to be saved must seek solitude" (Chrysostom *Oppug.* 1.7; 47.328). But this ideal, if presented as the goal for all Christians, as indeed it was by many churchmen in this period, posed enormous problems for married Christians, who lived in a society bound by the ties of custom, education, and intermarriage. Among this class Christianity had the least success (Liebeschuetz 1972, p. 225). Yet it was to this class that John belonged and to which he felt the greatest responsibility, especially as a young man. Though they were members of the Church, the lives of these people often as not consisted of a conventional pagan lifestyle concealed under a thin veneer of Christianity. Hence, when John returned from his years in the desert, he felt acutely the contrast between the Christianity he had learned from the monks and the lifestyle of his Christian friends in the city. This tension was heightened when other young men like John were attracted to the monastic life and their parents saw their traditional way of life jeopardized.

Urban Society and the Monks

John's early work *Against Those Who Oppose the Monastic Life* (*PG* 47.319–86), written while he was a deacon, i.e., sometime before 386, was directed to parents, pagan as well as Christian, whose sons were contemplating a monastic vocation. The book is a sharp attack on the values of Antiochene upper-class urban society written by someone who is a member of that class.

The book begins as a defense against the maltreatment of the monks in Antioch. All over the city, says John, in the baths, in taverns, in public places, people mistreat the monks and boast of it. In the squares, people stand around bragging to others of their exploits. "I was the first to lay hands on a certain monk and beat him," says one. "I was the first to find his cave before anyone else" says another (*Oppug.* 1.2; 47.322). Even some "who call themselves Christians and have already been baptized" are hostile to the monks. The reason for their hostility is that they are offended to "see men who are free and well-born and able to lead a life of luxury pursuing such a harsh life" (*Oppug.* 1.2; 47.321).

The chief topic of the book, however, is not mistreatment of the monks but the clash between their ascetic lives and the lifestyle of the upper classes, both Christian and pagan. John cites passages from the gospels to stress the radical demand of Christianity: "Seek first the kingdom of God." To which his friends reply: What does this injunction mean for those who live in the city? How can people who remain in their homes, living with their families, involved in the life of the city, be expected to carry out what Jesus commands? John's response is uncompromising. One cannot be a genuine Christian and live in the city. I wish that this were not so, he says, and that monasteries were not necessary and life in the city were conducive to piety, but the city is filled with disorder and injustice, and the "desert blooms with the fruit of philosophy [i.e., Christian piety]." The city, like a burning house in the night, is "unsuited for philosophy." Who would blame someone who woke the sleepers within urging them to flee? Likewise, who would accuse someone who led its inhabitants "to take refuge on the heights of the mountains" (*Oppug.* 1.7; 328). His friends ask: "Are all those living in the city lost?" (ibid. 1.8; 329). Must one seek solitude to be saved? Must we sacrifice our homes, financial security, family name (for if a son does not marry, we will have no heirs) for the sake of the uncultured, boorish life of the monks? "Is it impossible to be saved if one lives in a city and has a household?" (ibid. 3.13; 372). "Will all who are married perish?" (ibid. 3.15; 376).

In fourth-century Antioch, the conflict between Christianity and Hellenistic culture took a new and quite specific form due to the rapid spread of monasticism in Syria. Most of the clergy had some contact with the monks, and some, like John, joined their ranks for a time. To John only the monks fully believed the gospel and acted on it. To the members of the upper class of Antioch, the monks were men "without a hearth," Libanius *Ep.* 1367.4), rustics, anti-city, anti-culture, anti-Greek, anti-traditional. It was the monks who "removed altars from the temples," says Libanius (*Or.* 30.8). The monks are "models of sobriety only as far as their dress is concerned" (*Or.* 2.32), men who hide their misdeeds "under an artificial pallor" (*Or.* 30.8), barbarians, "vapid men" who "pretend to converse with the creator in the mountains" (*Or.* 30.48). The monks "pack themselves tightly in caves" to avoid the city (*Or.* 2.32).

Monasticism accented the conflict between Christianity and the traditional culture. Greek culture was "eminently urban and linked in principle to the phenomenon of the city," whereas the monks were often ignorant peasants, unlettered, unable to speak Greek, schooled only in the Scriptures (Festugière, 1959, p. 239). John's advocacy of monasticism as the ideal Christian life irritated and annoyed wealthy Christians who were "rich, admired by others, wielders of power, owners of fields and houses, possessors of great wealth" (*Oppug.* 2.2; 47.333). He mentions a Christian father who was a high-ranking military officer with high aspirations for his son. This man, says John, insisted on a "literary education" for his son, even though he was to follow a career in the military (*Oppug.* 3.12; 369). Elsewhere he mentions a pagan father, "rich, of good reputation, illustrious," who lamented his son's attraction to Christian monasticism (*Oppug.* 2.10; 348). Monasticism threatened familiar patterns of life, and most parents from this class opposed the monks. Those whose sons gave up careers to go into the desert were ridiculed by friends and associates (*Oppug.* 2.10; 348).

An underlying problem, and part of the reason for John's hostility to the educational system, was homosexuality (Festugière, pp. 195–200). It was not uncommon for a young boy's teacher of rhetoric to establish a homosexual relation with the boy—what John calls a "new and unnatural love" (3.8; 360). Homosexuality was neither new nor unnatural to the Greeks, but John singles it out as another reason why boys should leave the city to learn asceticism from the monks. But it is clear that homosexuality was not the primary problem; what provoked John was the unwillingness of parents to allow their sons to pursue a monastic life beyond the bounds of family, education, and society.

The opposition of Christian parents comes out clearly in part three of the work. Parents say that if a boy goes off to the mountains before his education is completed, he will never be able to make up what was lost. They propose that he "first learn letters and when he has mastered the literary skills, then let him pursue philosophy," that is, the monastic life (*Oppug* 3.11; 366). But, counters John, a boy does not finish his literary studies until his late teens; by that time he is already lost. If someone can assure me that they will not be corrupted, I agree that they should not be removed from the city because this hurts the city, he says. But if we cannot be assured of this, what purpose is served by handing over our children to teachers from whom they learn to pursue lesser ends? (*Oppug.* 3.11; 367).

Parents realized, however, that without a literary education, a young man could not have a career. What John urged, then, was not simply a singular way of life; he was undermining the social order. "Are we to destroy the schools?" parents ask (*Oppug.* 3.11; 367). "How can we have heirs and become grandparents if our sons flee to the desert and refuse to marry?" (*Oppug.* 3.16; 376). Though John presents his argument in narrow moral terms (ibid. 3.7; 360), the choice did not lie in simple moral alternatives. At issue was the maintenance and transmission of the received values and institutions of the society in the face of an uncompromising Christian ideal. John's defense met the same resistance from parents that it met when his friend Theodore gave up the monastic life on the death of his father to assume the role of head of the family (*Thdr. lapsum* 2.1; 47.309).

The resistance of Christian parents to John's entreaties is reminiscent of the reaction of the educated Christians of twenty years earlier to Julian's "school laws." Julian required that schoolteachers be examined not only for their "eloquence," but also for their "morality." Rhetoric, he explained, does not consist in elegant language alone, but in the transmission of beliefs and values. Anyone who does not share these values should not be allowed to teach in the schools. If teachers are to be real interpreters of the ancient classics, let them "first imitate the ancients' piety toward the gods. If they think the classics wrong in this respect, then let them go and teach Matthew and Luke in the church" (*Ep.* 61c [36] Bidez). Gregory of Nazianzus complained that Julian "barred us from rhetoric [*logoi*] as though we were stealing someone else's goods" (*Or.* 4.5).

Here was the dilemma. Without a rhetorical education, the sons of the wealthy could not make their way in society; but if a child went through the schools, he absorbed the values of the pagan culture. The flight of men to the desert heightened the tension. Not only did they offer an alternative system of education based on the Scriptures, but they enticed away the children of the better families. Flight from civic responsibility is a recurring fact of life throughout the fourth century; now a new avenue of escape, besides the army, the bar, and civil service, was opened up, draining off men who could provide the money, leadership, and will to maintain the life of the city (Jones 1964a, p. 745; Kopecek 1974).

Not Yet the Christian Era

It is evident that how one views Christianity in Antioch during the lifetime of John Chrysostom depends on many different factors, among which are the number of Christians and pagans in relation to the size of the city, the strength of Christianity and paganism among the different classes, the viability of the traditional institutions and culture, the social background of the higher clergy, the role of Christian monks, and the divisions within the Christian community itself. How one assesses the place of Christianity within the city's life—its influence and its strength, its capacity to form the lives of its adherents—will depend on which of these factors one chooses to emphasize. For purposes of this book, a study of conflict between two religious groups, Christians and Jews, I have stressed three factors: divisions within the Christian community, the continuing influence of Hellenism, and the attraction of monasticism.

In the Christian tradition, John Chrysostom is revered as a saint who was driven from the patriarchate of Constantinople by the evil scheming of the empress Eudoxia and the self-serving plots of Theophilus, the patriarch of Alexandria. Driven from his office by his foes, harshly maltreated by imperial guards, he was abandoned to die in lonely exile in a forsaken village on the eastern edge of the Black Sea. His courage in the face of persecution and abuse, his unselfish devotion to his flock, and the nobility of his death quickly caught the imagination of Christians. Few other figures from Christian antiquity spawned as many biographies and panegyrics as did John. Already in the early fifth century, only eight years after his death, the first biography appeared, written by Palladius, the bishop of Helenopolis.

John's personal holiness and asceticism, his moral earnestness, and his elegant and graceful literary style have won him an honored place in Christian hagiography, but the reverence bestowed on him as a saint of the Church has obscured the memory of his earlier years when he was a presbyter in Antioch and a partisan figure. Palladius's life of John mentions only briefly the years in Antioch. John came to maturity in a competitive religious environment, in which the loyalties and allegiances of Christians were constantly shifting. Much of his time during his early years as deacon and presbyter was devoted to winning and holding the allegiance of the mercurial throng of Christians who crowded the churches on festivals and holy days, but at other times could be found joining other assemblies.

Besides these divisions within the Christian community in Antioch, John's social and religious world was formed by the continuing and pervasive presence of paganism in the life of the city. In his sermons he thunders against popular pagan amusements, the theater, horseraces, and the revelry surrounding holidays. Reminiscent of the modern mania for football, John says in one sermon, "If you ask [Christians] who is Amos or Obadiah, how many apostles there were or prophets, they stand mute; but if you ask them about the horses or drivers, they answer with more solemnity than sophists or rhetors" (*Hom. 58 in Joannem* 9:17; 59.320). Fickle, easily diverted, John's congregation was quickly bored with the jejune moralizing they heard from the pulpit and easily distracted by horseraces or the religious practices of their neighbors.

The full impact of paganism, however, can be seen not in popular amusements or pagan holidays; its most significant impact was on the upper classes, on the way they educated their children, in the web of traditional values that formed their lives and behavior. The influence of Christianity was not commensurate with the number of its adherents. John says that the "greater part of the city is Christian" (*Jud.* 1.4; 849), but Libanius says it is a "dwelling place of the gods" (*Or.* 11.115). Each exaggerates. John was speaking to a Christian congregation to persuade them to avoid the Jewish festivals, Libanius was celebrating the values of the traditional religion in a literary form that self-consciously avoided any mention of Christianity. The temptation is to say that the truth lies somewhere in between; but that is too simple an answer.

Paganism and Christianity were not on equal footing in Antioch. Hellenism set the tone, undergirded the institutions, inspired the art and literature. In the schools the "air one breathed" was Greek, not

Christian (Festugière, p. 240). It is commonly thought that by the end of the fourth century, especially after the conversion of Constantine and the accession of an orthodox Christian emperor, Theodosius I, to the imperial throne in 379, the Christian religion had come to dominate the society. From the perspective of later history such an interpretation is understandable, but to those living through this period, things did not appear that way. In the opening paragraphs of his work *On Those Who Oppose the Monastic Life*, written most likely after 379, John bemoans the mistreatment of Christian monks while an orthodox Christian sat on the imperial throne. Later in the same work, he observes that some people, contrary to the experience of monks, think that a good reason for becoming a monk is that monks will receive honor and respect from Christian rulers. Don't count on it, says John. Not only are monks mistreated under a Christian emperor; there may come a time when "policies will change" or "unbelievers will be our rulers" (*Oppug.* 2.9; 344). John did not expect that the emperors would always be Christians or that the policies of the present emperor would necessarily continue. He anticipated a time, perhaps on the death of Theodosius, when a non-Christian emperor would ascend the throne.[6]

Since the time of Constantine, there had been Arian emperors, emperors indifferent to Christianity, even a pagan emperor, Julian. Valens, emperor in the east from 364 to 378, was an ardent Arian who vigorously supported pagans and Jews in Antioch (Theodoret *Hist. eccl.* 4.21). This memory was still fresh in John's mind. Even the orthodox Theodosius was ambivalent toward paganism during the first twelve years of his reign. He banned sacrifices, but he allowed other forms of pagan worship, such as the offering of incense. In 386 he ordered that pagans be appointed to the high priesthood in Egypt, since they alone would look after "the temples and the solemn rites of the temples" (Jones 1964a, p. 167). In a frieze in the temple of Hadrian in Ephesus, the orthodox Christian emperor Theodosius is pictured with his family flanked on one side by Artemis Ephesia and on the other by Athena. In the west, when Eugenius, a nominal Christian, usurped the throne on the death of Valentinian, he restored the altar of Victory in the senate house and was feared to be a new Julian by some Christians (Piganiol, p. 266).

Theodosius promoted influential pagans to high office, for example, Proclus as prefect of Constantinople. When his fanatical praetorian prefect Cynegius died in 388, he was replaced by a pagan, Flavian Tatianus, who had held office under the Arian emperor Valens. In a mat-

---

6. A generation later, Cyril of Alexandria spoke of the rulers of the empire as "foster-parents who look after those who believe in Christ" (*Comm. in Isa.* 49:22–23; *PG* 70.1076d).

ter of high symbolic importance, especially for citizens of Antioch, Theodosius forbad that the sacred cypress grove near Antioch be felled, with the argument that the ancient traditions not be transgressed (*CT* 10.1.12). It was not until 391 and 392 that a more aggressive anti-pagan policy was initiated.

In spite of the gains made by Christians over the course of the century, the Christian movement still had to contend with paganism as a rival. A viable way of life for some citizens of the empire, paganism was an aggressive critic of the Church. The euphoric days under Constantine early in the century had long been forgotten. Unlike Eusebius, John did not celebrate the emperor as a "mighty victor beloved of God," a king who had "wiped away all tears and cleansed the world of hatred of God" (Verosta, pp. 190–94). In his "own generation," John could remember an "emperor who exceeded all who preceeded him in impiety" (*Pan. Juv.* 1; 50.573). The conflicting, often contradictory, experience of enthusiastic support by one emperor and outright persecution under another had tempered the outlook of John's generation. The high hopes of an earlier age had not been realized; John could remember martyrs "from recent times" (*Pan. Juv.* 1; 50.571).

John's ascetic and unyielding piety, learned at the feet of the monks in the desert, only reinforced his experiences as young man growing up in Antioch. Intemperance, obduracy, impatience in the face of acculturated Christians set the tone of his early writings and preaching. As a young man, John felt himself besieged by foes, on the defensive. In his view, the Church had but a fragile hold on the allegiance of its followers.

Unlike Eusebius or Prudentius, the Latin poet who could sing of Rome shaking "the dark mist from her wrinkled face" and "placing herself under the rule of Christ" (Markus, p. 28), the youthful John Chrysostom had no conception of a Christian empire. The Church, in John's view, was "not dependent on the good will of the rulers" (*Oppug.* 2.9; 47.344). To the historian of this period, the events of the fourth century seem to be moving inexorably to the formation of a Christian civilization, but few who lived in the fourth century saw this far ahead. And, if some did, John was not among them. "The contemporaries of Chrysostom did not yet know they were opening the Christian period," writes the historian Elias Bickerman.

> Julian was yesterday, the persecutors the day before yesterday. Ambrose knew some magistrates who could boast of having spared Christians. At Antioch the Catholics had just endured the persecution of Valens (375–377 C.E.) and unbelievers of every sort dominated the capital of Syria. The army, composed

of peasants and barbarians, could acclaim tomorrow another
Julian, another Valens, even another Diocletian. One could not
yet, as Chrysostom says somewhere, force [people] to accept
the Christian truth; one had to convince them of it.
[Bickerman, p. 82][7]

7. Citation apparently from *Pan Bab.* 2.3 (*PG* 50.537).

· II ·

The Jews of Antioch

In the summer of 386, six months after he had been ordained, John began what was to have been a series of sermons against the Arian party in Antioch. For weeks the Arians had been goading John to respond to their attacks, but he had hesitated and made excuses. "I realized that many who are sick with this disease [Arianism] would take such pleasure in hearing me," he tells us. The temptation, however, was too great for the young presbyter, and John succumbed. Since the Arians "keep begging me" and "making a nuisance . . . I have entered the arena and stripped for battle" (*Incomprehens.* 1.6; 48.707). The metaphor is commonplace, but in this case accurate. When John stepped up on the pulpit, he would be met by an eager and partisan crowd, his friends ready to cheer and applaud every turn of phrase, his foes anxious to jeer and boo any blunder.

Both friends and foes were disappointed, however, because John preached only one sermon. Abruptly terminating his assault on the Arians, he immediately began a new series on the Judaizers within the Church, noting that,

> Sermons against the Anomoaeans [Arians] can be delivered
> at another time; the delay will work no harm. However, if

34

those who are sick with Judaism are not healed now when the Jewish festivals are "near, at the very door" [Matt. 24:33], I am afraid that some, out of misguided habit and gross ignorance, will share in their transgressions. Then sermons about such things would be pointless. If the offenders aren't present today to hear what we say, later we would prescribe medicine in vain, because they would already have committed the sin. This is the reason I am eager to take up this matter before the festivals begin. [*Jud.* 1.1; 48.845]

In 386 C.E. Rosh Hashannah fell on September 9–10. Already at the end of August, the Jews in Antioch had begun to make preparations for this festival as well as for Yom Kippur and Sukkoth, which would follow in quick succession as John observes in the opening lines of the sermon (*Jud.* 1.1). Since the Jews lived intermingled with the other inhabitants of the city, their preparations were visible to their neighbors, among whom were Christians. Some Christians planned to join the Jews in their celebrations. "Many who belong to us and say they believe our teaching, attend their festivals and even share in their celebrations and join their fasts," complains John (*Jud.* 1.1; 844). Who were these Jews whose festivals attracted Christians and prompted John to launch an attack on judaizing Christians?

The Jews in Ancient Antioch

When the city of Antioch was founded in the early third century B.C.E. by Seleucus, a general in the army of Alexander the Great, Jews were among the first settlers.[1] The original nucleus may have come from mercenaries in Seleucus's army, but as the years passed they were joined by Jews from elsewhere. Antioch's proximity to Palestine as well as its accessibility to Persia, where large numbers of Jews lived, rapidly established the city as a Jewish center. In later Jewish tradition Syria was considered an extension of Palestine [the rabbis debated whether produce in Syria was subject to the same laws as produce from Eretz Israel (*Mishnah Hallah* 4.7)] and the Lake of Antioch on the plain northeast of the city was considered one of the seven lakes surrounding Israel (Kohut). As Antioch's importance as an administrative center of the Seleucid Empire grew, so did the Jewish community residing there, attracted by the comforts of urban life as well as the commercial and cultural opportunities. Located on the main road to

---

1. For the history of the Jewish community in Antioch, see Krauss, 1902; Downey, 1961, passim; Kraeling; Lurie; and Meeks and Wilken, 1978.

central Asia Minor, and easily accessible to the Jewish communities in western Asia Minor via its fine port at Seleucia Pieria, Antioch became a convenient stopping place for Jews traveling to cities along the Aegean coast and in the valleys of Asia Minor.

According to the Jewish historian Josephus, who is our chief source of information for the early history of Antiochene Jewry, the Jews there prospered during this period. From the middle of the second century B.C.E. at least, and perhaps earlier, the Jews were recognized as a distinct group within the city with the right to practice their religion, follow their ancestral customs, and keep their own laws (Josephus *AJ* 12.119; *BJ* 7.44). Josephus says the Jews were called "Antiochenes," but the precise legal and political significance of this term is unclear (*Ap.* 2.39).

As the community grew, a synagogue was constructed and participation in the city's life deepened. For a short time in the second century under the "mad" king Antiochus IV (165–64 C.E.), the Jews of Antioch may have been harassed. Josephus mentions that Antiochus's successors "restored to the Jews of Antioch all such votive offerings as were made of brass to be laid up in their synagogue" (Josephus *BJ* 7.44), implying that Antiochus had initiated repressive measures against the Antiochene Jews. And it is possible, some would say likely, that the martyrdom of Eleazar, the seven brothers, and their mother (the Maccabean martyrs, 2 Macc. 7) under Antiochus IV took place at Antioch rather than at Jerusalem.[2] What is certain is that the remains of the Maccabean martyrs were later venerated at Antioch and a synagogue was constructed over the tomb (Downey 1961, p. 110; Bickerman).

Whatever difficulties the Jews of Antioch experienced during the reign of Antiochus IV, after his death the community quickly recovered. They received favorable treatment from later monarchs and the "Jewish colony grew in numbers . . . and constantly attracted to their religious ceremonies multitudes of Greeks, and these they had in some measure incorporated with themselves" (Josephus *BJ* 7.44–45). No doubt Josephus, writing for a Roman audience, wished to present the Jews as exemplary citizens from whom the rulers had nothing to fear, but his description is probably close to the truth. The Antiochene Jews were able to pursue their way of life in peace and tranquility. By the end of the Hellenistic period, they constituted a sizeable, well-organized, and visible part of the city's life.

Besides the community of Jews within the city proper, there were at

---

2. Schatkin, 1974, argues that "there is overwhelming evidence that the martyrdom took place at Antioch" (p. 98).

least two other settlements of Jews in the vicinity of Antioch. We do not know when these communities were established, but they are present in the fourth century C.E. and may date from the Hellenistic period. One was in Daphne, the suburb on the plateau south of the city. Rabbinic tradition mentions Daphne as the site of a meeting between King Nebuchadnezer and the Sanhedrin (*p. Shekalim* 6:3; 50a). This account is no doubt legendary, but the mention of Daphne as the place of meeting indicates that the community in Daphne was significant enough to be accorded such an honor and to have won for itself a place in Jewish memory. At least since the time of the emperor Tiberius (14–31 C.E.), there had been a Jewish synagogue in Daphne (Malalas *Chronographia*, p. 261). In the fourth century, there was still a Jewish synagogue in the suburb (*Jud.* 1.6; 852).

Jews also lived outside of the city in a rural community. The precise location of this settlement is unknown, but it seems to have been located on the great plain northeast of the city. According to rabbinic sources, this area was called Hulta and the Jews who lived there grew rice. Because of the proximity of Syria to Eretz Israel, some rabbis thought this rice was subject to the laws that applied to produce from Israel (*Tosefta Demai* 2.1). Jewish commentaries on the Bible from the late Roman period give several versions of a story about visits to the area by rabbis to collect money for the Jews in Israel (*Deuteronomy Rabbah* 4.8; *Leviticus Rabbah* 4.3). From these accounts, it is clear that the rabbis came regularly to the area to collect funds. The Jews both outside of and in the city, as we shall see shortly, maintained continuous ties with the Jews living in Palestine.

Libanius also mentions a settlement of Jews who lived outside of the city. "Some Jews—of that famous people—who have worked our land for a long time, four generations, were seized with the desire to be no longer what they had been. They took it upon themselves to shake off the old yoke and henceforth to dictate the terms by which we were to employ them. Since we could not tolerate that, we sued them" (*Or.* 47.13). Whether these Jews were part of the community mentioned in rabbinic sources is uncertain, but the coincidence is intriguing. Those who have examined the texts are inclined to identify the two communities (Harmand, pp. 72–87; Kraeling). The most likely place to locate the settlement is on the plain of Antioch north and east of the city. Further, both the rabbinic sources and Libanius's account indicate that these Jews had been living in the area for a long time. This community, however, was quite unlike the community of Jews in the city itself. In Antioch, as we shall see later in this chapter, the Jews came from different economic classes, including the wealthy, but the Jews living on the plain of Antioch were tenant farmers, bound to the land

by custom and law and, like other peasants in Syria, poor. They were
not, however, serfs. They, too, had rights before the law and were not
subject simply to the whim of the landowner. With the help of a
powerful military patron, they were able to bring pressure on Libanius
and to force him to litigate their dispute with him in the courts. The
Jews won the case.

In sum, then, there were at least three Jewish communities in Antioch and vicinity, two of which traced their history back to Hellenistic
times before the arrival of the Romans, and one that in the fourth century had been known to contemporaries for at least four generations
and may have existed longer.

Antioch Under the Romans

The arrival of the Romans in Syria in 64–63 B.C.E. and the annexa-
tion of Syria to the Roman Empire brought administrative changes to
the area, but the policies of the new rulers had no immediate effect on
the Jews living in Antioch. If the analogy of other Jewish communities
within the empire is used, (for example, of communities in Greek-
speaking cities in Asia Minor that had recently come under Roman
rule), the integrity of Jewish life and the protection of Jewish institutions and traditions were guaranteed. In cities of which we have information, the Jews were allowed to organize themselves in accordance
with their customs, to follow their own laws on matters pertaining to
their lives, to maintain relations with the Jews in Palestine, and even to
send funds to Jerusalem. Cicero complained about this practice of
sending gold from the provinces to Jerusalem (*Pro Flacco* 66–67), but
his opposition seems not to have altered Roman policy (Safrai 1974,
pp. 186–90).

Several decrees from the city of Sardis in western Asia Minor illustrate the privileges accorded Jews living in Greek-speaking cities under Roman rule. The city council of Sardis declared that the Jews who
had "continuously received many great privileges from the people,"
had requested that "since their laws and freedom have been restored
to them by the Roman senate and people, they may, in accordance
with their accepted customs, come together and have a communal life,
and adjudicate suits among themselves, and that a place be given them
in which they may gather together with their wives and children, and
offer their ancestral prayers and sacrifices to God." The decree also acknowledged the difference between Jewish customs and those of other
citizens. "On stated days," Jews were allowed to come together "to do
those things which are in accordance with their laws." It was even said

that suitable food should be provided for them in the marketplace (Josephus *AJ* 12.147–53; 14.259–61). Decrees of this sort are known from other cities in Asia Minor and elsewhere, and it is reasonable to assume that the status of the Jews in Antioch during the first century B.C.E. and the first century C.E. was similar to that of the Jews living in cities from which we do have information. No doubt Josephus has rewritten the language of the decree to accentuate the privileges granted the Jews (ancient historians commonly rewrote documents included in their histories), but there is no reason to doubt the authenticity of the decree (Schalet). Epigraphic and literary evidence from the period, particularly from cities in the same geographical area, confirm the statements of Josephus (Kraabel 1968; Stern 1974, pp. 143–55).

There was another side to the story. As successful as Jews were in establishing communities outside of Israel and practicing their way of life among foreign peoples, their unique customs (observing the Sabbath, abstaining from the eating of pork) and beliefs (in one God), generated misunderstanding, disapproval, and, at times, outright hostility. People were attracted to the Jewish religion, but because the Jews remained aloof, a people apart, refusing for example, to marry non-Jews, they were often resented. Reflecting popular attitudes the satirist Juvenal wrote:

> Some, whose lot it was to have Sabbath-fearing fathers,
> Worship nothing but clouds and the numen of the heavens,
> And think it as great a crime to eat pork, from which their parents
> Abstained, as human flesh. They get themselves circumcised,
> And look down on Roman law, preferring instead to learn
> And honor and fear the Jewish commandments, whatever
> Was handed down by Moses in that arcane tome of his—
> Never to show the way to any but fellow believers
> (If they ask where to get some water, find out if they're foreskinless).
> But their fathers were the culprits: they made every seventh day
> Taboo for all life's business, dedicated to idleness.
>
> [*Sat.* 14. 97–106]

As early as the third century B.C.E., legends began to circulate ascribing dubious origins to the Jews. The Egyptian writer Manetho, whose account of the Jews influenced Tacitus, claimed that Jews were originally lepers who had been expelled from Egypt. In the famous chapter in his *Histories* where Tacitus describes the war between the Jews and the Romans, he gives a highly tendentious account of the origin and practices of the Jews. Moses, writes Tacitus, led the Jews out of Egypt and established for them a "novel religion quite different from those of the rest of mankind. Among the Jews all things are profane that we hold sacred; on the other hand they regard as permissible what seems to us immoral." They prohibit the eating of pork, fast often, celebrate a meal with unleavened bread, and sit idle one day out of each week. Their practices are "sinister and revolting." The Jews are wicked, given to lust, and look on other men and women as enemies. They even introduced the practice of circumcision "to show that they are different from others." Their proselytes despise the gods of the Romans and eventually shed all patriotism to Rome. In short they are a most criminal people (*sceleratissima gens* [*Hist.* 5.4–5]).

An even better insight into popular attitudes toward Jews in this period can be found in the *Acta Alexandrinorum* (Acts of the Pagan Martyrs), a collection of papyri giving reports of Alexandrian embassies to Rome and conflict between Roman officials and citizens of the city of Alexandria. Anti-Semitic language and epithets appear in a number of the papyri, and it is generally thought that they reflect the actual situation in Alexandria during the first centuries of the common era. The word "Jew" is used as a term of opprobrium. In one scene, a citizen of Alexandria accuses the Roman emperor of having Jews in his "privy council," knowing that the term Jew would be "offensive" (*Acta Hermaisci*; Musurillo, p. 45). At times popular feelings, reflected in writings such as these, led to open conflict. In 38 C.E. the Greeks of Alexandria, with the acquiescence of the Roman governor Flaccus, mounted a savage attack on the Jews of Alexandria. They demanded that statues of the emperor be placed in Jewish synagogues, looted shops and houses, forced Jewish women to eat pork publicly, and murdered many Jews. Although the ancient world was not inclined to religious intolerance or racial hatred in the modern sense, the severity of anti-Jewish feeling and the violence catch one up short.

But my purpose here is not to chronicle the attitudes toward Jews in the ancient world or assess the reasons for anti-Semitic feelings. The matter is extremely complex and in some ways paradoxical. As the Jewish scholar Isaac Heinemann has observed, "The roots of hate and love were the same." Antipathy and sympathy stood side by side. As a religion, Judaism had great success among the peoples of the Greco-Roman world, appealing strongly to the religious instincts of large numbers of men and women. Even critics respected Jews for the antiquity of their traditions. But alongside of this admiration and esteem for the Jews, and the privileges they were granted under the law, there was an undertone of hostility and ill-will that cannot be ignored.

In light of this situation, it is understandable that as Roman rule was extended into Palestine tension would increase. For Palestine was the land of the Jews and some still hoped to establish a Jewish kingdom once more. Conflict between Romans and Jews in the Jewish homeland also had an impact on Jewish life in neighboring Syria. The proximity of Antioch to Palestine, as well as its strategic importance for Roman generals in the east, drew Antiochene Jewry into the conflict. Close ties between Syrian Jews and the Jews of Palestine, illustrated by the practice of rabbis traveling to Syria to collect tithes on produce, or Syrian Jews traveling to Jersualem for the high festivals, served to heighten tensions in Antioch. Though there were no indications that Antiochene Jews were disloyal, the Romans realized that Jews in the diaspora had a stake in events unfolding in Palestine, especially if the Jewish state were restored.

Resentment toward the Jews began to build during the years before the war in 66−70 C.E. The emperor Caligula ordered his statue to be placed in the temple in Jerusalem and the decree was transmitted to the Roman authorities in Palestine via the governor of Syria. In response to the order, Jews from Palestine traveled to Antioch (where they may have been joined with Antiochene Jews) to meet with the governor. They pleaded with the governor not to carry out the order, but he replied that the army was "ready at hand" if they resisted and would "strew the land with the dead." On hearing this speech, the Jews, according to Philo, "stood riveted to the ground, incapable of speech." As tears poured from their eyes, they moaned that they were unfortunate to see "what none of our forefathers saw in the past" (Philo *Ad Gaium* 222−24; Josephus *AJ.* 18.262−72). Stripped of its dramatic element, this story illustrates how the Jews of Antioch were drawn into events occurring three hundred miles from their city. The Roman governor made his headquarters in Antioch (Bowersock 1973), forcing Jewish leaders from Palestine to travel to Syria to consult him, thereby drawing Antiochene Jews into the conflict. Josephus also reports that, on his way from Antioch to Jerusalem, the governor met crowds of Jews protesting his action, suggesting that Jews throughout the area were united in their opposition to Caligula's provocative decree.

During this period, some citizens of Antioch charged the Jews with unrest and sedition and asked the governor to revoke their Sabbath privileges. (Traditionally, the Jews were not required to engage in business or legal affairs on the Sabbath.) Believing the charges to be groundless, the governor refused the request. In another incident, after the war in Palestine, the victorious emperor Titus marched north toward Antioch displaying the spoils of his victory, among them Jewish prisoners. When he reached Antioch, a large crowd met him and demanded that the Jews be driven from the city. According to Josephus,

Titus refused. "But their own country to which as Jews they ought in any case to be banished, has been destroyed, and no other place would receive them. Now that their city is destroyed there is no place for them to live but where they do live." The people renewed the request and again Titus refused. He ordered that the Jews should be allowed to enjoy the same privileges they had had previously (Josephus *BJ* 7.100–111). It is, however, difficult to fit this report in with other sources, which give a somewhat different impression. Malalas, a late Antiochene chronicler, reports that Vespasian set up bronze figures, possibly cherubim from the temple at Jerusalem, outside the southern gate of the city in the vicinity of the Jewish settlement and that a theater was constructed on the site of a Jewish synagogue in Daphne with the inscription: FROM THE JEWISH SPOILS (Downey, 1938–39).

After the war between the Romans and the Jews of Palestine, the Romans imposed an onerous tax, the *fiscus Judaicus*, an annual payment of two denarii, formerly sent to Jerusalem but now to be sent to Rome. It was collected from all Jews, including those living in the diaspora. In other ways, however, it is unlikely that the war with the Romans altered Jewish life in most cities of the diaspora in any fundamental way. There were exceptions, of course, notably Egypt and Cyrene in North Africa.

In the case of Egypt, bad feelings between the Jews and the local citizenry persisted, but these difficulties had less to do with the presence of the Romans than the "incessant strife" between Jews and others (Josephus *BJ* 2.487). Cyrene was another story altogether. A genuine Jewish revolt broke out in Cyrene in 117 C.E. to coincide with Trajan's campaign against the Parthians on the eastern frontier. This revolt, initially directed against the local inhabitants, turned into a full-scale war, spilling over into Egypt and the island of Cyprus. Alarmed by the spread of the revolt, the emperor Trajan sent one of his ablest generals, Marcius Turbo, to quell the resistance. Thousands of Jews were killed, annihilating Jewish communities in Cyrene and most of Egypt. In the city of Teucheira in Cyrene, evidences of Jewish life simply cease at the beginning of the second century. As an indication of the feelings of the local population toward the revolt, ninety years later, in 119–20 C.E. an annual festival was still celebrated at Oxyrhynchus in Egypt to commemorate the victory over the Jews (Schuerer, 1:531). As papyri from Egypt amply demonstrate, Jewish life and activities went into steep decline in this period. Only in Alexandria is there evidence of the continuation of Jewish life, but the community was much smaller and less influential than it had been a century earlier and its intellectual activity was nil, judging from the absence of any literary remains (*Corpus papyrorum Iudaicarum* 1.85–93; Applebaum 1961).

In 132–35 C.E. Jews in Palestine, led by Bar Kochba, revolted against the Romans and for a brief period reestablished a Jewish state. This revolt was soon crushed and the Romans gained control of the country. Some Jews from Palestine fled to other parts of the empire (Justin *Dial.* 1), and the emperor Hadrian imposed new restrictions concerning circumcision. He also cleared the city of Jerusalem of Jews and founded a Roman colony, Aelia Capitolina, on the site, with a new temple dedicated to the Capitoline gods, Jupiter, Minerva, and Juno. He forbad Jews to enter the city of Jerusalem. Now the center of Palestinian Jewry shifted to Galilee, where the patriarchate was established and Jews sought to restore the remnants of their religious life after the loss of their most important religious symbols, the city of Jerusalem and its temple.

From this unhappy account of Jewish fortunes during the first two centuries of the common era, it may seem that the Jews would cease to play a significant role in the life of the Roman Empire, and that the Jewish religion had lost its appeal. But this overlooks the tenacity of the Jews and the capacity of Jewish leaders to reinterpret their ancient traditions in the light of radically new circumstances. Already under the new emperor Antoninus Pius (138–61 C.E.), the ban on circumcision was modified and relations with the Roman rulers began to improve (Harris; Avi-Yonah, pp. 39–42).

The History of the Jews
and the History of Christianity

In the second and third centuries of the common era, after the Bar Kochba war, the sources for the Jewish community in Antioch are very meager. Whether the paucity of information should, however, be taken to suggest a decline in the status and size of the Jewish community in Antioch is doubtful. Much of our knowledge of the cities of the Roman world is uneven and erratic, due to historical accident. What *is* significant about the history of the Jewish community in Antioch, however, is that the later fourth century, the time when John Chrysostom was living there, is the best documented of any period. When the Jews of Antioch again come to light after an interval of several hundred years, the Jewish community is large, well established, highly respected, and influential. The most likely explanation is that the status of the Jews in Antioch underwent little change during the intervening

centuries and, what is more likely, the community grew and prospered. By drawing on what is known about the Jews in other eastern
cities such as Sardis in Asia Minor, Caesarea in Palestine, and elsewhere, we are able to construct a plausible picture of Jewish life in the
Roman Empire before substantial information again becomes available for Antioch.

Because one of the purposes of this book is to show that the Jews
were a factor in Christian history during this period, and that we miss
an important dynamic in the history of Christian thought if we overlook the Jews, I should like, before turning to the situation in Antioch
in the late fourth century, to say something about the way historians
of Christianity have viewed this period in Jewish history.

A perusal of histories of Christianity in the ancient world will show
that the Jews are almost wholly ignored after the first century. This is
particularly puzzling because the Jews play a major role in the study of
primitive Christianity and the New Testament. In the first century of
the Roman Empire, when Christianity began, it is estimated that the
Jews numbered four or five million, and most studies of Christianity
during this period give extensive attention to Jewish life and thought,
in Palestine as well as in the cities of the empire. Yet within a few decades the Jews mysteriously disappear from the scene as though they
had ceased to exist and therefore need not be taken into account to
understand the history of Christianity.

The neglect of the Jews during this period of Christian history is a
result of the interpretation of early Church history in the nineteenth
century, notably under the influence of the great historian of dogma,
Adolf von Harnack, whose views also dominated the historical work
of the first half of the twentieth century. In his work *The Mission and
Expansion of Christianity*, Harnack argued that, after the Bar Kochba
revolt, the Jews abandoned their efforts to relate constructively to the
larger society, as Jews had done earlier; instead they became preoccupied with internal problems, shut themselves off from the stimula-
tion of outside influences, and as a result Judaism atrophied. "Intercourse with pagans was confined within the strictest of regulations,
and had to be given up as a whole" (Harnack, p. 18). Christianity, on
the other hand, was thought to enter a period of growth and of recep-
tivity to Hellenistic influences, a time in which the emerging Christian
movement, originally a sect within Judaism, adapted itself to the larger
culture and society. As a consequence of this view, the early centuries
of the Roman Empire are seen as a time of the ascendancy and adapta-
tion of Christianity to Hellenism and the precipitous decline and with-
drawal of Judaism from the life of the Roman world. Even the new
edition of the classic work of Emil Schuerer on the history of the Jews,

completely reedited and published in 1973, perpetuates this interpretation. In the period after the Bar Kochba revolt, the Jews are said "to become more and more strangers in the Gentile world, despite the many surviving bonds linking them to it" (Schuerer, 1:556).[3]

The reasons behind this view are many and complex. One reason is the powerful impact that the destruction of the city of Jerusalem and the ravaging of the temple had on Christian perceptions of Judaism in the years after 70 C.E. The destruction of Jerusalem and the cessation of temple worship appeared to signal the end of Judaism. The coincidence of the rise of Christianity and the destruction of the city of Jerusalem, already noted by Origen in the third century (*Contra Celsum* 4.22), seemed to confirm this view. Another reason is the widespread ignorance of Jewish sources among non-Jewish historians. Most historians in this period are familiar with Greek and Latin but not Hebrew and Aramaic, the languages in which many of the Jewish sources are written. Yet another factor is the influence of Christian theology. With the emergence of Christianity and the compilation of the Christian Scriptures, the Jewish Scriptures became known as the "Old Testament," because the "splendor" seen in the face of Moses, as St. Paul puts it, had given way to a far greater splendor, so great that "what once had splendor has come to have no splendor at all" (2 Cor. 3:7–10). Christianity, which would soon begin calling itself the "true Israel," had, in the view of Christians, taken the place of the old Israel, Israel "after the flesh" (Gal. 4:21ff.).

Ideas such as these, symbolized in the dating of all events (secular and religious) by reference to the birth of Jesus, eventually came to dominate the historiography of Western civilization. This "majority history" has had a profound influence on the way the Jews are presented in standard historical works and college courses on the history of Western civilization.

> That history is a seamless web, that any scheme of periodization is an arbitrary convenience to suit a point of view, these are well known propositions. Yet the most influential of all periodizations, that which divides history before the Incarnation from history after, is as unmodifiable as our sense of historic time itself. It orders the passing years for agnostics and Communists as for Christians. For the Jews the standard is dual, yet the Christian scheme is by far the more influential. If for some members of the majority the Christian ordering is a reflection of God's providence, while for others it is a mere convenience,

---

3. The editors, realizing that something was wrong with this statement, added a qualifying footnote (p. 556).

for many in both camps the Incarnation still corresponds to the one real division in history, whether that cesura be seen providentially or secularly. [Langmuir, p. 343]

Though Judaism has a continuous and illustrious history from the ancient world through medieval times into the modern period, that history is not part of the public record of our civilization. In spite of the obvious fact that late antiquity was the formative period in the history of Judaism, a time of intense spiritual activity that led to the editing of the Mishnah and the compilation of the Palestinian and Babylonian Talmuds, many historians still insist on calling the Judaism that existed when Christianity began "late Judaism" [*Spätjudentum*]. Judaism, as it is presented in most colleges and universities [except where programs in Jewish studies have been established], is chiefly a pre-Christian phenomenon, the religion of the Old Testament. Even the study of the Hebrew language falls under the same strictures. Until fifteen or twenty years ago, the only Hebrew studied in American and European universities was biblical Hebrew, though there is a vast body of Hebrew literature extending over the past two millennia. "Before the first century the Hebrews were of great historical importance," writes Gavin I. Langmuir, but "after the emergence of Christianity a reprobation falls on the Jews, and a dark night of ignorance conceals their activities from the historical consciousness of most western society until Dreyfus, the Balfour Declaration, or Hitler once more draws historical attention to the Jews" (Langmuir, p. 343).

Nowhere is this cultural bias more evident than in the study of the later Roman Empire, the period that concerns us in this book. A fresh consideration of the place of the Jews in the history of the Roman Empire and in early Christianity will show, however, that the Jews continued to be a significant factor throughout the third and fourth centuries, and they cannot be ignored even later, during the Byzantine period (Bowman; Scharf). The third and fourth centuries were a time of new life and vitality within the Jewish communities of the empire, of material prosperity and economic growth, of spiritual creativity and intellectual productivity. Resurgence of Jewish life and institutions can be documented not only in the communities of the diaspora, but also in Palestine, particularly in Galilee, as archaeological investigations are demonstrating.

With the recognition of the Jewish patriarch as the official link between the Jews and the imperial authorities in the third century, the Jews were able to maintain cordial relations with the Roman government (Applebaum 1958). The emperor Septimius Severus (193–211 C.E.), for example, encouraged Jewish participation in city councils

(*Digesta Justiniani* 50.2.3.3.; Linder 1974, p. 13), and the practice was continued in the fourth century. From inscriptions and literary allusions, we know that Jews actually served on the councils of cities in Palestine, for example, in Tiberias (*p. Shekalim* 7.2; 50c) and Sepphoris (*p. Peah* 1.1, 16a; Alon 1977, p. 469; Linder 1974, p. 111), and in cities of the diaspora such as Antioch in Pisidia (*CIJ* 772),[4] Acmonia (*CIJ* 770), Corycus in Cilicia (*CIJ* 788), and in Caesarea (Levine, p. 65). This participation was based on laws from the time of the emperor Septimius Severus, whom Jewish inscriptions praise (*CIJ* 972, 677), and it is clear that the rationale behind such legislation was that the Jews, like other citizens, were needed to help support the cities. The Jews were subject to the same laws as other citizens, bore their share of responsibility in the cities, and benefited from the laws (Linder 1974, p. 98–99).

Even in Palestine, where devastation had been the greatest, Jewish life recovered rapidly, as evidenced by the large number of synagogues constructed during this period (Meyers, Kraabel, and Strange, pp. 14–16; Groh, pp. 78ff.). Drawing on information in the Palestinian Talmud, Saul Lieberman has shown that Jewish life continued as normal in the third and fourth centuries, and there is no evidence of persecution either from pagan or Christian emperors (Lieberman 1974, pp. 125, 180–89). During this same period, the Jewish community in Caesarea, a Greek city on the Mediterranean coast, flourished (Levine). Origen, who lived in Palestine for several decades in the third century, had extensive contacts with Jewish scholars (DeLange, pp. 29–38) and was impressed by the strength of the Jews and the "great power of the patriarch granted by the emperor." He differs, said Origen, "little from a true king" (*Ep. Africanus* 14).

Attitudes toward the Jews had also changed. Tacitus, writing in the early second century, described the Jews as vulgar and superstitious. But a century later another historian, Dio Cassius, observed that the Jews, who have "frequently been persecuted," had prospered and

> succeeded in winning the right to observe their laws freely. They are distinguished from the rest of mankind in practically every detail of their way of life, and especially in that they honor none of the other gods, but show extreme reverence for one particular deity. They never had a statue of him even in Jerusalem itself, but believing him to be unnamable and invisible, they worship him in the most extravagant way among hu-

---

4. *CIJ* 772, a funerary inscription, comes from Apollonia in Phrygia but it refers to the dead person's ancestors who exercised public responsibility in Antioch.

mans. They built him a large and splendid temple . . . and
dedicated to him the day called the day of Saturn of which,
among many other most peculiar observances, they undertake
no serious occupation. [*DC* 37.17]

What Dio Cassius says in this passage, as John Gager observes, is interesting not only for what it tells us about the actual situation of the
Jews in Dio's time, namely the freedom to pursue their way of life
without disturbance, but also for his attitude toward them. "The tone
of the passage is significant for its combination of neutrality, accuracy,
and even a certain admiration for the Jewish cult. The memory of early
hostilities has all but disappeared" (Gager, p. 92). Elsewhere in his
history, Dio has more negative things to say about the Jews, the inju-
ries they did to Rome (*DC* 49.22), and about Jewish treatment of cap-
tives in Cyrene (*DC* 68.32), but in those passages he is describing military campaigns. The overall impression one receives is that of respect,
toleration, and curiosity. Not surprisingly, as public opinion of the
Jews began to shift, some Jews began to look more favorably on Roman rule, viewing it as providential or at least professing neutrality
(Glatzer).

At the very beginning of the period after Bar Kochba, the Jews of
Sardis in western Asia Minor purchased a large building from the city
and transformed it into a synagogue and educational center. This
building, the largest synagogue of antiquity to be excavated, was situated alongside the main road through the city and was adjacent to its
central ceremonial square. All the inscriptions, except one, were written in Greek. Of the Jews mentioned in the inscriptions, nine out of
twenty-seven males were members of the city council. Three use the
epithet *Sardianos*, and three others were members of the provincial
Roman administration. One was a financial officer in the imperial administration. The one Hebrew inscription includes only the letters
BYRS. Some have suggested that this be read BEROS, i.e., VERUS,
which could refer to Lucius Verus, co-emperor with Marcus Aurelius,
who visited the city in 169 C.E. On the occasion of the emperor's visit,
the Jews of Sardis, like other residents, may have presented a tribute to
him (Kraabel 1980, pp. 483–88).

From other inscriptions, we know that Jews enrolled their children
in the gymnasia in the cities of the empire. Jewish names appear on
lists of ephebes (Applebaum 1974, pp. 112–13), the adolescent boys
who had completed the athletic and educational course in the gym-
nasium and were presented in a public ceremony involving games, pa-
rades, sacrifices to the traditional gods, and even service as "choir
boys" in some cities to sing hymns to the gods (Nilsson). Jews served

as watchmen; as clerks in the market; in municipal waterworks; as police officers; in the military; and in other positions in the cities (Linder 1974, pp. 112–13). And as we shall see in discussing the Jewish patriarch later in this chapter, Jews educated their sons in Greek schools and sought the same kinds of careers in public or private life for their children as did wealthy pagans and Christians. Yet these same Jews also built synagogues that served as places of worship as well as educational centers for the Jewish community in the cities. Indeed, it is the remains of the synagogues that give us much of the information we possess about the participation of Jews in the life of the cities. These synagogues show that the Jews maintained their traditional way of life, cultivated Jewish customs and passed on Jewish institutions, and that they had the financial resources to construct (or purchase) substantial buildings, to decorate them according to the fashions current in the society, and to maintain them as centers of Jewish life.

On the basis of epigraphic as well as literary sources, there seems to have been little disruption in the continuity of Jewish life in most of the cities of the diaspora during the second and third centuries. One important exception, as we have noted, was the Jewish community in Egypt. There the large and prosperous Jewish community did go into a period of decline after the conflicts of the first century, and it is not until much later that the community begins to recover. Yet the situation in Alexandria was unique, brought about by local factors that were not present in other cities. In Palestine, where the Jewish population suffered the ravages of war with the Romans, the loss of the city of Jerusalem, and then the devastation following the Bar Kochba revolt, Jewish life had begun to stabilize and by the third century was entering upon a time of recovery and growth.

Roman Law and the Jews

If it is the case that the third and fourth centuries were years of renewal within the Jewish communities of Palestine after the ravages of the wars with the Romans, and of stability and growth of the communities in the disaspora, it might be asked what impact the accession of a Christian emperor, Constantine the Great, to the imperial throne in the early fourth century had on these communities. For centuries both popular and scholarly historiography have presented Constantine as the founder of Christian Europe, the creator of a policy of exclusion of the Jews, the man who laid the legal foundations for the repression of the Jews. The "victory" of the Church, it is assumed, caused a rapid deterioration in the legal status of the Jews throughout the Roman

Empire.[5] But is this really the case? Let us consider the legislation on the Jews in the early fourth century, one body of evidence usually thought to support this view.

Beginning with Constantine, there is a marked change in the way Jews are referred to in the laws. Judaism is called a "feral" or "nefarious" sect, while Christianity is referred to as the "worship of God" (CT 16.8.1). Further, some legislation begins to show a marked bias in favor of Christianity and against Judaism (CT 16.8.5). The tone of Constantine's legislation leads one to think that the legislation on the Jews was a direct result of the influence of Christian bishops at the court. Such an interpretation, however, oversimplifies the situation. One must consider not only the language of the legislation but also the specific content of the laws. When they are compared with earlier legislation, it is clear that most of the laws of Constantine fall within the bounds set by his predecessors. In his letters to bishops, Constantine uses sharp, hostile language to describe the Jews, but his laws remain, in the main, within Roman legal tradition. Indeed, like earlier emperors, Constantine responded to concrete situations and problems; he does not exhibit a thoroughgoing and uniform policy toward the Jews (Linder 1974, pp. 142–43).

Constantine encouraged Jews to participate in the councils of the cities in which they lived. "By a general law we permit municipal senates to nominate Jews to the municipal council" (CT 16.8.3). Here Constantine's rescript is guided by legal precedent and the fiscal situation of cities that needed the support of wealthy Jewish citizens. This law might be seen as a revocation of traditional privileges enjoyed by Jewish leaders, namely exemption from service on the councils, but the action is not motivated by anti-Jewish feeling. The concern is economic and social. In another law, he granted new privileges to the Jewish "clergy." "If any persons with complete devotion should dedicate themselves to the synagogues of the Jews as patriarchs and priests and should live in the aforementioned sect and preside over the administration of their law, they shall continue to be exempt from all compulsory services that are incumbent on persons, as well as those that are due to the municipalities" (CT 16.8.2). Later in the century, the councils of several cities clamor to have these privileges revoked, not because of anti-Jewish sentiment, but because Jewish support of the city council was desperately needed to keep the cities financially solvent.

These laws dealing with the leaders of the Jewish communities es-

5. For a recent statement of this view, see Reichardt; for the view developed here, see Linder, 1974, and Vogler. For a discussion of older literature, see Linder, pp. 95–97. Linder has also written a major work on Roman laws dealing with the Jews, to be published by the Israel Academy of Sciences in Jerusalem.

tablished important precedents that were to be followed by emperors later in the fourth century; as Amnon Linder has shown, they made possible a system of Jewish self-government that strengthened Jewish life and identity (Linder 1974, pp. 125–26). The laws also gave the Jewish clergy a status similar to that of the Christian and pagan clergy (*CT* 12.1.99).

The one area where the influence of Christianity is most apparent is in the laws dealing with proselytism and the protection of converts from Judaism to Christianity. In the former case, Constantine builds on the legal tradition set by his predecessors, who in the second century had prohibited the circumcision of non-Jews. But one can also see that Constantine's laws are more explicitly designed to dissuade people from affiliating with Judaism, especially through marriage or through slavery—for example, the purchase of a Christian slave by a Jew (*CT* 16.9.1). Furthermore, Constantine introduced legislation that prohibited any retribution by Jews against those who left Judaism for Christianity. "Jews shall not be permitted to disturb any man who has been converted from Judaism to Christianity or to assail him with any outrage" (*CT* 16.8.5). In these cases, Constantine uses the law to favor Christianity against Judaism, and, as Linder observes, such laws come from the latter period of Constantine's life (324–37 C.E.), when he was sole ruler and the influence of Christian bishops at the court was greatest (Linder 1974, pp. 109–10).

Constantine also introduced new legislation concerning the relation of the Jews to the city of Jerusalem. Since the time of Hadrian, Jews had been forbidden to enter the city of Jerusalem (Justin *Apol.* 1.47), but Constantine must have relaxed the prohibition because an early pilgrim to Jerusalem reported that Jews visited the city once a year, on the ninth of Ab, the day the temple was destroyed, to mourn its loss (*Itinerarium burdigalense*, ed. Geyer, p. 22). This was no doubt less a concession to Jewish piety than a subtle way of confirming Christian religious claims. Jews mourning at the ruins of the temple underscored the victory of Christianity over Judaism. It does appear, however, that Jews began to return to the vicinity of Jerusalem during this period, since they are to be found in Bethlehem later in the century (Jerome *Ep.* 84).

The laws on proselytism are the most significant for determining the status of the Jews in the empire, because they restrict Jewish activity. But the effect of these laws was much less than the legislation itself would suggest. Later legislation reiterates some of the same laws, and this may mean that the laws had had little effect or were not widely enforced. As is always the case in using laws as historical sources, one must place them within the framework of what is known from other sources. They must be set against the backdrop of the archaeological and literary evidence.

Constantine's legislation on the Jews must be seen not only in light of what his predecessors did, but also in light of the legislation of his successors. The laws of Constantius, Constantine's successor, reiterate Constantine's legislation on the conversion of slaves owned by Jews (*CT* 16.9.2), forbid the marriage of Christian women to Jews (*CT* 16.8.6), and reaffirm protection of converts from Judaism to Christianity (*CT* 16.8.1). It is noteworthy, however, that all legislation on the Jews by the emperor Constantius comes within two years after Constantine's death, and the law codes record almost no legislation on the Jews until the end of the century, a period of over forty years.

The absence of legislation during the years from 340 to 380 suggests that Constantine's impact on the status of the Jews was less profound than is usually supposed. Even if there was a conscious effort under Constantine to restrict Jewish activity and to protect Christians from Jewish proselytization, that policy was not carried through in the years after his death. Indeed, one has the distinct impression that a great gulf lies between the time of Constantine and the age of Theodosius I. Eventually the Roman world would become a Christian society, and the Jews would be made into second-class citizens, but it is a long way from the time of Constantine to that day. Constantine was not the architect of Christian Europe.

Legislation from the time of Theodosius, a thoroughly orthodox emperor, who came to power in 379 C.E., exhibits genuine respect for the Jews and their traditions. The abusive language that appeared in some of Constantine's laws is absent. No doubt the intervention of Julian's reign had made an impact. In one of his letters, Julian says that he has restored the rights taken away from the Jews (*Ep.* 204[51] Bidez). But we have no record of Julian's actual legislation. Whatever the situation under Julian, however, Theodosius affirmed and protected Jewish rights under the law, and insisted that the Jews, like other citizens of the empire, had obligations as well as rights. In a case when Jewish leaders complained that local officials had interfered in internal matters of the Jewish community, Theodosius defended against his own governors the Jews "who, by the decision of their Most Noble and Illustrious Patriarchs, manifestly have the right to pronounce sentence concerning their own religion" (*CT* 16.8.8). In another, quite different case, involving a group of Jews who had been exempted from the obligation to transport grain to the capital (i.e., to serve as *naviculari*), he reaffirmed the right of these Jews (and Samaritans) as "not lawfully summoned to the compulsory public service of shipmasters" (*CT* 13.5.18).

In 393, in a rescript to the count of the east, Theodosius ruled that the "sect of the Jews is forbidden by no law." From the explanation accompanying the law, the rescript was prompted by the efforts of some Christians in the east to "destroy and to despoil the synagogues" (*CT* 16.8.9). This rescript is particularly interesting and significant because it was issued after the famous incident of the synagogue at Callinicum, a military station on the Euphrates on the eastern border of the Roman Empire.

In the summer of 388, some Christians in Callinicum set fire to a Jewish synagogue and destroyed a gnostic chapel. When Theodosius heard of the incident, he sent orders that the synagogue be rebuilt by the Christian bishop of the town and the monks punished. When Ambrose, the powerful bishop of Milan, heard of the matter, he immediately sent a letter to Theodoius (*Ep.* 40) in which he asserted that a Christian bishop should not rebuild a synagogue and requested an interview with the emperor. Theodosius refused to see him, but he did, however, decide to rescind his order. Later, when Theodosius was in church, Ambrose challenged him on the matter, refusing to continue with the celebration of the Eucharist until the emperor had promised to rescind the order. Since Theodosius had apparently already done this, a clash between emperor and bishop was averted.

This incident is sometimes taken as evidence of the changing status of the Jews in the fourth century, but its importance lies less in what it tells us about the status of the Jews, than in what it says to us about Ambrose and his conception of episcopal authority. What is significant is that five years later, while Ambrose was still bishop, Theodosius issued the rescript cited above, which not only affirmed the right of Jews to assemble and to own synagogues, and reiterated that the practice of Judaism was not forbidden by any law, but also prescribed punishments for those who despoiled Jewish synagogues. "The logic of his [Theodosius's] thought was not applied to the Jews, despite the pressure Ambrose brought to bear on him" (King, 1960, p. 50).

Another incident from the same period can perhaps be cited to illustrate what was the more typical situation of Jews. As I mentioned earlier in this chapter, Libanius had dealings with a group of Jewish peasants who had worked his family's land for four generations. These peasants were poor Jews, tenants of the most restricted sort, not serfs, but people who were very much dependent on the landowner. In an effort to change the conditions of their relationship to the landowner and, according to Libanius, "to dictate the terms by which we were to employ them," they turned to the military officer in the area as a powerful person who could take their side against the landowner. With the help of this patron, the Jews forced Libanius to take the matter to court, where he lost, even though on the face of it, his case appears to have been strong. This incident is significant for what it tells us about the Jews in the fourth century. Libanius had to file suit against his own workers, even though he was wealthy, influential, well connected, and a friend and correspondent of the most powerful men in the empire, including the emperor. It is clear that the Jews were protected, like other citizens, by Roman law; at no point in the dispute does Libanius hint that the Jews are to be treated any differently from others because they are Jews (Libanius *Or.* 47.13–17).

Even after Theodosius's death in 396 C.E., the traditional Sabbath privileges of Jews were affirmed: "On the Sabbath day and on all other days at the time when the Jews observe the reverence of their own cult, we command that no one of them shall be compelled to do anything or be sued in any way, since it appears that other days can suffice for fiscal advantages and for private litigation" (*CT* 2.8.26). The privileges of Jewish clergy were continued (*CT* 16.8.13), and people who harmed Jews were liable to punishment (*CT* 16.8.12).

Looking back on the fourth century from the perspective of the Middle Ages, it seems that the status of the Jews in the empire was changing rapidly during this period, but, if so, these changes were probably not perceptible to the people living at that time. The laws do not follow a consistent pattern; they are designed to respond to specific situations and problems, one sometimes contradicting another. Further, the significance of the legislation is not always clear. Some laws, e.g., on proselytizing, can be seen, on the one hand, as evidence of Christian efforts to restrict the Jews; on the other hand, that the same laws are repeated over the course of seventy or eighty years can be seen as evidence that Jews continued to seek and to win converts to their religion. The laws come in the form of rescripts directed at particular imperial officials in specific localities. It is doubtful whether a rescript sent to Cologne in the far west of the empire was enforced in the cities of the east.

What appears to have been happening in this period is that, while monks and some lay Christians were becoming hostile to the Jews, no doubt because of the strength of Jewish communities in their cities and the success Judaism had as a rival to Christianity, the imperial authorities continued to affirm Jewish rights and to issue laws protecting them. Cases of open hostility between Jews and Christians must be seen as the exception, not the rule. In some cases, citizens realized how important Jews were in the life and economy of the cities. In a city in southern Italy, for example, the residents petitioned the emperor to rescind the exemptions from public financial obligations (liturgies) enjoyed by certain Jews, not because the city wished to penalize the Jews, but because without Jewish support the city would slide into financial ruin (*CT* 12.1.158).

In recent excavations at Khirbet Shema', a village in Upper Galilee approximately ten miles west of Safed and close to Meiron, the excavating team discovered that the greatest prosperity and the most extensive economic relations between the small community and the larger cities on the coast, such as Tyre, as well as Antioch (where many coins were minted), occurred in the fourth century C.E. The number of coins gradually increased to a high point in the fourth century and remained high until the site was devastated by an earthquake in the early fifth century (Meyers, Kraabel, and Strange, pp. 167–79). In the conclusion to their report, the excavators observe that their findings point to a revision of the standard accounts of post-Constantinian Jewry. "The great flowering of Jewish material culture in this same period— usually thought to be a time of stress and growing tension between Jews and Christians—seems to suggest that the restrictive legislation against Jews had a far more limited impact than was thought heretofore" (Meyers, Kraabel, and Strange, p. 269). It is possible that the Jewish towns and villages were part of a general economic revival. If so, this in itself is significant, for it shows that the Jews were not excluded from the larger society. They benefited from the prosperity of all.

Antiochene Jewry in the Fourth Century

Let us now return to the Jewish community in Antioch during the years when John Chrysostom was growing up in the city and entering upon his career as a presbyter. As we have seen, our knowledge of Antiochene Jewry from the second century to the latter part of the fourth century, though meager, does correspond with the picture we have from other cities. According to Malalas, the chronicler of Antiochene history, Antioch had a Jewish magistrate in the late second century (*Chronographia*, p. 290). As a member council, this magistrate would have come from the upper classes and would have received a traditional Greek education. We also know of a wealthy Jewish woman from this period, Cornelia Salvia, whose will, designating a bequest to the Jewish community in Antioch, was brought before the emperor Antoninus (Caracalla) for adjudication (*Codex Juris Civilis* 1:9.1). The date was 213 C.E., one year after citizenship had been conferred on all the inhabitants of the empire. The matter was brought before Roman authorities because, with the change in citizenship, Roman requirements concerning the making of wills had to be met. No doubt the reason the legal status of the will was taken up was due to the size of the bequest.

Such sparse evidence would hardly be worth mentioning were it not for the information we have from the later fourth century. In 391 C.E., the Jews of Apamea, a Greek-speaking city in Syria on the Orontes River fifty miles from Antioch, constructed a new synagogue. This in itself is significant. It shows that ten years after the empire became officially Christian, the Jews had enough confidence in their status, and in the future, to make such an investment. Another sign of the importance of Apamean Jewry is that the bishop in the later fourth century, Polychronius, the brother of Theodore, bishop of Mopsuestia in neighboring Cilicia, responded to Jewish interpreters in his biblical commentaries, all of which he wrote on books from the Old Testament. He may also have known some Hebrew (Bardenhewer, pp. 41–43).

The Jewish community in Apamea had close ties with the Jews of Antioch. Large sections of the mosaic floor of the Apamean synagogue were contributed by wealthy Antiochene Jews. From formulas set in the floor, written in Greek in the same style as dedicatory formulas in Christian churches built in the same period, we learn the names of the Antiochene Jews who donated the floors: "At the time of the most honored archisynagogoi Eusebius and Nemios and Phineos, and Theodoros the gerousiarch and the most honored presbyters Eisakios and Saulos and the rest, Ilasios, archisynagogos of the Antiochians, donated the mosaic entryway, 150 feet, in the year 703, the seventh of Aydynaios [January 7, 391]. Blessing on all." A second inscription mentions other members of the same family. "Ilasios son of Eisakios, archisynagogos of the Antiochians, for the well-being of Photion his wife and his children, and for the well-being of Eustathia his mother-in-law, and in memory of Eisakios and Edesios and Hesychios his ancestors, donated the mosaic entryway. Peace and mercy on all your holy people."[6]

The Ilasios mentioned in the inscription as archisynagogos of the Antiochians was the grandson of Edesios, about whom we have further information. By a happy coincidence, another series of inscriptions, not from Syria, but from Palestine, mentions this same family. In the famous burial ground of Beth She'arim in Galilee, for a time the seat of the Sanhedrin, there are tombs that can be identified with particular families or locales. Jews from other parts of Palestine, as well as from communities in the diaspora, bought spaces at Beth She'arim. The possession of tombs at Beth She'arim by Jews from the diaspora

6. Text and translation of the inscriptions on Meeks and Wilken, 1978, pp. 53–55. For a similar inscription in a Christian church from the same period, see Meeks and Wilken, p. 56.

ensured that they would be buried in the land of Israel. From the inscriptions found in the caves, some in Hebrew, but most in Greek, as well as from the iconography, we get yet another picture of the mixture of Jewish tradition and Greco-Roman culture. The iconography in the tombs combines Jewish symbols, such as the Menorah, Ethrog, and Lulab, with animal figures, birds drinking from bowls, human heads, and explicitly pagan symbols. As puzzling as this combination may appear to one schooled in rabbinic tradition, it was commonplace among Jews of this period. Indeed, one reason why the two sets of symbols stand side by side is that the coffins were purchased from non-Jewish craftsmen and Jewish symbols were added later (Urbach 1959, pp. 149–65).

One of the rooms at Beth She'arim, comprising six tombs, was owned by the family of Edesios. "Apse of Edesios, head of the council of elders of Antioch," reads one inscription in Beth She'arim (Meeks and Wilken 1978, p. 55). Other inscriptions mention the names of family members buried there. Moreover, other Jews from Antioch also arranged that members of their families be buried in the land of Israel. An inscription found at Tiberias, the famous city on the sea of Galilee, a center of Talmudic learning, and seat of the patriarchate for a time during this period, mentions another Antiochene Jewish family. Though the inscription is very fragmentary, the name "Antiochians" and parts of the names of family members can be made out. Moise Schwabe, a specialist in Jewish epigraphy, has shown that the inscription dates from the late third or early fourth century and commemorates a woman named Leontine, who was buried in Tiberias and had been married to Thaumasios, an *archisynagogos* from Antioch (Schwabe 1949). Her father, Samuel, had been gerousiarch (head of the council of elders), in Antioch. Like those in the apse of Edesios, this inscription too was written in Greek.

These inscriptions give us a glimpse of the life of the Antiochene Jewish community in the fourth century. Among its members were a number of wealthy families who had close ties with Jews living in the neighboring city of Apamea. The families also cherished their ties to the land of Israel, exemplified by the desire to be buried there. Their language was Greek, as, no doubt, was the language of the Jews living in Antioch. In Greek-speaking cities, even in Palestine, the Jews prayed in Greek (*p. Sotah* 7.1; 21b) and used Greek as the language of instruction. Many rabbis had extensive knowledge of Greek (Levine, p. 197; Fischel, pp. 885–87). Certainly they also saw to it that their sons were educated in Greek schools, as did Christians and pagans from the same social background. The Jews who have left us these inscriptions were immersed in the society and culture in which they lived.

Just how thoroughly at home some Jews were in the Hellenic culture of the later Roman Empire can be seen in a series of letters preserved in the correspondence of Libanius. Between 388 and 393, Libanius carried on an extensive correspondence with the Jewish patriarch, most likely Gamaliel VI, and eight of these letters are still extant.[7] They not only show that the patriarch was on intimate terms with one of the most famous teachers of rhetoric at the time, but that they shared a similar rhetorical education and love for the Greek classics. Like educated Greeks and Christians, the patriarch fretted about his son's education and career. In contrast to Libanius's oration *On Patronage*, which deals with Jewish tenant farmers, Libanius's social inferiors, these letters were written to his social equal, a man who belonged to the same class and shared the same education and many of the same values.

Among these letters is a charming epistle to the patriarch concerning his son, who had been a student of rhetoric under a man named Argeus, a student of Libanius's. After finishing his studies with Argeus, the patriarch's son was supposed to go to Antioch to study with Libanius. The young man lost interest in books, however, and set out on his own to see the world. When the patriarch learned that his son had not arrived in Antioch as expected, he wrote Libanius. We have Libanius's reply to the patriarch. "Your son," he writes, "came with ability to learn; indeed through the rhetorical power of Argeus, he had something in common with me even before he saw me." Libanius then tells the patriarch that it might "be profitable for him [the son] to see many cities—as it was for Odysseus" and asks the angry father to be tolerant of his son's disobedience: "I entreat you to forgive his flight and not to treat him harshly or to make him despair" (*Ep.* 1098).[8]

The young man was in his late teens, away from home for the first time, fascinated by the world he had discovered. Under Argeus he had been closely supervised, but now that he was old enough to travel alone to Antioch, he took the opportunity to enjoy the cities through which he passed. Libanius, as an acquaintance of the patriarch's, tells the boy's father that the young man will no doubt return to his studies, and to make his point he alludes to the story of Odysseus, assuming that the allusion would be familiar to a man who knew the Greek classics. The letter reveals cordial relations between Libanius and the

7. Text of the letters in Foerster; text and Hebrew translation in Schwabe; English translation in Meeks and Wilken, 1978. Text with English translation and extensive notes most recently in Stern, 1980, pp. 580–99.

8. The identity of the addressee of this letter is problematic. The previous letter is addressed "to the patriarchs" and this letter is addressed "to the same" [singular]. See Stern, 1980, p. 596.

patriarch and a common familiarity with the classical rhetorical education.

In other letters to the Jewish patriarch, Libanius makes allusions to figures from Greek legend. In a letter about Hilary, a proconsul in Palestine, Libanius entreats the patriarch, who had apparently criticized something Hilary had done, to use his influence to restore Hilary to good standing. To make his point, he alludes to the story of Achilles and Telephus: "Since he [Hilary] was destined to fall into this situation by ill fortune which compelled an intelligent man to sin—for a man like you, who avoids treating people badly but is accustomed rather to doing good, would not have publicly accused him without cause—become then, Achilles to his Telephus and by your kindness heal the results of anger" (*Ep.* 1105). Telephus was king of Mysia, an island where the army of Achilles inadvertently landed on the way to Troy. Achilles wounded Telephus with his spear and the wound would not heal. When he sought advice from an oracle, he was told that the one who caused the wound should also heal it. When Telephus told Achilles what the oracle had said, Odysseus explained that the spear that had caused the wound would become the instrument for healing it. The scrapings from the spear were thereupon applied to the wound and Telephus was healed. In his letter to the patriarch, Libanius assumed that he need only mention Telephus and Achilles for the patriarch to understand the allusion without further explanation. In another letter, he simply mentions the "son of Lysimachus," and he knew that the patriarch would understand he meant Aristeides, though he does not mention the ancient Athenian statesman by name. All of this is conventional among the rhetors of the fourth century, and it illustrates that educated Jews shared fully in the conventions of fourth-century society.

Men educated in the traditional rhetorical schools took great pride in their letters, choosing vocabulary, literary allusions, and stylistic ornaments with great care. Letters were read and reread, passed on to friends and associates, treasured not for content but for style. Libanius addresses the patriarch as one who belongs to this cultured world. If you respond to my request, he writes, "my profit will be your letter." I shall gain two things, says Libanius: a letter that can be enjoyed as literature and the fulfillment of my request (*Ep.* 1084).

Not only do the letters of Libanius to the Jewish patriarch show that the latter inhabited the same social world and was educated in the same way as any other hellenized intellectual (Schwabe 1930b, p. 108), but they also tell us that the patriarch was an influential man who was also respected and revered by non-Jews. The letters of Libanius to the patriarch are not simply cordial, they are deferential (Schwabe 1930b,

p. 88). We also know from other sources that the patriarch was an influential figure. Jerome says that Gamaliel was able to influence Theodosius to condemn a certain Hesychius to death because he was caught stealing papers from the imperial archives (*Ep.* 57.3). In imperial rescripts, the patriarchs were given the honorific title *vir clarissimus et illustris* (*CT* 16.8.8), terms used for persons with the rank of praetorian prefect. In one letter, Libanius speaks of the power of the patriarch as similar to that of the provincial governor: "Next to Fortune, it is you and the governor who have this in your power; you do especially, more than someone who has the responsibility of governing" (*Ep.* 974).

The letters of Libanius to the Jewish patriarch thus confirm the impression gained from archaeological sources—namely, that in the fourth century a significant segment of the Jewish community in the east was well educated, wealthy, influential, and at home in the culture and society of the later Roman Empire. From laws in the Theodosian code, we know there were "Jews instructed in liberal studies" who acted as "advocates" (*CT* 16.8.24) and who served on city councils because of the "prerogative of birth and splendor of family." Like other wealthy citizens, Jews contributed to the upkeep of the cities (*CT* 12.1.157–58) and they owned slaves (*CT* 3.1.5).

Among Libanius's letters there is another written almost a generation earlier than the letters to the patriarch, prompted by a disturbance within the Jewish community in Antioch concerning leadership. Libanius had been asked to intervene in the dispute:

> Some disturbance has arisen among the Jews who live among us because [of a rumor that] a certain wicked old man is going to come into office, whom they had expelled when he held it previously, because he had made the office into a tyranny. They are of the opinion that the chief of their officials will order this done [again] at your behest. For [they think] that you accepted the old man's petition without knowing his character, which not even age has been able to amend. Those who are agitated believe the matter to be as stated, and, while they were unable to convince me of it, they did succeed in compelling me to write. Please forgive both me and them—me for having yielded to so many, them because they suffered what is common to crowds, to be easily satisfied. [*Ep.* 1251]

The addressee of the letter is unnamed. It could have been Priscianus, a long-time friend of Libanius's, who had recently become proconsul of Palestine, or a certain Callistio, who was assessor for the praetorian prefect Salustius (Seeck, p. 103). Whoever the recipient was, he knew the Jewish community well and was on intimate enough terms with the leaders of the community to intervene in their affairs. The specific point at issue concerned membership on the council of elders, headed by the gerousiarch. In the cities of the east, the Jewish community was governed by a council composed of representatives from the various synagogues of the city and headed by the gerousiarch. Edesios, for example, the man mentioned in the Beth She'arim inscriptions, was gerousiarch of the Antiochene Jews.

The old man mentioned in the letter had once been a member of the council of elders, but due to abuses under his administration he had been deposed. Now he was attempting to regain his position, and some of the members of the community were trying to prevent him from doing so. In an effort to advance his cause, he appealed to a non-Jew who knew the situation well and who could put pressure on the gerousiarch. At this point Libanius was asked by some of the Jewish leaders to write his friend, the recipient of the letter, because they had heard that Libanius's friend had used his influence to assist the old man.[9]

It is possible that the old man was friendly with one of Libanius's friends, but it is also possible that they did not know each other and that Libanius's friend had been approached through the normal circle of contacts available to men of the upper classes. He knew someone who knew someone. That the old man was successful in his attempt to get the attention of an important official shows that he moved easily among influential and powerful men. What is equally interesting is that the petition assumed that Libanius's friend was capable of exerting influence on the internal affairs of the Jewish community, not because he was a Jew, but because the leaders of the community were acquaintances, men of the same class and background. The old man, then, was simply following the long-accepted practice of the powerful, using social and political influence to attain one's ends. Libanius wrote letters for dozens of people to advance their careers, to help them out of difficult situations, to recommend their children or relatives for jobs. Here he was asked to use his friendship with another influential man to prevent a Jew from gaining a position on the Jewish council. The correspondence illustrates the informal relations of power and in-

9. Schwabe, 1930b, argues that the "old man" or "elder" was a delegate of the patriarch in Tiberias, but it seems unlikely, as Gedalia Alon has argued, that the patriarch in Palestine could exercise such authority over the internal affairs of a Jewish community in the diaspora (Alon 1970, 2:315–16). Stern, however, in his recent edition of the letters of Libanius, revives the discussion and provides new arguments in favor of Schwabe's view (Stern 1980, p. 599). However one decides the issue, the letter nevertheless gives further evidence of the close ties between Jewish leaders and the educated upper classes of the Roman world.

fluence existing in fourth-century Antioch, a series of relations in which the Jews were as much a part as Christians or pagans. It is not a matter of the weak appealing to the powerful, but of men of equal status using friends and acquaintances to wield influence and power.

Not all Jews in Antioch were as well placed as the friends of Libanius. The Jews who worked Libanius's land were poor, landless, bereft of influence and power, and dependent on the patronage of soldiers and governors. John mentions Jewish shopkeepers (*Hom. in Rom.* 12:20.3; 51.176) who, like their pagan and Christian counterparts, would have been subject to the trader's tax and to the harsher legal penalties faced by members of the lower classes. Elsewhere in Syria, inscriptions mention other Jews from this class: goldsmiths, perfume makers, manufacturers, and traders in silk (Applebaum 1976, p. 714), but our information about this class of Jews is meager. This hardly means that the majority of the Jews in Antioch were wealthy and highly educated, but that the lower classes, who seldom wrote, left fewer clues as to their activities.

If we use a city such as Caesarea in Palestine as an analogy, we can gain a fuller picture of the diversity of the Jewish community in Antioch. Caesarea, like Antioch, was a large Hellenistic city with a sizeable Jewish community. Even though it was located in Palestine, there are enough similarities to Antioch to make comparisons. In Caesarea the Jews used Greek as the language of instruction and worship, as they no doubt did in Antioch. In Caesarea Jews served on the city council, some had close ties with the provincial governor, and one held a position in the municipal waterworks (Levine, p. 70). But we also know that Jews in Caesarea were bakers, bathhouse attendants, workers in metal, and weavers. Some even worked in the theaters and participated in athletic events. Some Jews were so poor they had to do without light on the Sabbath because they could not buy oil. Rabbi Abbahu is said on one occasion to have paid the debts of a poor Jew lest he hire himself out as a gladiator. Some Jews were forced to eat carob and others were derided for their poverty (Levine, p. 69).

If the wealthy and well-educated Jews were active participants in the Hellenistic high culture of late Roman society, the lower-class Jews participated fully in other aspects of the city's life, sometimes drawing their livelihood from the theater, the races, the baths. Rabbi Abbahu once asked a poor Jew in Caesarea: "What is your occupation?" To which the man responded, speaking of himself in the third person: "This man commits five sins every day; he adorns the theater, engages the hetaerae [whores], brings their clothes to the bath-house, claps hands and dances before them, and clashes the cymbals before them" (*p. Ta'anith* 1.4, 64b; Lieberman, 1942, p. 31). Here and there in the

Palestinian Talmud, and in inscriptions from Beth-She'arim, there are references to Jews who made their living as gold or silversmiths, a trade that they learned from gentiles and, more often than not, was used to adorn objects with pagan symbols. Some rabbis said, "None may make ornaments for an idol, necklaces or earrings or finger-rings." But R. Eliezer says, "If for payment it is permitted" (M. Abodah Zarah 1.8). One Jewish craftsman was challenged because he made idols. "What use is this to you? It cannot see or hear, eat or drink, do good or harm, nor can it speak. . . . Why, then, do you make such things?" He said, "It is my livelihood" (p. Berakoth 9.2, 12d; Urbach 1959, p. 158).

Neither the Jewish community in Caesarea nor that in Antioch was unique. As we have seen, there were strong Jewish communities in many cities in the east, particularly in the vicinity of Antioch. We have already mentioned Apamea, but one should also include other cities such as Ihmestar (Socrates Hist. eccl. 7.16), Aleppo (Sauvaget, pp. 60–61), Emessa, and Cyrus, where Theodoret the bishop responded to Jewish objections in his biblical commentaries (McCollough). There one would have found Jewish communities as diverse and as much immersed in the life of the cities in which they lived as the Jews of Antioch. The Jews who inhabited the cities of the later Roman Empire were no less assimilated to their culture than Jews had been before the war with the Romans in the first century or before the Bar Kochba revolt in the second century.

In a recent essay on the Jews and Hellenistic culture, Professor Ephraim Urbach of the Hebrew University in Jerusalem argues that the old generalizations about Judaism becoming ossified, preoccupied only with internal problems and a narrow interpretation of the Torah, simply do not fit the evidence we now have at our disposal. There is little evidence that Judaism entered on a period of isolation or that it set up "hedges" to protect Jews from the inroads of the larger culture. The Jews continued to be as much a part of the social and cultural world of late antiquity as they had been prior to the loss of the temple and the city of Jerusalem. Indeed, Urbach goes on to say that most Jewish leaders, even with particularistic views about Jewish identity, did not oppose proselytism, but welcomed it (Urbach 1981).

The openness of Jews to the society in which they lived did not mean that Jews were absorbed by the larger culture. Jews who were receptive to Greco-Roman culture did not cease being Jews. One sign of the identity of the Jews of Antioch was the desire to be buried in the land of their fathers. For a fourth-century Jew living in Antioch this desire was an act of piety, for his ancestors had been living in Antioch for centuries. Their home was Antioch, yet they wished to be buried in

Eretz Israel. Being buried in Israel was considered an act of atonement (Meyers, pp. 73–94). "As soon as they are buried in the land of Israel or even a handful of soil of the land of Israel is placed on them it will make expiation for them as it is said, 'And his land shall make expiation for his people'" (*Pesikta Rabbati* 1.6). Furthermore, as we saw earlier, the Jews of Antioch also looked for a restoration of the temple and a return of Jews to Jerusalem (Chrysostom *Jud.* 7.1; 48.916).

In various ways, Jews in Antioch and Syria maintained close ties to the land of Israel. John mentions that Jews in Antioch sent money to the patriarch in Palestine (Chrysostom *Jud. et gent.* 16; 48.835), and from other sources we know that the patriarch sent messengers to cities in the diaspora to collect money to be brought to Israel (Juster, 1:388). On occasion rabbis also came to Antioch to adjudicate legal questions on difficult cases. In the third century, Rabbi Simlai is reported to have rendered a decision concerning a *mamzer* (a child of a prohibited union) in Antioch (*b. Kiddushin* 69a). This may have been an exceptional case because it seems that the Jews of Antioch had their own Jewish tribunal (*p. Sanhed.* 3.2, 21a).

On occasion Palestinian rabbis came to Antioch to engage in exegetical disputes. According to an account in *Genesis Rabbah* (19.4), Tanhuma bar Abba, who flourished in the latter part of the fourth century, had a dispute in Antioch about the verse in Genesis 3:5 "For God knows that when you eat of it your eyes will be opened, and you will be like God, knowing good and evil." The dispute centered on the word "knowing," which in Hebrew is plural. Tanhuma's opponents argued that the subject of the verb "know" in this verse is "God." In Hebrew the term for God, *Elohim*, is plural. Since Christians frequently defended the doctrine of the Trinity on the basis of an appeal to the plural Hebrew form of God (Chrysostom *Jud.* 7.3; 48.919), it is likely that the dispute was with Christians. The Palestinian Talmud (*p. Berakoth* 9.1, 12d) mentions a similar dispute over the plural name for God.[10]

The Jews of Antioch celebrated the major Jewish festivals and observed the Sabbath (*Hom. in Rom.* 12:20; 51.176). In the fall they celebrated Yom Kippur and Rosh Hashannah as well as Sukkoth (Chrysostom *Jud.* 1.1; 48.844). In the spring they celebrated Passover (*Jud.* 3.2; 48.864). In one of his sermons preached in the fall, John mentions that the Jews were at present building the *sukkoth*, the little huts without roofs in which the Jewish males eat during the week of the festival (*Jud.* 7.1; 48.915). The Jews practiced circumcision (*Jud.* 2.1; 858) and kept some of the food laws (*Jud.* 6.3; 907). How strictly

10. On disputes over the plural name for God, see Segal, pp. 121–34, 220–33.

other laws were observed, we cannot say, but the existence of a rabbinical court in the city, and the mention of a dispute concerning a *mamzer* would suggest that other halakic regulations were observed of which we have no information.

John mentions that the Jews of Antioch practiced ritual bathing. He even admits that the Jewish ritual baths are "more solemn than . . . [ordinary] baths," though he is quick to add that such baths are inferior to Christian baptism (*Catech. ad Illum* 1.2; 49.225–26). This mention of Jewish ritual baths is significant, for it occurs in a series of baptismal homilies delivered to men and women who were about to be baptized. No doubt they wondered whether Christian baptism was as efficacious as were Jewish baths. The matter troubled John, since he mentions Jewish baths several times in other homilies. A generation later, Theodoret of Cyrus, a native of Antioch, indicates that the Jews of his time continued to practice ritual bathing (*Comm. in Heb.* 6:4; *PG* 82.717). The Jews also wore scriptural texts sewn into their clothing (Chrysostom *Hom.* 53.3 *in Jo.* 8:20; 59, 296). John is probably referring to phylacteries, the black leather boxes containing scriptural passages, bound to the head for morning prayer. He could, however, have had in mind amulets with scriptural texts, the carrying of which was a practice common among Jews and Christians of the time. Elsewhere he mentions phylacteries (*Hom. in Matt.* 72:2; 58, 669). He also says that Jews had the custom of dancing on the Day of Atonement (Chrysostom *Jud.* 1.2; 846), a custom attested in the Mishnah (*M. Ta'anith* 4.8).

By the end of the fourth century, Jews had been living in Antioch for over six hundred years, sharing the city's good fortunes, suffering through its wars, its earthquakes, its economic woes. Yet, while sharing in the city's culture and its way of life, the Jews stood apart. They belonged to an ancient and venerable people whose customs were an object of curiosity and whose way of life was a source of wonder and admiration. Libanius speaks of them with respect, and John says that many people "have a high regard for the Jews and think that their present way of life is holy" (*Jud* 1.3; 847). It was this community of Jews that attracted the Christians of Antioch.

· III ·

The Attraction of Judaism

During the many centuries Jews lived in Antioch, they cultivated cordial, often intimate, relations with their neighbors and with the larger society. Yet they did not lose their distinctive identity as Jews. They celebrated the major Jewish festivals, observed the Sabbath, read and studied the Jewish Scriptures, and maintained close ties with Jews in neighboring cities and in the land of Israel. John Chrysostom, a hostile critic, acknowledged, albeit reluctantly, that the fervor of Jewish piety discredited the Christians:

> You Christians should be ashamed and embarrassed at the Jews who observe the Sabbath with such devotion and refrain from all commerce beginning with the evening of the Sabbath. When they see the sun hurrying to set in the west on Friday they call a halt to their business affairs and interrupt their selling. If a customer haggles with them over a purchase in the late afternoon, and offers a price after evening has come, the Jews refuse the offer because they are unwilling to accept any money. [*Hom. in Rom.* 12:20.3; 51.176][1]

1. The Migne editors (*PG* 51.174–75) place this homily, *Si esurierit inimicus tuus, ciba illum*, in Constantinople, but there is nothing in the text to support this view. The

Jewish customs and Jewish religious rites had a powerful impact on Christians living close by, even when they caused inconvenience. By awakening curiosity, by bearing witness to another way of life drawn from the same ancient tradition, Judaism attracted Christians, some to the point where they actually joined with the Jews to celebrate Jewish festivals and adopted Jewish customs. In the early fall and again in spring (prior to Passover), when Jews bought and prepared special foods, decorated their homes and synagogues, constructed *sukkoth*, the tiny huts for prayers during the festival of Sukkoth (Chrysostom *Jud.* 7.1; 915), closed their shops at unexpected times, and on some occasions danced in the public squares of the city (*Jud.* 1.2; 846), some Christians (John says "many") forsook the cheerless moralizing of Christian preachers to go to the synagogue or the homes of the Jews to celebrate Rosh Hashannah or Passover.

Accordingly, with the approach of the Jewish festivals, Christian leaders became restive. In the fall of 386, John, already put on the defensive by the taunts of the Arians, now saw the precarious unity of his followers threatened by the allure of Jewish rites. "Many who belong to us and say that they believe in our teaching, attend their festivals, and even share in their celebrations and join in their fasts" (*Jud.* 1.1; 844). A year later he makes the same lament. Some of "our members who consider themselves yoked to us participate in their religious rites" (*Jud.* 4.3; 875). Unlike the Arians, who had their own presbyters and bishops, and who formed a distinct group among the Christians (John called them "outsiders" [*Jud.* 1.1; 844]) the judaizing Christians were "our brothers" (Chrysostom *Incomprehens.* 2.1; 48.709), refractory members of the Christian group to which John belonged.

John's sermons, usually entitled *Against the Jews*, were preached against these Judaizers, not against the Jews,[2] and were prompted by the specific circumstances in Antioch prior to the celebration of Jewish festivals. All the homilies except for one, Homily 3 on Passover, were preached in the fall, when, as John notes in the first sermon, the Jewish festivals "follow one after another in succession" (*Jud.* 1.1; 844).[3]

---

references to people staying away from church (PG 51.171–72), to the heat, to the agora, to the large church (174–76) fit Antioch as well as Constantinople. Further, the references to the Jews, and the use of the term *akairos* with respect to Jewish observance of the law (176) are more characteristic of John's Antiochene period. On *akairos* and John's homilies on the Judaizers, see Malkowski.

2. The recent English translation by Paul Harkins, 1977, entitles the homilies "Discourses Against Judaizing Christians." See also Ritter, pp. 78–80; Simon, 1936.

3. Homilies 1 and 2 were preached in early fall 386; Homily 3 in winter 387 (before the beginning of the forty-day fast leading to Easter); homilies 4–8 in fall 387. For dis-

John's visceral response to judaizing Christianity in Antioch can, however, be fully appreciated only if we place the situation there in a larger context. Judaizing Christians were not simply a local phenomenon. They were to be found in other cities in the east, and their numbers and influence seem to have been increasing at the end of the fourth century. Furthermore, judaizing Christians had existed from the beginning of Christianity, and in spite of four centuries of opposition by Christian leaders, they continued to be a visible presence in the Church (Simon 1964, pp. 356–93). Judaizing Christians disquieted other Christians, for by observing Jewish law and claiming that Christianity had an abiding relation to Judaism, they threatened the claims of orthodox Christianity. "If you admire the Jewish way of life, what do you have in common with us? If the Jewish rites are holy and venerable," says John, "our way of life must be false" (*Jud.* 1.6; 852).

Jewish Christians and Judaizing Christians

Christianity, which emerged as a religious movement distinct from Judaism at an early date, never completely severed its ties with the religion that had given it birth. Even after the emergent Church had created its own literature and sacred book, the apostolic writings, Christians continued to read and appeal to the Jewish Scriptures. When the Christian canon of Scripture was codified, it included both the writings of the evangelists and apostles and those of Moses and the prophets. In the second century, Justin Martyr claimed to have been converted to Christianity by reading the Hebrew prophets (*Dial.* 7). The Jewish Scriptures continued to be read in Christian worship, and during the patristic period as many (if not more) Christian commentaries were written on the Jewish Scriptures (the Old Testament) as were written on the distinctively Christian writings, the New Testament. Christians studied the history of ancient Israel, told and retold the stories of its holy men and women, set the lives of patriarchs and prophets before the eyes of fellow Christians as models to emulate, and sought within the Jewish Scriptures signs pointing to Jesus as the

---

cussion of the chronology, see Schwartz; Rauschen; and Harkins, 1977, pp. 1–lix. Homily 3, "Against Those Who Keep the First Paschal Fast," is unique in that it is directed at Christians who celebrate a Christian festival, Easter, on the date of the Jewish Passover, rather than Christians who observe Jewish festivals. However, this practice is another form of Judaizing, and it is likely that the same people who celebrated Jewish festivals in the fall celebrated Easter on 14 Nisan in the spring. For this reason, Homily 3 should be considered along with the other homilies on the Judaizers (Ritter, p. 79, n. 34).

Christ. Christian clergy and monks learned the Psalms by heart, and in Christian worship the Psalms became the Christian prayer book par excellence. Wherever Christians established churches, they carried with them the books of ancient Israel.

For many, indeed most, Christians, however, the Jewish tradition they espoused had become so thoroughly Christianized that it bore little resemblance to what Jews practiced and believed. Although Christians used the books of the Jews, worshipped the one god of Abraham, Isaac, and Jacob, repudiated the gods of the pagans, and were perceived by outsiders, especially in the early centuries, as belonging to the same "school"[4] Christians and Jews viewed each other as rivals, not allies, preferring to assail each other than to mount a common front against the gods of the Greeks and Romans. The social axiom that the closer the relation, the more intense the conflict (Simmel, p. 67) was never more true than in the enmity between Jews and Christians in antiquity. This hostility emerges early, especially where Jews and Christians were in close contact, as, for example, in the city of Sardis, where the Jews owned a large synagogue and where the nucleus of the Christian community was probably drawn from Jewish converts to Christianity (Wilken 1976). To a third party the similarities between Jews and Christians were often more striking than their differences, but to the Jews and Christians themselves the affinities were chimerical and superficial.

Nevertheless, this attitude of mutual hostility between Jews and Christians, which can be documented in Christian (Simon 1964, pp. 166–213) as well as Jewish sources (Segal, pp. 84–155) throughout the Roman period, was not shared by all. From the very beginning of Christianity and throughout its first five centuries, there were always to be found Christians who believed that adherence to Christianity did not mean the repudiation of Jewish ways, and Jews who thought that belief in Jesus did not mean one ceased being a Jew. For these people it was axiomatic that certain aspects of Judaism should continue to be observed by the followers of Jesus, as Jesus himself had taught. "Do not suppose that I have come to abolish the Law and the prophets: I did not come to abolish, but to complete. I tell you this: so long as heaven and earth endure, not a letter, not a stroke, will disappear from the Law until all that must happen has happened" (Matt. 5:17–18).

In discussing this phenomenon in early Christianity, it is customary to distinguish between judaizing Christians and Jewish Christians.

4. See, for example, the comments of Galen on Christianity and Judaism (Walzer, pp. 10–16).

Jewish Christians are said to be Jews who believe in Jesus yet continue to observe Jewish law. Judaizing Christians, on the other hand, are thought to be those Christians, usually gentiles, whose acquaintance with Judaism was mediated through Christianity; who, in contrast to the majority of Christians, adopted certain aspects of Jewish law, even though before becoming Christians they had not observed it. As useful as this distinction is for certain purposes, it obscures one significant fact: the chief identifying mark of both groups was the same: observance of Jewish law. This was not lost on Christian leaders who had contact with the various forms of "judaizing" Christianity. In contrast to the Arians or the Gnostics, the distinctive characteristic of Judaizers was not teaching or doctrine, but observance. This can be illustrated by reviewing some of the evidence from Christianity's first four centuries.

Already in the first century, gentile converts to Christianity were urged by some Christians to adopt Jewish practices—for example, to be scrupulous in what they "ate or drank" and to observe "a festival, new moon, or sabbath" (Col. 2:16). In the mid-second century, both Christian and pagan writers knew of Christians who observed the requirements of the Law.[5] Asked if he could have fellowship with such people, Justin, with a tolerance shared by few others, said he considered such people "kinsmen and brothers" as long as they did not urge others to keep the Sabbath, be circumcized, or observe other Jewish ceremonies (Dial. 47). At approximately the same time, the pagan writer Celsus noted the presence in the Church of Jews who "accept Jesus although they still want to live according to the law of the Jews like the multitude of the Jews" (Origen Contra Celsum 5.61). A generation later, Irenaeus knew Christians who "practice circumcision, persevere in the customs which are according to the Law and practice a Jewish way of life." To which he adds that they use only Matthew, repudiate the apostle Paul, and "adore Jerusalem as if it were the house of God" (Adv. haer. 1.26.2).

In the third century, Origen, writing in Caesarea in Palestine, knew of "Jews who believe in Jesus and have not left the law of their fathers. For they live according to it" (Contra Celsum 2.1). In the fourth century, Jerome and Epiphanius also had first-hand knowledge of Jewish Christians who observed the Law. One group, called the Nasoraeans, says Epiphanius, "lived according to the preaching of the Law as

5. Early in the second century, Ignatius, bishop of Antioch, came into contact with judaizing Christians in western Asia Minor (Ignatius, Magn. 9.1), and observance of the Sabbath was one of the matters of dispute. It is possible, however, that his opponents were Judaizers only in that they were fascinated by the Jewish Scriptures (Schoedel 1978, p. 105).

among the Jews," and read the Scriptures in Hebrew. Epiphanius believes these people are "Jews and nothing else," though he admits they are hated by the Jews. Midway between Jews and Christians, they do not agree with the Jews, because they "believe in Christ," and they differ with Christians because they are "constrained by the Law, by circumcision, the sabbath, and other things" (*Panarion* 29.7). Jerome also knew "Jews who believe in Christ" (*Ep.* 112.13), and who "want to be both Jews and Christians." They "believe in Christ and keep all the commandments of the Law" (*De situ* 112; *PL* 23.888).

These latter reports come from Palestine, but Christians who kept the Jewish law could be found elsewhere in the empire, for example, in Asia Minor, in Africa, and particularly in Syria (Simon 1964, pp. 382–93). The third-century church order *Didascalia apostolorum*, less a liturgical handbook than guidelines for church discipline and personal conduct, gives much information about judaizing Christians. From the author's description, it appears that many were former Jews, but they seem not to have constituted a distinct sect; rather they imported Jewish practices into the Church. Here, too, the issue centered on observance. In reading the Scriptures, the author wrote, "beware of the *deuterosis*"—that is, the ritual and ceremonial law (*Didasc.* 2). Only observe the decalogue, not the other laws that Jews continue to observe (*Didasc.* 26). This document shows that Christians were observing certain laws concerned with ritual purity, such as taking a ritual bath after touching a corpse or following certain prescriptions concerning menstruation. The *Didascalia* warns against "distinctions of meat," and "purifications, sprinklings, baptisms" (*Didasc.* 26). It also urges that Christian observance of the Pasch be distinct from the Jewish Passover (*Didasc.* 21). This group of Christians was celebrating the Christian Pasch at the same time as the Jewish Passover, a practice that is documented in Cappadocia, Cilicia (bordering Syria), and Syria (Athanasius *Ad Afros* 2; Socrates *Hist. eccl.* 5.22).

Admittedly, the *Didascalia* gives evidence of an extreme case of judaizing, but, when placed in context, the practices it describes do not appear uncommon. In a sermon preached on a Saturday, a bishop in the fifth century once apologized for delivering a homily on the Sabbath, lest someone think that, in worshipping on Saturday, he and his congregation were, "judaizing" (*PG* 28.144). Throughout the fourth century, when conciliar acts first become available, we find legislation from various parts of the Roman Empire attempting to restrain judaizing Christians. A council in Elvira, Spain, ruled that the Sabbath should not be considered a special day and prohibited the blessing of the fruits of the harvest by Jewish rabbis (Canons 26 and 49; Hefele, 1:235, 249). The council explicitly prohibited Christians from eating with Jews on the occasion of their festivals (Canon 50; Hefele, 1:250). Much closer to Antioch, the *Apostolic Constitutions*, a collection of ecclesiastical canons and prayers, some of which derive from the synagogue, forbad Christians from entering the synagogues of the Jews and urged them to avoid Jewish festivals (2.61; 5.17). Even bishops and presbyters fellowshipped with Jews. "If a bishop or another cleric fasts with the Jews or feasts with them or received gifts from their festivals, as unleavened bread or something else, let him be purified; if it is a layperson, let him be excommunicated" (*Const. app.* 8.47.70; 65). Another collection of canons from the fourth century, the Canons of Laodicea, prohibit "celebrating festivals with Jews," receiving gifts on festivals, and eating unleavened bread during the Pasch (Canons 37, 38; Hefele, 1.1019). One (Canon 16; Hefele, 1:1008) prescribes that if Christians gather for worship on Saturday, they should read the Gospels as well as other Scriptures. Other canons warn against Christians who "judaize" by resting on the Sabbath and working on the Lord's Day (Canon 29; Hefele, 1:1015).

From these ecclesiastical canons, one gains a picture of Christians and Jews living side by side, owning shops and stores on the same streets, drifting in and out of each other's religious rites. Anxious leaders, unable to stop the casual intercourse, could only plead with their followers to keep to themselves.

Christians who observed certain of the Jewish laws, had fellowship with the synagogue, and celebrated Jewish rites and festivals were most visible in Syria, Palestine, and Asia Minor, but were also to be found in Egypt, in Africa, and elsewhere. Indeed, what is striking about the evidence is that judaizing tendencies appear in unexpected places and in unlikely figures. For example, Apollinaris, the bishop of Laodicea, who is known in church history chiefly because of his christological views, was apparently attracted to Jewish practices. Basil attacks him in one of his letters for urging "the renewal of the temple and the observance of worship according to the Law" (*Ep.* 265.2; also 263.4).

From the point of view of Christian leaders, and of most Christians, the modern distinction between judaizing Christians and Jewish Christians is artifical. This distinction does, however, point to an important social fact. Judaizing Christians, as members of gentile churches, were disruptive of Christian communities. By attending the synagogue and celebrating festivals with Jews, they caused divisions in the Church. Jewish Christians, on the other hand, were members of the synagogue who adopted Christian ways while remaining Jews or they belonged to separate, sometimes Hebrew-speaking, Jewish Christian groups, and were isolated from gentile Christians. Jewish Christians were a concern for Christians, like Jerome or Epiphanius, who wrote against them; but their impact was felt most keenly in the synagogues. What troubled Christian leaders were members of the Church who adopted Jewish customs.

The most extensive evidence for judaizing Christianity comes from the fourth century. Due to the paucity of sources in the second and third centuries it is difficult to say whether the judaizing Christians of the fourth century were part of a continuous history extending to apostolic times. Though the evidence is insufficient to document such a history, it is likely that such a tradition of Christian practice and thought had existed without interruption from the earliest times (Simon 1964, p. 383).

The abundance of information in the later fourth century suggests that a resurgence of judaizing Christianity took place at that time. Julian's efforts to rebuild the temple in Jerusalem and return the city of Jerusalem to the Jews, though aborted by his untimely death, may have contributed to this resurgence. The Syriac writer Ephraem says that the "Jews were seized by a frenzied enthusiasm and sounded trumpets" when they learned about Julian's plan (*Contra Julianum* 1.16; 2.7), and Rufinus reports that some Jews thought that "one of the prophets had returned" and that the "times of the rule [of the Jews] has been restored" (*Hist. eccl.* 10.38). In several places in his commentaries on the prophets, Jerome says that the "Jews and our Judaizers" anticipated an imminent fulfillment of the prophecies that spoke of a restoration of Jerusalem and a return of the Jews to the city. The Jews and Judaizers, says Jerome, "anticipate entering Zion with gladness, the blood of sacrifices, the servitude of the gentiles" and, he adds, "beautiful wives" (*Comm. in Isa.* 35:10). The time is coming, he writes elsewhere, when, according to the Jews and Judaizers, all the precepts of the Law will be observed and "Jews will no longer become Christians but Christians will become Jews" (*Comm. in Zach.* 14:10–11).

Judaizers in Antioch

Stories about the restoration of Jerusalem were still circulating in Antioch a generation after Julian's death. In his homilies on the Judaizers, John says that Jews were still going about "whispering that the city [Jerusalem] will be returned to us" (*Jud.* 7.1; 916). And the "older members" of John's congregation remembered well the efforts of Julian over twenty years earlier (*Jud.* 5.11; 900). It is possible that John also had first-hand contact with Hebrew-speaking Jewish Christians during his years in the desert east of Antioch in the vicinity of Aleppo, a city with a significant Jewish population, as shown by the large synagogue that was standing in John's day (Sauvaget, pp. 60–61). According to Jerome, who had traveled through the area, there was a Jewish Christian community east of Antioch, and it possessed a Hebrew version of the Gospel of Matthew (*Vir. ill.* 3). Epiphanius also mentions the same group (*Haer.* 29.7.7).

But John did not have to go to Aleppo to meet Christians who observed Jewish law. In his own city of Antioch, and among the members of his own congregation, the rites of the Jews exerted a powerful attraction. Here is how he describes the situation in Antioch the year after he was ordained:

> Don't look around and say: "Look how many are fasting with the Jews, how many have been swept away." Rather make it your business to look after them. If there are many who are fasting with the Jews, don't parade it about, beloved, don't make a spectacle of the Church's misfortune. If someone says, "Many are fasting," shut him up so that the rumor does not spread. Say to him: "I haven't heard a thing. You're mistaken and not telling the truth. Perhaps you have heard of two or three who were snatched away and you are only saying that it is many." Then after you have muzzled your accuser, don't overlook those who have fallen, so that the Church will be doubly secure—rumors will no longer be noised about and those who were swept away will be led back to the sacred flock." [*Jud.* 8.4; 933]

Lest the rumors lead others to follow their errant ways, John urged his hearers to keep quiet about the Judaizers:

> Bridle your tongue and restrain yourself. Don't say to me that many have fasted; rather set them straight. I have not wasted so many words just to accuse the many, but to reduce the many to a few; or better, not to a few, [I have spoken] that you might rescue them. Don't parade one's failures about; correct them. Since there are many who go around talking about such things and who are interested only in this, even if the number is small, they make people think that many are involved. So, even if there are many defectors, the "big mouths" can be silenced, their sails trimmed, and those who are concerned about the defectors can easily straighten them out and no one will be harmed by the rumor." [*Jud.* 8.4; 933–34]

The louder John thundered from the pulpit against the Judaizers, however, the less he was able to contain his followers and prohibit them from adopting Jewish customs. In his final sermon on the subject, from which the above passage is taken, he admits that the talk among Christians about the Judaizers only had the effect of making people curious and attracting even more people to Jewish ways. No doubt his sermons contributed to this interest, for they called attention to the problem and prompted others to inquire what it was that friends and family members found so compelling about the Jewish rites.

What, then, were the Christians in Antioch doing with the Jews that so irked John? In the first sermon, preached immediately after a sermon against the Arians, John says that the struggle with the Jews "is related to the previous struggle with the Arians" (*Jud.* 1.1; 845). Both Arians and Jews, he says, accuse us of making Jesus, a man, equal with God; both deny the divinity of Christ. As we shall see in the final chapter of this book, from John's perspective there was a similarity at the doctrinal level between Arianism and Judaism. In the homilies on the Judaizers, this doctrinal question is mentioned only intermittently, however; the debate between John and the Judaizers does not center on theological matters, in the strict sense of the term, but on practice, on Jewish rites; in short, on matters of observance.

Judaizing Christians attended the synagogue of the Jews in Antioch on the Sabbath and on the high holy days (*Jud.* 1.5; 850; 8.8; 940). "Many among us keep the Sabbaths" with the Jews, says John (*Hom. in Gal.* 1.7; 61.623). They also went to the synagogue on Rosh Hashannah "to watch them blow trumpets" (*Jud.* 1.5; 851). On Yom Kippur they fasted with the Jews and went to the marketplace to watch the Jews "dance with naked feet" (*Jud.* 1.2; 846). Though Yom Kippur was traditionally a day of penance, in some places Jews danced to celebrate the day. When Rosh Hashanah and Yom Kippur had passed, the Judaizers made preparations to join the Jews in "pitching their tents"—that is, erecting huts for the festival of Sukkoth (*Jud.* 7.1; 915). Some seem to have practiced circumcision, though John acknowledges in a sermon dealing with circumcision that the guilty are "not present" (*Jud.* 2.2; 859). Others submitted to Jewish ritual baths, which John admits are more solemn than ordinary baths (*Catech.* 1.2–3; 49.225–26). Theodoret, a Christian raised in Antioch, later bishop in the neighboring city of Cyrus, also knew of Christians who underwent ritual baths with the Jews (*In Heb.* 6.4; *PG* 82.717). The *Apostolic Constitutions* also warn against participation in Jewish baths (*Const. app.* 7.44).

These Christians who participated in Jewish rites and observed Jewish law were not marginal renegades who came to church only infrequently. From John's comments, they appear to be regular members of his congregation who thought they could remain members of the

Church while observing Jewish rites and customs. In their minds, there was no contradiction between going to the synagogue on Saturday to hear the reading of the Law and coming to church on Sunday to participate in the Eucharist. They want, says John, to have fellowship with the Jews and "fellowship at the holy table sharing the precious blood." He warns them that they cannot have both. "If one who has this sickness [Judaizing] is a catechumen, let him be barred from entering the church doors; if he is one of the faithful and baptized, let him be barred from the Eucharist" (*Jud.* 2.3; 861).

Just how deeply judaizing practices had cut into the Church's life can be seen in the dispute over the celebration of Easter, a topic to which John devoted an entire sermon. This sermon was preached in the winter of 387 in anticipation of the celebration of Easter in the spring of that year. A group in Antioch celebrated Easter according to the Jewish calendar (i.e., the Sunday after Passover) with the result that they divided the Church (*Jud.* 3.2; 864). John's sermon is an attempt to persuade them to give up the practice and join with the rest of the Church. "The obstinancy of those who wish to keep the Pasch early forces us to devote our whole sermon today to healing their malady" (*Jud.* 3.1; 861).

The dating of Easter had long been a matter of dispute among Christians. Originally Christians had celebrated Easter as a Christian Passover on the same day as the Jewish Passover, but as the years passed the majority of Christians sought to disengage the Christian celebration from the Jewish feast. Unanimity in practice was, however, hard to come by. Even when Easter was clearly independent of Passover, the question still remained: how was the date to be computed? In some circles, it was set according to the Jewish Passover. In 325 the Council of Nicaea ruled that Easter was never to be celebrated on the same day as the Jews (Huber, pp. 61–75). If the fourteenth of Nisan, the day of Passover, fell on a Sunday, Easter was to be celebrated a week later.

Though the Council of Nicaea resolved the issue to the satisfaction of the assembled bishops, it did not stop the diversity of practices. Rome and Alexandria, for example, followed a different method of computation. And some Christians continued to compute the day according to the Jewish calendar. In 341 a synod in Antioch issued a new canon threatening those who followed the Jewish reckoning with excommunication (Canon 1; Hefele, 1:714). So incendiary was the issue that some Christians tried to prohibit Jews from calculating the date of Passover because judaizing Christians would use the information to set the date of their celebration (Lieberman 1974, p. 116). In certain areas of Asia Minor, such as Phrygia, Paphlagonia (Socrates *Hist. eccl.*

4.28), and Galatia (Socrates *Hist. eccl.* 7.18), Christians separated from the Church over the matter of the dating of Easter, insisting that it be reckoned "according to the Jewish custom." As late as the fifth century, some monks in Syria had not even heard of the decision of Nicaea and continued to celebrate Easter by the old method (Theodoret *Hist. relig.* 3.17).

In Antioch the canon of Nicaea prohibiting the practice was well known, as was the later canon from the local council at Antioch. But the judaizing Christians chose to ignore it, says John, thinking "the Jews to be wiser than the fathers of Nicaea" (*Jud.* 3.3; 865). Not only did they ignore the decree, but they argued that their practice was the older, authentic, practice of the Church in Antioch (*Jud.* 3.3; 866). "Why should it now be changed?" (*Jud.* 3.5; 869).

The year in which this homily was preached, 387 C.E., was a particularly troubling year to compute the date of Easter. The fourteenth of Nisan, the day Passover began, fell on a Sunday (*Jud.* 3.5; 869). If the Jewish calendar were followed, Easter would fall before the vernal equinox, making the celebration much earlier than usual. This calendrical confusion also created difficulties in churches elsewhere. In Asia Minor, for example, an unknown preacher delivered a homily on the problem of the date of Easter that year (Floeri and Nautin, pp. 35–77).

The conflict over the dating of Easter and the preceding period of fasting caused havoc in the Church in Antioch. While one group of Christians were celebrating the death and Resurrection of Christ, another would be fasting (*Jud.* 3.5; 869). Few things are more important to religious life than the calendar and the celebration of festivals on the proper dates. Even today, in the cities of the Middle East, where differing religious groups live side by side at close quarters, one can observe that the date of a festival, the performance of a particular ritual at a certain time, is a primary mark of religious allegiance. Even modern Westerners realize that birthdays, anniversaries, and national holidays lose their meaning if they are not celebrated on the proper day. This is why the debate over the date of Easter in the early Church was not simply a minor dispute over calendar. It was a dispute about religious and communal identity.

In Antioch, the Judaizers threatened the Church not by raising intellectual problems but by observing the rites of a rival religious group in the city. What caused the conflict and prompted John's sermons were not theological issues but religous practices, the determination of the calendar, the celebration of religious festivals. You divide the Church, John says to the Judaizers, "by running to the Jews," thereby depriving yourselves of the "Holy Scriptures, the assembly [of the

Church], blessings and prayers made in common during the days of the fast" (*Jud.* 6.6; 871). The Judaizers prefer to observe "fixed times" rather than to have "harmony in the Church," and to "keep fixed days . . . you divide the holy assembly in two" (*Jud.* 3.5; 869).

As John saw it, then, the issue was whether his followers would obey the decrees of the Christian fathers who had "set the day" (*Jud.* 6.6; 871–72) or the calculations of the Jewish sages who determined the time of the Jewish festivals. To the Judaizers the choice seemed unnecessary, because Jesus had observed the Jewish festivals. But to John Christians had to choose between the Church and the synagogue. Conflicting religious ideas may be able to coexist alongside of one another, and often do, but religious practices, by their very nature, force a choice. And if one chooses to celebrate one rite rather than another, it is apparent that the one that *is* celebrated is, by the very act of participation, rendered legitimate.

If Christians were going around the corner to attend the synagogue, this meant that the divine was more tangibly present in the synagogue than in churches. If churches were empty because the Jews were celebrating their high holy days, this suggested that the Jewish way was more authentic. If the Christians used the Jewish calendar to set the date of a Christian festival, this could only mean that the Jews had the true calendar. In such a setting there was no middle ground, no accommodation between Jews and Christians, because the claims of the two religions were being negotiated not in the tranquility of the scholar's study but in the din of the city's streets. When churches were empty and the synagogue filled, it was not a secret but public knowledge passed on in the shops and bazaars of the city. In a city such as Antioch, where the population lived cramped together in close quarters, rubbing elbows with neighbors as they made their way through the narrow streets, chatting with friends and acquaintances in the shops and stalls, everyone knew everybody else's business. The street was the living room of the ancient city (MacMullen 1974, pp. 62–65). Nothing could be kept secret for long, and rumors that Christians were going to the synagogue rather than to church spread quickly (*Jud.* 8.4; 933).

The adoption of Jewish ways by Christians called into question the truth of Christianity. "If you believe Judaism is true," John taunts the Judaizers, "why do you trouble the Church?" (*Jud.* 4.4; 876). Just as a Roman soldier cannot sympathize with barbarians or Persians, so a true Christian cannot have anything to do with the Jews (*Jud.* 1.4; 849). Perhaps the most telling fact, in the eyes of Christians, Jews, and, no doubt, onlookers, was that Christians were adopting Jewish ways, but Jews did not adopt Christian ways. "Go into the synagogues," says John, "and see if the Jews have changed their days of fasting, if they observe the Paschal Feast at the same time we do, whether they have ever taken food on that day? . . . When have they celebrated the Pasch with us? When have they celebrated the festivals of martyrs with us? When have they shared the day of Epiphany with us?" (*Jud.* 4.3; 375–76).

Holy Places and Holy Books

In the middle of the fourth century, by the time John was born, a Christian community had existed in Antioch for three centuries. The Jews, however, had been there much longer and their way of life and their Scriptures were known to have originated many centuries earlier, in the mists of antiquity. In the minds of Greeks and Romans, the Jews were an ancient people whose way of life commanded respect. In the ancient world, the older a religious tradition, the more authority it commanded. Newcomers lacked the religious power of the ancient religions. One of the critics of Christianity, the philosopher Porphyry, in his book *Philosophy from Oracles*, attacked Christianity by presenting the teachings of the ancient and venerable religions of Greece, Rome, Egypt, and also of the Hebrews (Wilken 1979). From its beginnings, Christianity was branded an "innovation," a latecomer, an upstart sect that had abandoned the ways of the ancients to follow its own novelties. The Jews at least had a tradition (Origen *Contra Celsum* 5.25). Even in the fourth century, when Christianity had been around for three hundred years, its critics repeated the same charge (Julian *Gal.* 43a). The antiquity of the Jews gave Judaism a spiritual potency that Christianity, in spite of its evident success, could not equal. One of the signs of this religious power was the synagogue, another was the Jewish Scriptures.

In Antioch people went to the synagogues as though they were "sacred shrines" (*Jud.* 1.3; 847). As proof of this, John tells the following story:

> Three days ago (believe me, I am not lying), I saw a noble and free woman, who is modest and faithful, being forced into a synagogue by a coarse and senseless person who appeared to be a Christian (I would not say that someone who dared to do such things was really a Christian). He forced her into a synagogue to make an oath about certain business matters which were in litigation. As the woman passed by she kept calling out for help, hoping someone would stop this lawless show of

79

force. Enraged and burning with anger, I roused myself and rescued her from this unjust abduction so that she would not be dragged into such lawlessness. When I asked her abductor whether he was a Christian he admitted he was. I reproached him severely. [*Jud.* 1.3; 847]

After censuring the man for coercing the woman, John importuned him with texts from the Gospel on the evils of oath taking. But he was curious as to why the man wanted to force the woman to do business in the synagogue in the first place. "I asked him why he had walked by the church and dragged this woman to a gathering place of the Hebrews. He replied that many had told him that oaths which were taken there were more awesome. When I heard this I shouted at him and was again consumed by anger" (*Jud.* 1.3; 848).

Oaths made in the synagogue were thought to be more binding and the parties less likely to renege at a later date. In the next paragraph of his sermon, John has to *offer an argument* to convince his hearers that churches "are *truly* places of awe and are filled with religious fear" (*Jud.* 1.4; 848). No argument was needed for the synagogue.

"Some think the synagogue is a holy place" says John, "because the Law and the books of the prophets can be found there." In antiquity books were objects of religious awe and wonder, and the books of the Jews were particularly mysterious (Leipoldt, cols. 695–98). Written in a strange script, read backwards, bound in a roll, and kept in a holy place (the Torah shrine, a prominent fixture in ancient synagogues), the Jewish books engendered fear and veneration (Goodenough, 4: 111–36). When they were read, they were ceremoniously carried from the shrine to the reading desk and solemnly unrolled. Christian books, on the other hand, were written in the vernacular and bound in codex form, similar to a modern book, a practice that already distinguished Christian books from Jewish books in fifth-century Syria (*PG* 82.853d).

All of this contributed to the numinous quality of the Jewish Scriptures. To the simple and uneducated, the books had magical powers and were capable of working wonders and miracles. It was not unusual, for this reason, for oaths to be taken before the Torah scroll (*b. Shevu'oth* 38b). Furthermore, the books contained arcane ancient wisdom and stories about the creation of the world. According to Jewish legend, the emperor Hadrian once asked the Jewish proselyte Aquila: "What do you see in [the Jews] that you want to become a convert to Judaism?" He responded, "Even the youngest among them know how God created the world; what was created on the first and on the second day, and how much time has elapsed since the world was created and on what the world stands. And their Torah is true" (*Exodus Rabbah* 30.12).

It was public knowledge that the Christian Old Testament was not a Christian but a Jewish book. To the men and women of the ancient world, the Bible appeared much differently than it does to a civilization formed by the Christian tradition. Today most people, except for Jews, know the Jewish Scriptures not as an independent collection of Jewish books but as the "Old Testament"—that is, as part of the Christian Bible. But in the Roman world these books were known first and foremost as Jewish books, the "Scriptures which are guarded by them," as John puts it (*Jud. et gent.* 2; 48.415). In debates with pagan critics of Christ, says Augustine, we point them to the prophecies in Isaiah, Daniel, Jeremiah, and other prophets. But they reply: "You [Christians] have forged these for yourselves, you have seen them come to pass, and have written them in what books you pleased, as if their coming had been predicted." To which Augustine responds, "We produce books written by the Jews." To silence critics "let the book of Isaiah be produced by the Jews," and see whether what we claim is written there. Through the book of "one enemy," says Augustine, we vanquish the other enemy (*Comm. Joannem* 35.7).

It was the "Jew who was the bearer of the books from which the Christians believe" (Augustine *Ennar. in Ps.* 56.9). Furthermore, Christians only had copies written in Greek or Latin. Even when the Jews used Greek in the synagogue, the Hebrew text of the Scriptures was present and was often read before the translation into Greek. Hence it was apparent to all, Jews, pagans, and Christians, that the books of the Christian Old Testament were "their Scriptures," the Jewish Scriptures (Eusebius *Demon. evang.* 3, Preface, 87a). For this reason, pagan critics attacked Christians for deriving their teaching from the "Jewish Law" (Origen *Contra Celsum* 2.4). Julian claimed that he could cite "ten thousand passages" proving that Christians had transgressed the ancient law of Moses as recorded in the Jewish Scriptures (*Gal.* 238b).

That Christians only had copies of the Jewish books, that few Christians knew Hebrew, and that Christians read and studied the Bible only in translations put them on the defensive. Possession of the original books was no small matter, for rightful possession implied that one understood their contents. In the second century, orthodox Christian leaders had argued against the Gnostics that the latter had no right to the Christian books and therefore could not claim to know what they meant. "We must first discover," wrote Tertullian, "who are the rightful owners of the Scriptures" before we can discuss what they mean (*Praescr.* 15). Just how significant rightful possession was can be illustrated from a medieval text in which Jews charge Christians with only possessing copies:

> You [the Christians] have not kept a single sign or testimony, as if you were thieving and ashamed of your descent. On the contrary, you have left us the lineage and nobility. For we keep all those—the law, the script, the language of the Book of Torah, which is the conclusive and main evidence for the Jewish faith. You have left with us the original and taken for yourself a copy. This is impossible, for surely there is no avoiding mistakes with copyists: civil contracts need court attestation of the correctness of a copy. We want to see that Torah scrolls are without error, we take three men who read in three scrolls, though the language is the same, so that if one fails, the second or third will correct him, for from the mistake of a single scribe a thousand books may be copied. It is written "God's Torah is whole" and "Ye shall neither add nor subtract." In conclusion, it is axiomatic that if the Messiah has come and they are the believers and we, God forbid, the infidels, and they of the true sons of Israel—they would not have left us the original, the script and the language, and taken for themselves translations without the original and would not have changed their language too. On the contrary, they would have compelled us to change our language and the script of our Torah, since the power is in their hands. [Ben-Sasson, p. 382]

A similar problem existed in John's day. For centuries Christians had been content to read the Bible in a Greek translation, the Septuagint, or translations based on the Septuagint, but precisely in this period, Jerome began to translate the Bible into Latin directly from a Hebrew text. After much discussion and many arguments with Christians, Jerome had become convinced that the only Bible Christians could use in disputes with the Jews was the original Hebrew text. As J. N. D. Kelly, Jerome's recent biographer, writes,

> It had become translucently clear, to himself and certain close friends, that their only hope of demolishing the arguments of Jewish critics was to take their stand on a text of the Old Testament which both parties agreed was authentic. "It is one thing," he declared, "to sing the psalms in churches of Christian believers, quite another to make answer to the Jews who cavil at the words." His whole object, he claimed, in sweating over this translation from a strange tongue was to stop the Jews

once for all from taunting the Church with the falseness of its Scriptures. He wished to deprive them of their present vantage-point for deriding Christians, and to refute them on their own ground by appealing, when controversy arose, to a version which they had to acknowledge as indisputably accurate and which nevertheless spoke unmistakably to the coming of Christ. [Kelly 1976, pp. 159–60]

Paradoxically, the only person from whom Jerome could learn Hebrew was a Jew; the only copies of the Hebrew text available to him came from the Jews; and, when he met with difficulties in his translation, he turned to a learned Jew from Tiberias for assistance. If Christians had to go to Jews to obtain the Hebrew text, nothing showed more clearly that they were dependent on copies and that the Jews alone were the rightful owners of the original version.

John, unlike Jerome, was not a scholar. He did not know Hebrew. In the face of the Jewish possession of the Scriptures and the allure of the Jewish books, he felt helpless. "This is the reason I hate the Jews," he says, "because they have the law and the prophets: indeed I hate them more because of this than if they did not have them" (*Jud.* 6.6; 913). He calls the Jewish Scriptures "bait to deceive the simple," the Law a "snare for the weak" (*Jud.* 6.6; 913). "Don't say to me that the Law and the books of the prophets can be found in the synagogue. That is not enough to make the place holy" (*Jud.* 1.5; 850).

In John's case, the dispute over the Scriptures was much less intellectual than it was with Jerome. Jerome wrote learned commentaries on the Jewish Scriptures, patiently dealing with textual, historical, and theological matters. From time to time, John drops hints that exegetical topics were discussed with Jews in Antioch (*Jud.* 7.3; 919) and Jewish sources mention rabbis who disputed with Christians in Antioch (*Genesis Rabbah* 19.4). But the dispute over the Jewish books and the holiness of the synagogue is less a matter of the correct interpretation of the books than it is an effort to dispel the mysterious power of the books to draw Christians to the synagogue.

Jewish Magic

If the Jewish festivals and the Jewish books were not sufficient to torment the young presbyter, yet another problem vexed him, Jewish magic. When sick, Christians ran to the Jews to be healed by "charms, incantations and amulets" (*Jud.* 8.5; 935; 8.7; 937–38). Here, too, the Jews seemed, at least to John, to have the edge; their magic was more powerful than Christian magic. John admits that Christians were being healed by the Jews (*Jud.* 8.7; 937). Faced with his intelligence, he was driven to the doubtful expedient of telling his followers it was better to remain sick than to be cured by Jewish magicians. Unimpressed, they promptly hurried to the Jews with the excuse, "My body hurts and the pain oppresses me" (*Jud.* 8.6; 935).

Christians wore gospel texts around their necks encased in small boxes and they used amulets and charms to ward off demons, to protect themselves from harm, and to heal their ills (Eckstein and Waszink, pp. 407–19). Even Christian leaders had on occasion to be warned not to dabble in magic. "Neither higher nor lower clergy may be magicians, conjurors, mathematicians, astrologers, nor make amulets" (*Canons of Laodicea*, 36; Hefele, 1:1018). In popular Christian piety, the apostles and martyrs were sometimes revered as magicians because of their ability to work wonders, and the relics of martyrs were thought to work miracles (Augustine *Civ. Dei* 22.8).

Though Christian leaders warned the faithful against the use of magic and Church councils passed resolutions condemning its use, neither the exhortation of the clergy nor the legislation of councils could stop the practice. Furthermore, magic was not simply a fringe phenomenon, the dark and secretive activities of a coven of witches. Magic was practiced by faithful Christians who attended church and participated in the Eucharist, and was presented as a technique to aid the divine. John mentions a Christian woman in Antioch who had resisted the suggestions of a magician who had told her, "This is only a charm, not idolatry." To John, however, his charm was a "device of Satan," by which he cloaked his wiles in deceit and offered a "noxious drug in honey" (*Hom. 8.5 in Col.* 3:5; 62. 357–58).

John's "stern, uncompromising religious theory" (Barb, p. 106) met with little success among the Christians of Antioch. No doubt the reason for this was that most Christians could not distinguish such gestures as the making of the sign of the cross from the practices of the magicians. Each seemed to have the same purpose: to heal the sick or put the devil to rout. In his sermons, John urged his followers to use the "sign of the cross" as a talisman to ward off demons and to heal the sick (*Hom. 8.5 in Col.* 3:5; 62.357–58). In one of the sermons on the Judaizers, he recommends that Christians who go to the synagogue make the "sign of the cross on their brows" to fend off the evil powers dwelling there (*Jud.* 8.8; 940). The question was which talisman, which amulet, which incantation was the most effective.

Among Jews the situation was no different. The practitioners of magic were faithful Jews who attended the synagogue, celebrated the Jewish festivals, and in other ways participated in Jewish life. Some

Jews saw magic not as a capitulation to paganism or idolatry but as a complement to more traditional and accepted religious practices. What distinguished Jewish magic, at least in the minds of many people in the ancient world, was that Jewish magicians were more successful.

It is likely that the success of Jewish magic derived in part from the use of Hebrew phrases and Hebrew names. Even non-Jews used Hebrew as a language for incantations and spells. The unusual alphabet and the strange practice of writing in the opposite direction from other languages in the Mediterranean basin set Hebrew apart. Among the magical papyri, widely dispersed throughout the Greco-Roman world, almost two hundred texts from the Hebrew Bible were used as omens or spells (Goldin, p. 124). The phrase "I exorcise you in the Hebrew language" is a familiar magical formula (*PGM* 1.38). Moses was seen by many as a magician (Gager 1972, pp. 134–61). The term *Iao*, a transliteration of the Hebrew Yahweh, occurs frequently in the magical papyri, as does another Hebrew word for God, Adonai (Smith, p. 223). In the index of the collection of magical papyri, three full columns refer to Iao, more references than to any other divine name. Even the rabbis on occasion approved amulets with biblical verses and the names of angels (*b. Shabbath* 61b).

A good example of Jewish magic is an early fifth-century amulet, written in Aramaic from Aleppo (Beroea), approximately fifty miles east of Antioch. This amulet mentions Yahweh, Yah Shaddai, and several non-Jewish deities, as well as the planets, stars, the sun and the moon. "Good amulet on which is written the following. Holy one, among the great and among the saints, your name is holy. Supreme God, exalted, my Help, Lord Ehjeh, Ahmah, Yah Shaddai. . . . God of heavenly aid, in the name of Agrith . . . in the reign of the moon . . . I abjure you by the rose and the cold, by fire and clouds" (*CIJ* 819). The distinction here between religion and magic is a very fine one. It is likely that the person who wrote and used the amulet was a Jew who felt no contradiction between his Jewish piety and the practice of magic.

An unusual glimpse into the intimate link between Jewish piety and the practice of magic in the late Roman world can be found in the recently published *Sefer Ha-Razim* [*Book of Mysteries*], edited by the talmudic scholar Mordecai Margolioth from a manuscript he accidentally discovered in a Cambridge, England, library. The discovery surprised Margolioth (Margolioth, pp. ix–xvi) because the book was written in elegant Hebrew, and its author was at home in rabbinic language and expression, yet its religious outlook seemed thoroughly out of step with rabbinic Judaism. The author was certainly a Jew who believed in the one God of Israel, for the work ends with a beautiful hymn of praise to the transcendent God who dwells unapproachably in the seventh heaven on a throne of glory surrounded by light:

> He alone is seated in the heaven of his holiness. He deals out judgment, evens the scales of justice, judges in truthfulness and speaks in righteousness. . . . His appearance is hidden from all, but the appearance of all of us cannot be hidden [from Him].
> . . . He sits upon a throne of light and the power of light surrounds Him . . . . Blessed is His name and the preciousness of His praises is to be blessed forever and ever, for all eternity and forever, for there is no God except Him and there is no God beside Him. [*Sefer Ha-Razim* 7.6–13, 23–25][6]

Most of the book, however, is concerned not with the one God of Israel but with countless legions of angels and heavenly beings, many of whose names are drawn from the magical papyri. The purpose of the book is to provide magical formulas to fit every occasion, such as how to win at horseracing, how to avoid paying a debt, how to find favor with a beautiful woman, how to impress an officer or the head of a city, how to heal sickness.

> If you wish to perform an act of healing, arise in the first or second hour of the night and take myrrh and frankincense in your hand. Place [the incense] upon the burning embers of a fire [while saying] the name of the angel who rules over the first encampment, who is called ORPaNI'eL, and say seven times [the names of] the seventy-two angels that minister to him, then say: "I *X* the son of *X* demand from you that you will bring success upon my hands in healing *Y* the son of *Y*." And anyone for whom you ask, whether in writing or verbally, will be healed. Purify yourself from all impurity and cleanse your flesh from all carnality and then you will succeed. These are the names of the angels of the second encampment who minister to TIGRaH: 'aKSaTaR MaRSOM BeBKIB KaMSO 'aSTIB KeRIt'eL. . . . [1.28–34]

The author lists the names of eighty angels. The *Sefer Ha-Razim* was probably written in the third or fourth century. Where it was written is conjectural. Since it is in Hebrew, it may come from Palestine, but it could just as well come from Syria, or even Egypt.[7] While I do not wish to draw a direct connection between the *Sefer Ha-Razim* and the Jewish community in Antioch, this handbook of magic provides us

6. My translation of the text of *Sefer Ha-Razim* relies on Morgan.
7. Levine (p. 198, n. 133) believes it was written in Caesarea in Palestine.

with a glimpse of the kind of practices that could be found among Jews in the later Roman Empire. The Jews in Antioch, like the author of *Sefer Ha-Razim*, used "magical tricks, spells, and potions" to heal (*Jud.* 8.5; 935), and Jewish sorcerers came to the homes of Christians with potions (*Jud.* 8.6; 936).

The *Sefer Ha-Razim* helps us understand how magic could be associated with the synagogue. It is quite conceivable that the same Jews who were welcoming Christians to the Jewish festivals were also healing their sicknesses with magic. We miss the significance of the *Sefer Ha-Razim* if we see it as a deviant form of Judaism. The book is at once a Jewish book and a book of magic. Although the author prays to Helios, to angels, and to other ministering spirits, he is nevertheless a believer in the one God of Israel. "For him they are all not divinities but angels, in other words, ministers and emissaries of the Supreme God" (Goldin, p. 135).

In the ancient world, magic was seen as a test of religious power. The Christian historian Sozomen tells a story about a man whom wonder-workers tried to free from the possession of the devil. "Neither the pagans nor the Jews could by any incantations and enchantments deliver him from his affliction." It was only a Christian healer who could deliver the man. "Hilarion [a Christian], by simply calling on the name of Christ, expelled the demon, and Alaphion, with his whole family, immediately embraced Christianity" (*Hist. eccl.* 5.15). Obviously the story is self-serving, designed to promote Sozomen's religion, but it illustrates the religious power of effective magic.

The success of Jewish magic lay in drawing people away from churches to the synagogues. Hence Chrysostom presents Jewish magic as the work of the devil, and warns Christians that, if they rely on Jewish magicians, they will be found guilty on judgment day and plagued with a guilty conscience during their lives. "How will you defend yourself before Christ? How will you call on him in your prayers? Afterwards, with what kind of conscience will you enter the church? With what eyes will you look at the priest? With what hands will you touch the holy table? With what ears will you listen to the reading of the Scriptures?" (*Jud.* 8.7; 937).

John's sermons make it clear that the friction between himself and the Judaizers in Antioch was not primarily the result of ideological difference, though this was surely part of the dispute, but chiefly between competing religious loyalties. John's polemic was directed at what the Judaizers *did*—participate in the rites of a rival religion. Their actions made other Christians wonder: Whose religion is more powerful? Whose rites are the most effective? Consequently, John's primary goal in the sermons was to win back the Judaizers to the Christian rites—

to the Eucharist, to the "sign of the cross" (*Jud.* 8.8; 940) which can ward off demons, and to the "martyrs and holy ones, God's friends," whose bones can combat the power of Jewish magicians (*Jud.* 8.77; 937).

The Efficacy of Religious Rites

Martyrs, particularly the Maccabean martyrs, were another source of conflict between Jews and Christians in Antioch. Seven Maccabean brothers, their mother, and the scribe Eleazar were martyred during the reign of Antiochus IV (Epiphanes) in the second century B.C.E., the occasion being their refusal to eat pork, according to 2 Maccabees 6–7. As mentioned in Chapter 2, their martyrdom may have taken place in Antioch. Whatever the historical setting however, the remains of the martyrs were buried there (Bickerman). By the first century of the common era, a synagogue had been built at the burial site and the Maccabean martyrs had become an object of veneration among the Jews.

In the fourth century, however, the Maccabean martyrs began to stir the imagination of Christians in various parts of the Mediterranean world. A Christian cult of the Maccabees began to emerge and bishops preached panegyrics on the anniversary of their deaths (cf. Gregory Nazianzus *Or.* 15). Sometime during the fourth century, on the wave of devotion to the Maccabees, the Christians in Antioch were able to take possession of the synagogue and made it into a Christian martyrium (Augustine *Serm.* 300; Simon 1936, pp. 413–20). Exactly how and when this came about is unclear, but by the time John was ordained to the presbyterate, the relics seem to have been in the possession of the Christians. Chrysostom preached several sermons on the festival of the Maccabean martyrs, whose relics would soon become objects of pilgrimage (*Antonini Placentini Itinerarium* 190, ed. Geyer; Schatkin 1974).[8]

To fourth-century Christian piety, martyrs were local heroes, men and women who had given their lives in the name of Christ, whose tombs had become objects of religious veneration, and whose bones were thought to possess divine power. In some cities on the anniversaries of the martyrs, people brought meal cakes and bread and wine to their tombs (Augustine *Conf.* 6.2). One of the most famous Antiochene martyrs was St. Babylas, bishop from 237 C.E. to 250 C.E., who

8. On the Maccabean martyrs in Christian piety, see also Frend, pp. 19–21, and Rampolla.

was imprisoned and martyred under the emperor Decius. A church was named after him in Antioch and he was the subject of several of John's sermons. To the faithful, the bones of the martyrs were palpable symbols of divine power. In his sermons John stresses the experience of *viewing* the remains of the martyrs. In a sermon preached on the anniversary of St. Drosis, a young woman burned for her faith in Antioch, John vividly describes the experience of going to the tomb outside of the city and viewing the sarcophagi. The preacher leads the congregation "to *look* at the bodies abounding with spiritual grace." As one goes down through the door of the crypt, "many tombs *fall on one's eyes* and wherever one *looks* he *sees* urns, monuments, burial chambers of the departed." Looking at the tombs, says John, is not a small part of the life of philosophy (i.e., the Christian life) for the soul "through this *sight*" is stirred to faith (*Pan. Dros.* 1; 50.683–84).

Because the martyrs were individuals associated with a particular place, and were often men and women of recent memory (some from the time of Julian), each city had its own list. Constantia and Gaza, for example, two cities in Palestine not far apart from one another, each had its own martyr festivals (Sozomen *Hist. eccl.* 5.3). At these festivals the acts of the local martyrs were read, and these were the only books allowed to be read on such occasions besides the Sacred Scriptures. The martyrs were not universal Christian heroes or saints like the apostles, but were often unknown to people living in other cities. Most of the martyrs of Antioch—Juventius, Maximinus, Barlaam, Lucianus, Phocas et al.—are mentioned only in sermons preached by Antiochene clergy.

Honored as ensigns of the faith, the martyrs were witnesses to Christian perseverance under persecution, but their remains were also thought to possess supernatural power. Greeks laugh, says John, when we speak of the deeds of martyrs continuing after their death, but their bones can blind the eyes of the devil. When demons "see the bones of the martyrs they run away" (*Pan. Macc.* 1.1; 50.617–18). "What riches and gold were incapable of, the remains of the martyrs accomplished. Gold has never been able to drive away sickness, nor put death to flight, but the bones of the martyrs have done both things, some in the times of our ancestors, others in our own times" (*Pan. Dros.* 4; 50.689).

The bones of the martyrs had become a focal point of Christian identity in fourth-century Antioch, and John pits the Christian martyrs against Jews and pagans. When Christians celebrated the anniversary of a martyr, said John, "Gentiles are ashamed and Jews hide their faces" (*Pan. Bern.* 1; 50.629). "The bones of the martyrs lighten up the whole city; they shine more brightly than the rays of the sun"

(*Pan. Macc.* 1.1; 50.617). Not everyone, however, was convinced by John's rhetoric or by Christian devotion. Some said that the remains were just "ashes," or "dust," or "bones which have deteriorated with time." They do not see, laments John, the "power of God which accompanies them and the grace of the Spirit which surrounds them" (*Pan. Bern.* 1; 50.629).

In this environment, the question inevitably arose: to whom do the Maccabean martyrs really belong? Even though by John's time their remains were in the hands of the Christians, no one could deny that the Maccabean martyrs were Jews, and that they had given their lives for Jewish religious practices. The Jews chided the Christians that the Maccabees had died "for the Law and the prescriptions of the Law; they were slaughtered because of the flesh of pork." The Christians, on the other hand, claimed, though with little justification, that the Maccabean martyrs "poured out their blood for the sake of Christ" (Chrysostom, *Hom. de Eleazaro* 1; 63.525). Though the Christians had possession of the relics, the Jews had the better of the argument.

The Maccabean martyrs are only one more illustration of how Jews and Christians were put in competition with each other in the fourth century. Jewish festivals, Jewish martyrs, Jewish magic, Jewish books— all seemed to conspire against John to draw his followers away from the Church to the synagogues. Though John's sermons highlight the conflict in the years 386–87, the situation in Antioch at that time was not ephemeral. It reflected an ongoing problem. In the next century, another Christian preacher from Antioch, Isaac, faced a similar situation. He, too, complained about the attraction of Christians to Jewish magicians and sorcerers, to incantations that use countless names of angels and heavenly beings. The Jews realized the religious power of their rites and traditions. They "boast of their circumcision and the Sabbath which they observe" and they consider their way of life "superior" because they possess the Law (Kazan, p. 32). Isaac's sermons exhibit little of the stridency associated with Christian anti-Jewish polemic. Quite the contrary, Isaac appears envious of Jewish traditions and betrays a tone of spiritual inferiority: "I have a judgment with Jacob and a discourse with the Jews. If we all have one Father, why should anyone feel superior to the nations? I belong to the nations, and on behalf of my people I speak. What do you think, oh nation, did not the Lord create us as well as you?" (Kazan, p. 31).

In light of relations between Jews and Christians in fourth-century Antioch, the question inevitably arises: were the Jews actively proselytizing among Christians? In the years immediately after the war with the Romans in 70 C.E. and the Bar Kochba revolt in 132–35 C.E., the Romans severely restricted Jewish proselytism. But, as time went on, and relations with Rome improved, Jews began to proselytize as they had earlier.[9] The most important evidence for the continuation of proselytization by Jews is to be found in Roman law. It was common for slaves to adopt the religion of their masters. Jews were no exception in this respect, and laws were passed prohibiting Jews from coercing their slaves to become Jewish (*CT* 16.9.1). As late as 415 C.E., the emperors were passing laws prohibiting proselytization of slaves by Jews, a sure sign that the practice continued (*CT* 16.9.3).

Marriage was another way to gain converts, since a woman who married a Jew inevitably adopted the Jewish religion. Hence there are laws prohibiting marriages between Christian women and Jewish men (*CT* 16.8.6). Besides these specific cases, there are also more general laws prohibiting "conversion from Christianity to Judaism" (*CT* 16.8.7). And in the early fifth century, when Roman officials decided to abolish the patriarchate, one of the reasons they cited was that it encouraged proselytizing (*CT* 16.8.22).

Christian sources present the Jews as actively seeking Christians (Jerome *Ep.* 93), but it is more likely that the majority of the individuals who converted to Judaism during this period did so through the normal social conventions that encouraged people to change religious affiliation, for example, through marriage or slavery.[10] That Jews encouraged and welcomed such converts is without doubt, but that they mounted an active program of proselytization is less certain.

As far as Antioch is concerned, on first reading of John's sermons on the Judaizers, it appears that the Jews were actively seeking Christian converts. But a closer reading shows that John nowhere says that Jews sought out the Christians. Indeed, the whole point of the sermons is that it is the Christians who seek out the Jews. At the beginning of one sermon, he pictures the Jews as "surrounding our flock" (*Jud.* 4.1; 871) seeking to snatch the weak, but this is a stock image used over and over again by fourth-century rhetors to portray their foes.[11]

The threat in Antioch does not seem to be actual conversion to Ju-

9. A thorough and critical study of Jewish proselytism during this period does not exist. Bamberger and Braude are the most extensive, but their conclusions are drawn almost wholly from what the rabbis *said* about proselytizing. For a criticism of Braude for ignoring other evidence, see Alon, 1970, 2: 278–84. Most scholars would agree that proselytism continued during this period, as evidenced especially in legislation against proselytism, and that the attitudes of the rabbis were, on the whole, positive toward proselytes. See Avi-Yonah, pp. 181–83; Simon, 1964, pp. 314–55; Bamberger, pp. 149 ff.

10. For evidence that the Jews were zealous in seeking converts, see Levine, pp. 81–82.

11. See Chapter 4, below.

daism, though this must have taken place on occasion, but the loss of credibility that Christian leaders experienced in the face of a rival religion, and in the concrete effect that Judaizers had on attendance at Christian services and festivals. The Judaizers were dissidents who disrupted the unity of the Church by participating in the religious rites of a rival. Their actions had a powerful symbolic impact, for they called into question the truth of Christian teaching and practice as taught and observed by the majority of the Christians in Antioch.

As I have emphasized repeatedly in this chapter, the conflict between Judaism and Christianity in Antioch was a conflict over the efficacy of different rites. Christians had baptism, the Eucharist, Epiphany, Easter, the tombs of the martyrs, the Gospels; the Jews had circumcision, the Sabbath, Passover, Rosh Hashannah, Yom Kippur, Sukkoth, the book of the Torah. Whose traditions were the most authentic, and whose rites were more successful in ensuring the presence of the divine? Where was the "'divine power' . . . to be found on earth and . . . on what terms [could] access to it be achieved?" (Brown 1978, p. 11).

In the great cities of the Roman Empire the primary distinguishing marks of religious allegiance were ritual, the proper observance of festivals, and the calendar. In the ninth century, a Christian bishop of Damascus, in explaining Christianity to a Muslim, mentions first that Christians "observe the Sundays and Christian festivals" (Browne, p. 7). Only after he has mentioned these does he go on to refer to the creed, the Scriptures, the priesthood, and other marks of Christianity. What set Christians off from other peoples was that they observed Sunday as their day of worship rather than Saturday or Friday, and they followed a different calendar. There is a story of a medieval Russian merchant named Athanasius who was robbed of his books and was fearful, since he was traveling in a foreign land, that he could no longer be sure of the date of Easter (Baynes). Similarly, a medieval Jewish writer, Jacob ben Ephraim, when asked about a Christian sect that followed Jesus yet kept the Jewish calendar, replied: We do not repel those "who ascribe prophetical power to those who were no prophets, Jesus, Muhammad, and Abu Isa—because they agree with us about the festival calendar" (Ginzberg, p. 105). As long as they celebrated the Jewish festivals, they were considered Jews. Calendar was a primary mark of religious identity.

These observations, drawn from a later period, help explain the nature of the conflict between Jews and Christians in Antioch. As John often says, the Judaizers separate themselves from the "spiritual assembly" and "mutilate the pleasure of the holy feast." Though they may be united with us "in word and name," they act like Jews. By celebrating the Pasch at a different time, "what they consider a minor matter," they do themselves great harm (*Hom. 12 in Gen.* 2:4; 53.98). The *date* of the Pasch was not incidental. Here, then, was the nub of the issue: one had to choose either the Christian calendar or the Jewish calendar, between Christian Baptism or Jewish circumcision, between the Jewish Sabbath or the Christian Sunday. There was no middle ground. The legitimacy of the rites was measured not by theological arguments, but by participating in the ritual. If one participated in the Jewish festivals, the very act of doing so established the legitimacy of the rite.

Pagan rites did not hold the same attraction for Christians in Antioch as did the Jewish festivals. Furthermore, the pull of the pagan festivals, for example, the Kalends, does not seem to have sprung from their religious magnetism. The Jewish rites, however, definitely offered a spiritual attraction for Christians. As we saw earlier in this chapter, Christians were drawn to Jewish customs and observances precisely because they were Jewish, not because they were strange or alluring. It is also interesting that what drew pagans to Judaism, as is evident from the statements of pagans as well as Jews, were such things as the Jewish Scriptures and the Jewish teaching about one God; but Greeks and Romans were repelled by many of the Jewish laws, the prescription about circumcision, the ban on the eating of pork, the observance of the Sabbath.[12] In contrast, it was precisely the prescriptions of the law (circumcision, the Sabbath, the festivals) that attracted Christians.

It is because they are Christians that the Judaizers are drawn to the Jews, and it is as Christians that they justify their actions. A persistent, though seldom noted, theme in the writings on Judaizers from the early Church is that they sanctioned their observance of the Law by appealing to the example of Jesus, who as a Jew had kept the Law. Origen says in one place that Judaizers justify their practice with the argument that Christians should be "imitators of Christ" (*Matt. comm. serm.* 79) and other Christian sources confirm his statement. Epiphanius reports that Judaizers say: "Christ was circumcised; therefore you should be circumcised: Christ lived according to the law; therefore you should do the same" (*Haer.* 28.5.1). In Antioch the Judaizers defended their practices by appealing to the example of Christ. If Christ celebrated the Jewish Pasch, his followers would do likewise (*Jud.* 3.4; 866).[13]

Not only did the Judaizers participate in Jewish rites and appeal to

12. This is not to say that no gentiles were drawn to the ritual aspects of Judaism. For evidence from Jewish sources, see Marmorstein 1950, pp. 77–92 (Hebrew section).

13. See also Hippolytus *Haer.* 7.34. 1–2; *Chron. Pasch.* 6–7 (PG 92. 80–81).

the authority of Jesus to justify their practices, they also defended Jewish traditions to other Christians. John says that those who "worship with the Jews" are "always taking up cudgels in the Jews' defense" (*Jud.* 4.3; 875). For these reasons I am inclined to see the Judaizers in Antioch not as unlettered and uneducated Christians, "half-Christians" who indiscriminately mixed Jewish and Christian elements.[14] They seem rather to reflect, in inchoate form, a different type of Christianity, which claimed to receive its authority from Judaism and from the example of Jesus, not from the apostolic tradition as interpreted by the great Church. This is why they could not be ignored.

What happened in Antioch in the late fourth century was neither unique nor unprecedented in the early Church, though the intensity of the struggle there and the vehemence of John's response are singular. This was, no doubt, due to the size and prestige of the Jewish community, as well as its spiritual power. But the magnetism of the synagogue must be attributed not simply to the repute of the Jewish community or the numinous power of Jewish holy places or Jewish books; it was also due to the intimate relations that existed between Judaism and Christianity. The Christians who went to the synagogue and observed Jewish law believed that the Law given by Moses and recorded in Scriptures venerated and read by Christians placed an obligation on them.

Throughout the history of the early Church, when Christian leaders were faced with attrition in Christian ranks due to the presence of strong Jewish communities in the cities in which they lived, they prohibited intercourse between Jews and Christians; others put Christian rites in direct competition with Jewish rites, calling for a fast when Jews feasted, and a feast when Jews fasted, or insisting that Christians work on Saturday and attend church on Sunday. Others wrote treatises against the Jews. John Chrysostom met the Judaizers face to face, from the pulpit, armed solely with his voice and the skills of a rhetor.

14. For the view that the Judaizers in Antioch represented an "inconsistent and incoherent juxtaposition" of Judaism and Christianity, see Simon, 1964, p. 374.

· IV ·

Fourth-Century Preaching
and the Rhetoric of Abuse

In the cities of the later Roman Empire, speaking in public was an honored profession. "Hellenistic culture was above all things a rhetorical culture and its typical literary form was the public lecture" (Marrou 1956, p. 195). The rhetor was the darling of late antique society. When he walked the streets, he was ogled by the curious; when emperors came to town they sought him out. The wealthy and powerful invited him to their homes to impress their friends. On sarcophagi the cultivated man was pictured as a rhetor, declaiming before a crowd of admirers (Marrou 1938, pp. 199–200). Even if one's background were poor or servile, the ability to address a crowd on the great themes of life, to praise the city's heroes and vilify its enemies opened doors to fame and wealth. Without props or costumes, armed only with his voice, the rhetor exhorted, cajoled, amused; he told stories and recounted deeds of valor; he raised people's hopes in defeat and calmed their passions in times of crisis. With a range of vocabulary and expression, of tone and gesture known to us only on the stage, the rhetor enthralled his audience. He was an entertainer, a virtuoso, trained to dazzle the public no matter how grand the occasion or how trite his theme.

In a world in which the most casual communications are written on slips of paper, this ancient infatuation with oratory appears eccentric.

The modern captivity to the written language, our impatience with verbosity, makes us forget that language is first and foremost sound, and that few things give as much pleasure as the sound of one's own language spoken well. In antiquity the art of cultivated and elegant speech reached a level of excellence that has seldom been surpassed. To this day the study and practice of rhetoric, such as it is, still draws on the writings of the ancients.

Beginning in the second century c.e. and continuing to the end of the fourth century, rhetoric blossomed in the cities of the Roman Empire. This period—usually designated the "second sophistic" to distinguish it from the classical period (fifth and fourth centuries b.c.e) when men such as Prodicus, Gorgias, and Protagoras dominated ancient rhetoric—was a time of literary exuberance. The practice of rhetoric had an enormous impact on how intelligent men and women wrote, and, consequently, on how they thought. "The cities of the Greek world bloomed as their wealthy citizens lavished money and taste on libraries, gymnasia, statues, and shrines. . . . The scions of the rich sat at the feet of powerful professors. Literary activity, both sophistic and not sophistic, flourished in the congenial atmosphere" (Bowersock 1974, p. 1).

The term *sophist* as used in this period refers to the rhetor, the public speaker, as well as the teacher of rhetoric, not to the hucksters of specious reasoning. "Sophists were, in a word, orators. Their impressive and today their best known speeches were those efforts on ceremonial occasions when a great sophist appeared before an emperor, an assembly, or a religious festival" (Kennedy 1974, p. 17). The chief characteristic of the style of the sophists was archaism, imitating the language of the classical writers. But besides this archaizing tendency, sophists made extensive use of hyperbole, of arresting metaphors and striking comparisons. They also employed a whole range of technical literary and rhetorical devices, such as repetition of parallel phrases, play on words similar in sound but dissimilar in sense, alliteration, assonance et al., and an affective approach to persuasion and argumentation.

For the modern reader who comes to the speeches of the sophists after the prose of the Hellenistic period or the language of the New Testament, the shift in vocabulary, sentence structure, literary pretensions and affectation is dramatic. The language appears labored, artificial, burdened with metaphors, laced with literary artifices, ostentatious. Lucian, the second-century satirist, wrote a humorous dialogue, *Professor of Public Speaking*, offering advice to the budding rhetor. "Cull from one source or other fifteen, or anyhow not more than twenty, Attic words, drill yourself carefully in them and have them ready at the tip of your tongue—'sundry,' 'eftsoons,' 'prithee,' 'in some wise,' 'fair sir,' and the like. Whenever you speak, sprinkle in some of them as relish. Never mind if the rest is inconsistent with them, unrelated and discordant" (*Rhetorum praeceptor* 16). But Lucian, who, in the style of the rhetors, exaggerates, used the very devices common to the rhetorical tradition to criticize rhetorical abuse. For the rhetorical education was the backbone of ancient culture and every intellectual pursuit betrayed its influence—the writing of history, philosophy, poetry, theological polemics, biblical commentaries, and, eventually, preaching.

The Skill of the Rhetors

In the classical period of oratory, the rhetors distinguished three forms of speeches, the deliberative, used primarily in the council and assembly of the city; the judicial, used in the courtroom; and the epideictic, speeches for show, delivered in the theater or odeum. All three were used in classical times, but as the city states gave way to an empire ruled by a monarch, the first two diminished in importance and the epideictic speech, a rhetorical exhibition before a live audience, became the primary vehicle of the rhetor's art. These speeches were delivered at religious festivals, on the occasion of a great victory, at an audience before an emperor or other important person, or on the invitation of a neighboring city.

On occasion, rhetorical contests were held and the outstanding rhetors of the day were placed in competition with each other. In a delightful account of the triumphant return of the sophist Prohaeresius from exile, the biographer Eunapius, who wrote the *Lives of the Sophists*, describes the excitement generated by the speeches of the best orators. "Then from the chair the sophist first delivered a graceful prelude by way of preliminary speech, in which he extolled the greatness of extemporary eloquence." When Prohaeresius sighted two of his bitterest enemies, he told the proconsul to have them propose a theme. "They produced the hardest and most disagreeable theme that they knew of, that gave no opening for the display of fine rhetoric." Prohaeresius accepted on the condition that the proconsul granted two requests. The first was that shorthand writers be called in to stand behind him and take down the speech. "The second was even more difficult to grant. . . . 'There must be no applause whatever.'" After the proconsul had given the order,

> Prohaeresius began his speech with a flood of eloquence,
> rounding every period with a sonorous phrase, while the audience, which perforce kept a Pythagorean silence, in their

amazed admiration broke their restraint, and overflowed into murmurs and sighs. As the speech grew more vehement and the orator soared to heights which the mind of man could not describe or conceive of, he passed on to the second part of the speech and completed the exposition of the theme. But then, suddenly leaping into the air like one inspired, he abandoned the remaining part, left it undefended, and turned the flood of his eloquence to defend the contrary hypothesis. The scribes could hardly keep pace with him, the audience could hardly endure to remain silent, while the mighty stream of words flowed on. Then, turning his face towards the scribes, he said. "Observe carefully whether I remember all the arguments that I used earlier." And, without faltering over a single word, he began to declaim the same speech for the second time. At this the proconsul did not observe his own rules, nor did the audience observe the threats of the magistrate. For all who were present licked the sophist's breast as though he were the statue of some god; some kissed his feet, some his hands, others declared him to be a god or the very model of Hermes, the god of eloquence. [Eunapius VS 489–90]

Only a person with a highly disciplined training could deliver such a speech, for extempore speech requires close mastery of technique, gifts of memorization, and a storehouse of stock phrases and metaphors, as well as the skills of an actor. By the fourth century, the methods of instruction were firmly fixed, handed on from teacher to teacher, and available in handbooks where they can be read today.[1] This education consisted of three chief parts: theory, study of models, and exercises. First, the student learned the rules and principles of speech making, then he studied the classical writers—Demosthenes, Isocrates, Thucydides, Plato—to observe how the rules were exemplified. Finally he wrote and delivered his own speeches, always following a set pattern. The actual writing and delivery of a speech depended on five distinct skills: invention, arrangement, elocution, memorization, and delivery.

How a rhetor approached a speech can be seen by looking at one of these skills, invention. As the term suggests, invention was a technique for discovery, a device to prompt the memory and stimulate the imagination. This was done through a rehearsal of set categories, a list of topics that purported to canvass the main subjects in any given theme.

---

1. See, for example, Libanius's *progymnasmata* in vol. 8 of *Libanii Opera*, ed. Foerster, and the *progymnasmata* of Apthonius, Theon, Hermogenes, and Aristides in L. Spengel, *Rhetores Graeci*, vol. 3.

In a speech of praise (*encomium*), for example, the topics included the person's birth, family, environment, personal advantages, education, et al. An ancient rhetorical manual, composed by Theon, a second-century sophist, lists the topics as follows.[2]

I. Exterior Excellences
  A. Noble birth
  B. Environment
    1. Native city
    2. Fellow citizens
    3. Excellence of the city's political regime
    4. Parents and family
  C. Personal advantages
    1. Education
    2. Friends
    3. Fame
    4. Public service
    5. Wealth
    6. Children, number and beauty of
    7. Happy death
II. Bodily Excellences
  A. Health
  B. Strength
  C. Beauty
  D. Bubbling vitality and capacity for deep feeling
III. Spiritual Excellences
  A. Virtues
    1. Wisdom
    2. Temperance
    3. Courage
    4. Justice
    5. Piety
    6. Nobility
    7. Sense of Greatness
  B. Resultant Actions
    1. As to their objectives
      a. Altruistic and disinterested
      b. Good, non-utilitarian, or pleasant
      c. In the public interest
      d. Braving risks and dangers
    2. As to their circumstances

2. Text in *Rhetores Graeci*, 2.109; trans. Marrou, 1956, pp. 198–99.

    a. Timely
    b. Original
    c. Performed alone
    d. More than anyone else
    e. Few to help him
    f. Old head on young shoulders
    g. Against all the odds
    h. At great cost to himself
    i. Prompt and efficient

To the modern reader this list of topics appears stiff and wooden, but the rhetors understood that without such a structure the speech would be shapeless, diffuse, rambling from one topic to another. Imitation, contrary to the modern view, can incite creativity and originality. The disciplined training of the rhetors made it possible for them to speak with ease and confidence, and often with little preparation, on many and varied topics. It also gave them the freedom to improvise, to dwell on the tone of voice or the choice of a phrase, or to accent the dramatic impact of a story by the use of gestures.

Besides the encomium, students learned to write other set speeches, such as invectives or comparisons. Libanius's rhetorical handbook includes, among others, encomiums on Diomedes, Odysseus, Achilles, Demosthenes, justice, and farming, and invectives on Achilles, Hector, Aeschines, wealth, and anger (*Opera* 8.217–328). He provides examples of the comparison: Achilles with Diomedes, Demosthenes with Aeschines, the city with the country et al. (*Opera* 8.334–60). Other fixed exercises included *ethopoeiae* (character sketches); *ekphraseis* (extended descriptions), for example, of a land battle (*Opera* 8.461), a harbor or a garden, hunting wild beasts, or drunkenness (*Opera* 8.477); *chreia*, short anecdotes with practical significance; and theses, or discussions of set topics, such as "whether one should marry?" and "whether one should build a wall?" These exercises helped students acquire the skills necessary to develop whatever theme was called for, to intersperse speeches with suitable digressions, such as pleasing descriptions of natural phenomenon, and to draw suggestive comparisons.

The study of rhetoric could become an end in itself, especially when the rhetors lacked great themes for their speeches, or wrote elegant speeches on a fly (Lucian *Musc.*) or eulogies on a parrot (Philostratus *VS* 1.7; 487), much as baroque musicians turned the techniques of their art to similar frivolity. Artificiality, technical frills for their own sake, labored comparisons, verbosity—these were some of the hazards of the rhetorical tradition. This is not to mention vanity, conceit, and infatuation with the sound of the crowd. To win fame and wealth

as a rhetor, said Lucian, one needs only "effrontery and shameless-
ness." Away with "modesty, respectability, self-restraint. . . . You need
a very loud voice, a shameless singing delivery, and a gait like a mime.
. . . Let your clothing be gaily colored, or else white, a fabric of Taren-
tine manufacturer, so that your body will show through; and wear either high Attic sandals of the kind that women wear, with many slits,
or else Sicyonian boots, trimmed with strips of white felt" (*Rhetorum
praeceptor* 15).

Critics notwithstanding, the rhetorical schools flourished and the
rhetors prospered. If the rhetors were performers, the people liked
a show; if superficial, few claimed they were philosophers; if they
used empty phrases and vacuous metaphors, slapped their thighs and
swayed their hips, the people only clamored for more. And when rhetors became bishops, they carried their skills into the pulpit, which offered a new stage on which to perform. Christians began to idolize
their preachers the way pagans admired the rhetors. "In our time,"
wrote John, "a passion for oratory has taken hold of Christians" (*Sac.*
5.8; 48, 677).

Christian Rhetors

When the second sophistic penetrated the Church, it profoundly
transformed the preaching and writing style of those schooled in its
techniques. Its influence can be detected in the sermons and books of
many fourth-century Christian bishops. Noteworthy representatives
of this new style were John Chrysostom and three Cappadocians, Basil
of Caesarea, Gregory of Nyssa, Basil's younger brother, and Gregory
Nazianzus, all of whom received a similar literary and rhetorical
education.[3]

Basil, who was born in 330 C.E., first studied at the rhetorical
school in Caesarea in his native Cappadocia, under the tutelage of his
father, a teacher of rhetoric. After completing his studies, he went to
Constantinople, the bustling new city on the Bosporus where Libanius
was teaching (before his return to Antioch), and thence to Athens to
study with Himerius and Prohairesius, two of the most distinguished
fourth-century sophists. Only after he had achieved a reputation as
speaker and teacher, and had received offers to teach in several cities,
did he consider an ecclesiastical career, a step that, as we saw in the
Chapter 1, was well suited for one trained in rhetoric.

3. For the influence of the second sophistic on Christian preaching and writing see
Meridier; Bernardi; Ruether, 1969; and Kennedy, 1980.

How deeply the rhetorical tradition formed these men can be seen in Gregory of Nazianzus, an intimate friend of Basil's and the beneficiary of a similar education (Ruether 1969, pp. 18–28). Gregory spent ten years studying rhetoric, and, when he began to write theological works, he eschewed the literary forms Christian writers had evolved during the first few centuries. He wrote neither commentaries on the Scriptures nor theological treatises nor polemical tracts, and even avoided the sermon (typically a homily on a biblical text). Instead, he wrote poems, letters, and orations, accepted literary forms in the rhetorical tradition. His friends chided him that he preferred that name *rhetor* to that of Christian (*Ep.* 11.4). Later in his life, he claimed that all of his study of rhetoric was intended to "turn bastard letters to the service of those that are genuine" (*Carmen de vita sua*, lns. 113–14; *PG* 37.1037), but his writings belie this claim. As an old man, Gregory spent most of his time writing poems, one of which is a long autobiographical work consisting of 2000 lines of iambic trimeters.

Of the four mentioned, only Gregory of Nyssa exhibited a profound philosophical intelligence, a trait seldom found in sophists. Yet even Gregory, especially as a young man, took greater delight in how something was said than in what was said. Writing to Libanius to thank him for a letter, Gregory observed, "It was a custom with the Romans, after the custom of their fathers, to celebrate a feast in wintertime, when the days begin to lengthen as the sun climbs to the upper regions of the sky. Now the beginning of the month is esteemed holy, and by this day auguring the character of the whole year, they devote themselves to forecasting good fortune, gladness and wealth. Why do I begin my letter in this way? I do so because I too kept this feast, having received a present of gold like others." What is Gregory's present? A letter from Libanius. "For gold came into my hands, gold, not like that vulgar gold, which rulers treasure and which those who possess it give—that heavy, vile and lifeless possession—but that which is loftier than all wealth, as Pindar says, in the eyes of those that have understanding, the fairest mark of friendship, I mean your letter and the vast wealth which it contained (*Ep.* 14.2).

What gave Gregory such pleasure in the letter from Libanius was not so much its message as the beauty of language and the grace of expression—in short, its style. So delighted was Gregory that he called in his friends to read and reread the letter so that all might share in his pleasure. "And I, being overjoyed at the concurrence, threw open my treasure to all who were present; and all shared in it, each getting the whole of it without any rivalry. . . . For the letter by passing through the hands of all, like a ticket for a feast, is the private wealth of each, some by steady continuous reading engraving the words on their memory, and others taking an impression of them upon tablets; and it was again in my hands, giving me more pleasure than the hard metal does to the eyes of the rich" (*Ep.* 14). No doubt Gregory was as pleased with himself over the letter he was writing to Libanius as he was with the letter he had received. He hoped to charm the great rhetor with his style, as well as with the subject matter, for his letter urged Libanius to persuade a mutual friend to devote himself to the study of rhetoric. The writing of charming and graceful letters was taken very seriously by Christian sophists, as Gregory Nazianzus explains in one of his letters dealing specifically with the writing of letters (*Ep.* 51).

The extent to which a Christian thinker like Gregory was formed by the rhetorical tradition can be seen in his youthful work *On Virginity*. Gregory calls his treatise an "encomium" on virginity and explains that he has adopted this form rather than a "simple speech" because it is capable of "stimulating" the reader to practice a life of virtue (*De virg.*, Preface 1). In the style of ancient rhetoric, the book was designed not simply to persuade its readers of the benefits of virginity, but "to create in its readers a desire for the life of virtue" (*De virg.*, Preface 1). The book itself is prolix and pretentious, the youthful work of a man showing off his rhetorical training. Filled with excess, tedious in the heaping up of metaphors and comparison, pedantic in its deliberate choice of rare and unusual words, it is not untypical of the work of fourth-century rhetors. The spirit is captured in a short passage from its beginning, in which Gregory describes the perils of marriage:

> Let us take a marriage that is in every respect happy: noble birth, adequate means of support, suitable ages, the flower of youth, great affection, the very best that each can think of the other, pleasant rivalry in which each seeks to outdo the other in loving. Add to this popularity, power, reputation, and whatever one wishes. But observe that even beneath this array of blessings the fire of inevitable sadness is smouldering. I do not speak of the envy that springs up against those who are well born. . . . I omit this from the picture, as though envy against them were asleep. . . . What then is the sadness, you will say, when even envy of their happiness does not touch them? I say that this very thing—that their life is happy in every respect—is the spark that kindles suffering. For in so far as they are humans, mortal and perishing, they need only to look at the tombs of their ancestors to realize the fate that awaits them. So pain is

inseparably bound up with their existence if they have the least power of reflection. When the husband looks at the face of his beloved, inevitably the fear of separation comes upon him. If he listens to her sweet voice, he realizes there will come a time when he will not hear it. And when he is charmed by gazing at her beauty, then he shudders most of all over the anticipation of mourning her loss. When he marks all those charms that are so dear to youth and that the thoughtless pursue, the bright eyes beneath the lids, the arching eyebrows, the cheek with its sweet and dimpling smile, the natural red that blooms upon the lips, the hair bound in gold and shining in many-twisted masses on the head, and all that transient grace, then, though he may be little given to reflect, he must have this thought also in his inmost soul, that someday all this beauty will melt away and become as nothing, turned after all this show into loathsome and hideous bones, which wear no trace, no memorial, no remnant of that living bloom." [*De virg.* 3.2]

Gregory of Nyssa was not an ancient Ernest Becker, offering the specter of death as the motive force of human action. He was an ancient rhetor, appealing to the fears and dread of his readers, drawing on the emotive impact of language and images to inflame them with a love of virginity and a repugnance against marriage. The joyful, expectant marriage of a young, devoted couple, becomes, in the hands of the rhetor, the beginning of sadness and tragedy. One cannot read a work written by one skilled in the rhetorical tradition, especially by a young man, as one would read a theological or philosophical treatise presented in a discursive style. *On Virginity* was as much an exhibition of Gregory's skill as it was an argument for the virtues of chastity.[4] Not everything that he says should be taken with equal seriousness.

The greatest of the Christian sophists was John Chrysostom. Later generations called Gregory of Nazianzus "the theologian," but John they called the "golden mouth." In his own lifetime, and in the generation immediately after his death, Christians and pagans alike admired his language and style (Isidore of Pelusium *Ep.* 5.32; 2.42). To the Byzantines, he was the "full-toned trumpet of the Holy Spirit," the "golden lyre of the Holy Spirit." In modern times, classical scholars, whose appreciation of most Christian writers is restrained, have been unanimous in praising John. Wilamowitz-Moellendorf called his style the "harmonious expression of an Attic soul" (p. 96). With greater reserve, but no less admiration, the Swedish classicist Fabricius said that

4. For a compact discussion of the rhetorical features of *De virginitate*, see Aubineau, pp. 83–96.

John wrote a "flawless classical style" (p. 144). Like other rhetors, John was more at home on a pulpit or lecture platform than at a desk. As a young man, he wrote some treatises, but most of his writings are transcriptions of sermons. His "main effort was directed toward preaching, not writing. . . . The force of his personality and oratorical ability inspired such enthusiasm in his audience that they were unwilling to let his sermons go unrecorded. Stenographers therefore recorded his words[,] which were afterwards transcribed and circulated" (Goodall, p. 78). The pulpit was his forum. Today his sermons can only be read, but it must be remembered that they were designed to be delivered orally and that the response of his audience was an integral part of his preaching.

In the churches where John spoke, the pulpit stood in the middle of the nave, not perched at one end on the edge of a chancel. The pulpit was little more than a small stand, two or three feet high, with a platform on top. No podium, reading desk, or screen stood between the preacher and the congregation. People crowded around the pulpit, like crowds around a soap-box orator, looking up at the speaker, often close enough to touch him. The pulpit (*ambo*) simply provided a modest elevation, enough to lift the preacher a few feet above the crowd, to help project his voice and display his hands and face. With nothing between himself and the audience, the skillful preacher could move the emotions of his hearers at will.

Christians expected a performance in church equal to what they enjoyed in the theater. If dissatisfied, they booed and hissed; if delighted they clapped their hands and shouted. Most people, said John, "listen to a preacher for pleasure, not for profit, like critics at a play or concert" (*Sac.* 5.1; 48.673). The people had favorites, taking sides as to who was best, idolizing their heroes. They became "partisans, some liking this preacher, others another, listening to their words with favor or dislike" (*Sac.* 5.1; 48.672). Each time the preacher appeared, he was expected to top his previous performance, always offering something new, a conspicuous metaphor or a string of unusual or arcane words:

> If it happens that a preacher weaves among his own words anything taken from another, he falls into worse disgrace than a common thief. And often when he has borrowed nothing at all, he suffers, on bare suspicion, the fate of a convicted felon. But why mention the work of others? He is not allowed to repeat his own composition too soon. . . . The power of eloquence . . . is more desired in a church than when professors of rhetoric are made to contend against each other. [*Sac.* 5.1; 48.672–73]

Like the rhetors, the preachers expected a response of shouts and cheers, applause, stomping of feet. John complained about the love of applause (*Hom.* 30.3 *in Acts* 13:42; 60.225) but, like any other speaker, he sought and desired the adoration of the crowd. What greater disgrace, he says, than to walk from the pulpit "with blank silence," and what is more embarrassing than to be met by the faces of listeners "waiting for the end of the sermon as if it were a relief after fatigue" (*Sac.* 5.8; 678). In one sermon, when the congregation did not respond, John raised the emotional pitch of his language until finally the congregation shouted its approval and broke into applause (*Diab.* 1.1; 49.245). In the first homily on the Jews, he had the reverse experience. After only a few opening sentences, filled with hyperbole, his speech "set the people afire with enthusiasm" and the "congregation broke into thunderous applause" (*Hom. Jud.* 1.1; 843).

When John entered the pulpit, the people of Antioch always expected a stellar performance. The more gifted the rhetor, the more demanding the audience could be.

> If his sermon does not match the great expectation formed of the speaker, he will leave the pulpit the victim of countless jeers and complaints. No one ever takes into consideration that a fit of depression, pain, anxiety, or in many cases anger, may cloud the clarity of his mind, and prevent his production from coming forth unalloyed. . . . Being a man he cannot invariably reach the same standard or always be successful but will naturally make many mistakes and obviously fall below the standard of his real ability. People are unwilling to allow for any of these factors . . . but criticize him as if they were sitting in judgment on an angel. [*Sac.* 5.5; 48.675]

Nevertheless, John loved to preach, and year after year he preached two, three, sometimes four times a week. Words rushed from his mouth like a mighty torrent; his sermons fill over a dozen volumes in the tight-cropped columns of the Greek Patrology. Nothing else gave him such pleasure. When he stepped before a congregation, he came alive. "Preaching makes me well. . . . As soon as I open my mouth, all weariness is gone; as soon as I begin to talk, all fatigue is over. . . . For just as you are hungry to hear, so am I hungry to preach" (*Hom. post terrae* 50.713).

The Practice of Rhetoric

How did the preacher win and hold the attention of his audience? Preachers, said John, are like those who care for the sick. "We must not set before them a meal prepared haphazardly, but a variety of dishes so that the patient may choose what suits his taste. We should proceed in the same way in spiritual banquets. Since we are weak the sermon must be varied and embellished; it must contain comparisons, examples, elaborations, digressions, and the like so that we may select what will profit our soul" (*Proph. obscur.* 1; 56.165).

Of all the devices at the rhetor's disposal, the one that stands out is hyperbole, exaggeration. The rhetors overstate, they magnify, they use poetical and grandiloquent words for the simplest actions; everything is writ larger than life. "Callimachus withstood a shower of missiles of every kind . . . until he had exhausted all the arrows of Asia and fatigued the grand army of the king," proclaims the Greek rhetor Polemon (*Call.* 10; Hinck, p. 19). "The very theater of angels shouted aloud at the endurance of his soul and applauded him the victor," John declaims. Speaking of the absent bishop Flavian, he says, "When I look on that throne, deserted and bereft of our teacher, I rejoice and weep at the same time. I weep because I do not see our father with us. But I rejoice that he has set on a journey for our preservation. . . . Here is both an ornament to you, and a crown to him; an ornament to you that such a father has been allotted to you; a crown to him, because he is so affectionate towards his children" (*Stat.* 3.1; 49.47).

The first sermon on the Judaizers begins with two paragraphs of hyperbole based on a catena of scriptural citations. After citing four biblical texts, John says, "Although these testimonies were sufficient proof, I was not satisfied with the prophets; nor did I stop with the apostles. I went up to heaven itself and displayed to you the chorus of angels singing, 'Glory to God in the highest heaven, and on earth peace, good will to men.' Moreover you heard the seraphim, trembling and filled with awe, cry out, 'Holy, Holy, Holy. . . .'" (*Jud.* 1.1; 843). When he finished, the congregation broke into applause. Passages such as these are not lonely flights of rhetorical enthusiasm sprinkled here and there throughout his sermons; they are the very stuff of his preaching, and they fill page after page, frequently overshadowing the presumed topic of the speech.

Besides hyperbole, the rhetors used metaphors and similes, sometimes of genuine originality, but more often hack figures repeated over and over in different contexts. John usually begins his sermons with an extended metaphor leading up to the main theme. Here is the beginning of a sermon commemorating Drosis, a fourth-century Antiochene martyr, preached at her tomb in a field outside of the city:

Industrious shepherds, when they see how the sun's bright rays shining through the long winter have at length brought warmer weather, drive their sheep out of the folds to the usual pastures.

Imitating them, our worthy shepherd [Bishop Flavian] has led
this holy and spiritual flock of Christ to these spiritual pastures
of the saints. The sheep, it is true, get their fill standing at the
manger, but once outside the pen, they derive more benefit
from the meadows, bending down with great delight, nibbling
off the grass with their teeth, breathing the fresh air, looking up
at the bright and clear sunlight, and leaping along lakes,
springs, and rivers. The earth too, decked everywhere with
flowers, gives them pleasure. This is true not only of the sheep
but of us also. For us too, indeed, there is set within the church
a table full of spiritual viands, but going out to the graves of
the holy martyrs affords us great consolation and not less ad-
vantage, not because we breathe the fresh air, but because we
fix our gaze on the grand deeds of these noble heroes.

The introduction to this sermon is brought to a close with another
rhetorical device, *parison*, a string of parallel phrases:

> We leap with joy,
>> not by rivers of flowing water
>>> but by the streams of divine grace
>> not grazing with heads bowed to the earth
>>> but gathering the virtues of the martyrs
>> not contemplating the earth decked with flowers
>>> but looking at bodies teeming with spiritual gifts.

Earlier in the same passage, he uses a similar technique, a series of
verbs parallel to one another and all ending in the same sound:

> bending down [katakupt*onta*] with great delight
>> nibbling off [apokeir*onta*] the grass with their teeth
>>> breathing [anapne*onta*] the fresh air
>>>> looking [blep*onta*] at the bright and clear sunlight
>>>>> leaping [skirt*onta*] along lakes, springs, and river.
>>>>>> [*Pan. Dros.* 1; 50.683]

This technique can be used for a series of clauses, for a string of parallel words, or for a series of prepositional phrases, as in the following
passage from the homilies on the Judaizers. God, says John, shows his
solicitude for mankind,

> by the pliability of the law
>> by the abundance of his gifts
>>> by the threat of coming punishments
>>>> by the promptness of his chastising. . . .
>>>>> [*Jud.* 8.2; 48.929]

Sermon after sermon begins with a long, carefully worked out metaphor or series of metaphors. Such metaphors had a powerful effect on the hearer because they communicated the speaker's point with forcefulness and clarity. Though the metaphor is sometimes drawn out at length and cluttered with many details, often employing seldom used words, the point is always clear and the audience can enjoy the play of language without losing the main idea of the speech.

Occasionally, the rhetors employed detailed descriptions, not only to illustrate a point, but to divert the audience, and give it a rest before returning to the theme. Commenting on Luke 14, "When you are having a party for lunch or supper, do not invite your friends . . . or your rich neighbors . . . but ask the poor, the crippled, the lame and the blind," John says:

> Let us suppose two tables, and let one be filled with . . . the blind, the halt, the maimed of hand or leg, the barefoot, those clad with but one scanty garment, and that worn out; but let the other have rulers, generals, governors, great officers, arrayed in costly robes and fine linen, belted with golden girdles. Further at the table of the poor let there be neither silver, nor store of wine, but just enough to refresh and gladden, and let the drinking cups and the rest of the vessels be made only from pottery; but at the table of the rich, let all the vessels be of silver and gold, and the semicircular table, not such as one person can lift, but as two young men can with difficulty move, with the wine-jars lying in order, glittering far beyond the silver with gold, and let this table be smoothly laid all over with soft drapery. Let there also be many guests, elegantly dressed, and wearing loose trousers, men beauteous to look upon, in the very flower of life, plump, and well conditioned. . . . And let the one have costly meats, but the other only enough to appease hunger and inspire cheerfulness. . . . Have I said enough? Are both tables laid out with sufficient minuteness? Is anything lacking? I think not. For I have gone over the guests, and the costliness of the vessels, and of the linen and of the meats.
> [*Hom.* 1.4 *in Col.* 1:1; 62.304–5]

By the time John has finished this lengthy metaphor, the audience may well have forgotten why it was introduced. But that is hardly a drawback. The comparison of the dinner party had become a digression, what the rhetors called an *ekphrasis*, and its purpose was chiefly to delight the audience. When John returned to the main theme after the digression, he knew his hearers were refreshed, ready to take up the main point of the speech. And if the digression was too long and the people forgot the point, the comparison was pleasing in its own right, and the audience could be reminded of the theme.

John draws on an arsenal of standard metaphors, commonplace in the schools, drawn from athletics, the military, the sea, pastoral life, and medicine (Ameringer, pp. 56–57).[5] The Maccabean brothers look down on the martydom of their youngest brothers "like judges in the Olympic games," acting "not as arbiters of the struggle but exhorting the champion to win the crown" (*Pan. Macc.* 2.1; 50.624). Timothy "curbed the steed that was unmanageable" and "delivered him under complete control to the hand of reason, the charioteer" (*Stat.* 1.4; 49.21). On fasting: "Let us learn the laws of fasting that we may not run heedlessly, lest we beat the air and while boxing we fight shadows" (*Stat.* 3.3; 49.51). In this last case, John is probably alluding to St. Paul, who speaks of boxing "as one beating the air" (1 Cor. 9:26).

In sermons against the foes of the church, John's language abounds with military metaphors (Burns:6–62; Ameringer:29–41). The preacher must be "at once archer and slinger, captain and general, in the ranks and on the command, on foot and on horseback, in a sea fight and in a siege" (*Sac.* 4.4; 48.666). The mouths of the martyrs are "quivers with many arrows" (*Pan. Bab.* 2.2; 50.575). Describing the contest between martyrs and tyrants, he says, "Two armies, well entrenched, are arrayed against one another, bristling with weapons and armor. . . . From every side clouds of arrows are discharged, which obscure the light of day. Rivers of blood flood the ground [note the hyperbole] and many are cut down everywhere, like the crops at harvest time" (*Pan mart.* 3.1; 50.707–8).

Fourth-century rhetorical style encouraged excess, and John was sometimes unrestrained. Like other rhetors, he heaps up metaphors. In one passage, he offers ten metaphors for excessive love of wealth: "runaway slave, cruel murderer, untamable beast, sheer precipice, rock continually washed by billows, sea agitated by winds, imperious tyrant, despot crueler than barbarians, implacable enemy, irreconcilable foe" (*Saturn.* 2; 52.416). In another sermon, he shows off by listing a series of metaphors for foes attacking the Church: "Pirates surround your vessel, wolves beset your flock, robbers undermine the bridal chamber, adulterous hissing sounds about your bride, the serpent again breaks into paradise, the foundation rock of the Church shakes, the evangelical anchor is cast down" (*Pan. Rom.* 2.1; 50.613–14). Such prolixity seems to vitiate the value of metaphor, confusing the hearer and confounding the original point, but the rhetors were undaunted and the audience clapped its approval.

5. See also Sawhill's study of athletic metaphors and the material collected in Burns.

Besides metaphor, comparison, and hyperbole, the rhetors had at their command technical devices designed to titillate the ear and entertain the mind. These technical devices, too numerous to discuss in detail here, appear time and time again. After reading many sermons, one takes them for granted, but each had its own rules and required care and precision if it was to be used effectively. I have already mentioned *parison*, one of the more popular ornamentations. Others appear frequently. In *arsis*, an idea is first stated negatively, then positively: "It is not a time for judgment, but for mercy" (*Entrop.* 1.4; 52.396); "not that you may applaud what is spoken but that you may imitate the virtue of noble men" (*Stat.* 5.2; 59.70). In John's sermons this device occurs on the average of six times to every hundred lines. *Oxymoron* combines two or more terms that are ordinarily contradictory: "hostile friend, domestic enemy" (*Stat.* 2.5; 49.41). *Epanaphora* repeats the same word at the beginning of a series of clauses or sentences, often in the form of rhetorical questions: "Who has brought them together . . . ? Who has bound them? Who has bridled them? Who has held them together?" (*Stat.* 10.2; 49.113). *Antistrophe* employs the same word at the end of successive clauses: "We fear a childish fear, fearing (*dedoikotes*) death, but not fearing sin (*dedoikotes*). Little children fear (*dedoike*) masks, but fire they do not fear (*dedoike*)" (*Stat.* 5.3; 49.73; Burns, p. 30).

Besides these devices, John uses figures for dramatic effect, such as *asyndeton*, omission of connectives, and *polysyndeton*, accumulation of connectives. He employs figures of sound: *paronomasia*, similarity of sound with dissimilarity of sense, and *parachesis*, two words of different roots but with similar sound. (This latter device, one of the most artifical embellishments of style, is used five times more frequently by John than by his contemporary, Basil of Caesarea.) His sermons use *diaporesis*, pretended doubt: "How shall I begin this speech?" Or employing *paraleipsis*, he pretends to pass over a point in silence, while emphasizing that very point. He raises questions and provides answers, giving the semblance of a dialogue. He raises objections to his argument only to refute them in the next line.

All of these techniques were capable of being used for many different purposes: to praise and to censure, to encourage and to restrain, to comfort and to blame. They could be put at the service of instruction or exhortation, to comfort a bereaved widow or censure an apostate monk, to vilify a corrupt official or praise a saintly bishop. Extraordinarily pliable, the rhetorical tradition was ready to be molded to whatever ends the rhetor wished. As a consequence, the rhetors appear more interested in the effect their speeches had on their audience, in how things sounded and how people responded, than in the truth of what they said. Elegance of phrase was more important than logic, appearance than truth. As Robert Browning remarks, somewhat unkindly, about the rhetor Himerius: he displayed a "talent for saying nothing gracefully and at length" (Browning 1970, p. 516).

As a young man, John borrowed phrases from Libanius and put them to a different, and often contrary, use. Choice phrases that Libanius used to praise Julian, John's archenemy, are stolen from Libanius and used to praise Libanius's adversaries, the monks. Libanius calls Julian a man who "laid the foundation of freedom and has not allowed the tyranny of pleasure to dominate his soul" (Or. 12.101). John describes the monk as one who "keeps his mind free and has not allowed the tyranny of pleasure to dominate the soul" (Comp. 2; 47.388). Libanius calls Julian's table "modest and [his] companions the pupils of Plato" (Or. 13.44). John calls the monk's table "modest and his companions athletes of virtue" (Comp. 3; 47.389). Julian rises while the night is young and "addresses the gods much earlier than do the birds" (Or. 12.94). The monks, says John, "address the gods much earlier than do the birds" (Comp. 3; 47.389).

In themselves, these are innocuous borrowings, typical of the rhetor's style, but they do give a good insight into the practice of rhetoric in the fourth century. The rhetor was less interested in the veracity of his language, whether it conformed to some objective standard of truth, than he was in the effect his words would have on his hearers. This can be seen particularly in the *psogos*, or invective, a form of speech learned in the schools along with the encomium. Without any appreciation of the practice of invective, we cannot understand John's homilies on the Judaizers.

Sophistic Invective

The encomium was designed to glorify and honor, the invective to vilify and defame (Payr, col. 336). The technique for both speeches was similar. Each employed the same list of topics—birth, environment, personal life, bodily characteristics, virtues (or vices), and actions—and both used exaggeration (Alexander *Rhet. Graeci* 3.3; Hermogenes *Rhet. Graeci* 2.11). In the encomium the speaker used the list of topics to praise and honor the subject, whereas in the invective the topics were used to highlight the faults and expose the vices, in short to disgrace and malign the subject. In discussing a person's education in a *psogos*, the rhetor would say that his teachers were ignorant and corrupt; in speaking of his family, he would narrate the misdeeds of his father and the vices of his mother. "His father's cradle was a miserable village," says Libanius in an oration attacking an opponent (*Or.* 4.15).

The *psogos* was supposed to present unrelieved denigration of the subject. As one ancient teacher of rhetoric put it, the *psogos* is "only condemnation" and sets forth only the "bad things about someone" (Apthonius *Rhet. Graeci* 2.40). In the invective, the rhetor deliberately twisted the material to distort, to falsify, to condemn. If, in a *psogos*, one is speaking of Menelaus, Helen's husband, one says that Menelaus went off to war "not for the sake of great deeds" or because barbarians shamed Greece, but "because of a woman who was herself not very good" (Aristides *Rhet. Graeci* 2.506). In a *psogos*, the rhetor used omission to hide the subject's good traits or amplification to exaggerate his worst features, and the cardinal rule was never to say anything positive about the subject. Even "when good things are done they are proclaimed in the worst light" (Aristides *Rhet. Graeci* 2.506). In an encomium, one passes over a man's faults in order to praise him, and in a *psogos*, one passed over his virtues to defame him.

Such principles are explicit in the handbooks of the rhetors, but an interesting passage from the church historian Socrates, writing in the mid-fifth century, shows that the rules for the invective were simply taken for granted by men and women of the late Roman world. In discussing Libanius's orations in praise of the emperor Julian, Socrates explains that Libanius magnifies and exaggerates Julian's virtues because he is an "outstanding sophist" and a partisan supporter of Julian. Had Libanius been a Christian, he "would have magnified every ground of censure as is customary for a sophist" (*Hist. eccl.* 3.23). The point is that one should not expect a fair presentation in a *psogos*, for that is not its purpose. The *psogos* is designed to attack someone, says Socrates, and is taught by the sophists in the schools as one of the rudiments of their skills. It accomplishes its purpose not by sound reasoning, but by recourse to "sneer and contemptuous jests" and by "holding up to derision" someone's good qualities. "For anyone who enters into controversy with another, sometimes trying to pervert the truth, and at others attempting to conceal it, falsifies in every possible way the position of his opponent" (*Hist. eccl.* 3.23). Echoing the same rhetorical background, Augustine said that, in preparing an encomium on the emperor, he intended "that it should include a great many lies," and that the audience would know "how far from the truth they were" (*Conf.* 6.6).

In his handbook on rhetoric, Libanius included many stock speeches illustrating the various rhetorical genres. Among these speeches are several examples of the encomium and the *psogos*. In one case, that of

Achilles, Libanius provides both an encomium and a *psogos*, illustrating to his students that any subject, no matter how noble or vile, could be presented as an object either of praise or of censure. Here are some passages from his sample invective on Philip of Macedon, the father of Alexander the Great (*Opera* 8.296–301).

A speaker would be remiss, begins Libanius, if one were to overlook Philip's evils, for a tyrant is the "lowest degree among evil men" and Philip was the "worst of tyrants." "Who would say something good about him? His country? He was a barbarian. The greatness of his city? What could be more wretched than Pella? . . . His ancestors? Though they seemed to rule they were in fact slaves taking orders from the Persian king and bringing tribute to the Athenians." Philip was the child of Amyntas, "who was distinguished in no way." Raised in the customs of the barbarians, he prized "neither love of music, nor cultivation of wisdom, nor love of language, nor the pursuit of temperance, nor was justice esteemed, but he prized much wine, drunkenness, overeating, giving oneself over to pleasures and not shrinking from anything shameful." It was in such an environment that Philip grew to manhood (*Opera* 8.296–97).

As a young man, Philip was taken hostage by the Thebans. This showed his "father's weakness and his own ill fate." While captive, he was neglected, except for the attentions of Pammenes, his captor, who took him as lover. When Philip came to maturity and commanded his own army, he captured many cities, but "none with any beauty." He was a poor fighter, who achieved success only through "trickery and flattery." What was marvelous was "not his troops of soldiers, but the gold which came to the citizens" of the captured cities. "Such were his strategems, to grant favors, to deceive, to mislead." Cities looked to him as a deliverer from tyranny, but his rule "established a much worse tyranny." He desecrated the gods and altars of captured peoples. He made friends with traitors, but after they had served his purpose, he got rid of them. When he took a city, he did not plunder it, but instead "got drunk, danced licentiously, participated in lewd acts." "He was a man who sought peace when he should have gone to war, who waged war when it was a time for peace, an example of weakness and of evil." He brought destruction to the Greeks, the freest of men, and ruined their cities. Even his body was offensive. "One would shun it as an ill omen if one saw it; he limped, an eye was knocked out, many of his limbs were maimed" (*Opera* 8.298–300).

Such was the *psogos* as taught and practiced in the schools of the fourth century. In his orations and letters, Libanius used the techniques illustrated here to attack his opponents, such as the claque who disrupted the theater in Antioch (*Or.* 41.6–10), the monks who "ate like elephants" (*Or.* 30.8) and who were "sober only as far as dress is concerned" (*Or.* 2.32), the agents of the imperial bureaucracy, and political opponents in the city. The same charges are repeated over and over: lack of education, vulgarity, gross immorality, licentiousness, greed, drunkenness, exploitation of the poor, use of magic, murder, and the like. The charges are so predictable, so similar from situation to situation, that they become monotonous in their regularity.

Christian writers, trained in the same tradition, put the technique of the *psogos* to use not to deal with political foes or personal enemies, though on occasion they did this as well, but to assail religious opponents, chiefly heretics and Jews, but also pagans. Christians became as adept as the pagan sophists at heaping abuse on their foes, as the following passage from Gregory Nazianzus shows. The object of his attack is George, the Arian bishop who had replaced Athanasius when he was exiled by Constantius II:

> There was a monster from Cappadocia, born on our farthest confines, of low birth, and lower mind, whose blood was not perfectly free, but mongrel, as we know that of mules to be; at first he was a servant at the table of others for the price of a barley cake, having learned to say and do everything with an eye to his stomach, but in the end he sneaked into public life, filling its lowest offices, such as that of contractor for swine's flesh, the soldiers' rations. Then betraying this trust and proving himself a scoundrel for the sake of his stomach, he fled without any of his belongings, and after passing, as exiles do, from country to country and city to city, finally, in an evil hour for the Christian community, like one of the plagues of Egypt, he reached Alexandria. There, he ceased his wanderings, and he began his villainy. Good for nothing in all other respects, without culture, without fluency in conversation, without even the form and pretence of reverence, his skill in working villainy and confusion was unequalled. [*Or.* 21.16]

In another oration, this one on the emperor Julian, Gregory uses the same techniques to vilify the hated emperor.

> Hear me all nations. . . . Hear nations, tribes, tongues, every kind of man and every age . . . every power of heaven, all angels, whose deed was the putting down of the tyrant, who have overthrown not Sihon king of the Amorites, nor Og, king of Bashan, but the Dragon, the Apostate, the great mind, the Assyrian, the public and private enemy of all in common, him that has madly raged and threatened much upon earth, and

that has spoken and meditated much unrighteousness against heaven. [*Or.* 4.1]

How differently Julian could be portrayed can be seen in Libanius's lament for him.

> Alas, great indeed is the grief that has beset not just the land of Achaia, but the whole empire where the laws of Roman hold sway. Gone is the glory of the good; the company of the wicked and the licentious uplifted. . . . Hector has, and rightly, been called the "steadfast stay of Troy," for when he had fallen Ilium stood on rickety foundations soon to lie prostrate with him. But now there has fallen the pillar of not just a single town by Hellespont, nor yet a single province, but the empire of the descendants of Aeneas, the most glorious thing of land and sea, is stood on no sure foundation. [*Or.* 17.1−3]

Chrysostom's Rhetoric and the Judaizers

In the strict sense, John's homilies on the Judaizers do not follow the formal requirements of the fixed speeches of the rhetorical tradition. Nevertheless, the techniques of the *psogos* are apparent in the use of half-truths, innuendo, guilt by association, abusive and incendiary language, malicious comparisons, and in all, excess and exaggeration. In the opening paragraphs of the first sermon on the Judaizers, John's hearers would have recognized the familiar marks of a polemical speech:

> Today I wanted to finish the topic we were discussing recently.
> . . . Today I wanted to return to the same contest. For if the enemies of truth have not had their fill of blaspheming their benefactor, how much more have we not been satiated with honoring the supreme God? But what can I do? Another more terrible sickness beckons and our tongue must be turned to heal a disease which is flourishing in the body of the church. . . . What is this sickness? The festivals of the wretched and miserable Jews which follow one after another in succession— Trumpets, Booths, the Fasts—are about to take place. And many who belong to us and say that they believe in our teaching attend their festivals, and even share in their celebrations and join in their fasts. It is this evil practice I now wish to drive from the church. [*Jud.* 1.1; 48.844]

With these words, the audience's ears pricked up and the chatter subsided, for the congregation knew it was in for a performance. The young presbyter, who had already begun to make a reputation by his eloquence, was now going to display his gifts in a frontal attack on the Judaizers, most of whom were well known to the members of the congregation, and some of whom may even have been present.

They would not be disappointed. John's first tactic is to give the Judaizers a label: they are a "disease" infecting the Church.

> But if those who are sick with Judaism are not healed now when the Jewish festivals are "near, at the very door" [Matt. 24:33], I am afraid that some, out of misguided habit and gross ignorance, will share in their transgressions, and sermons about such matters would be pointless. If the offenders are not present to hear what we say today, afterwards medicine would be applied in vain because they have already committed the sin. This is the reason I am in a hurry to take up this matter before the festivals. That is the way doctors do things. They deal with the most urgent and acute sickness first. [*Jud.* 1; 48.845]

The metaphor of disease was commonplace among the rhetors, both pagan and Christian. As long ago as the time of Plato, the comparison was made between the physician of souls and the physician of bodies (*Politicus* 293b), and the rhetors used the image to refer to spiritual sickness. Christians used it to refer to their opponents who were infected with error (Theodoret *Hist. eccl.* 5.31), and pagans such as Julian used it to refer to Christianity (*Gal.* 327b; *Ep.* 20 [Bidez 89a]). It was used in the second century in Antioch by the bishop Ignatius (*Polyc.* 2.1). In John it is much overworked. He uses it in the opening paragraphs of his first sermons on the Judaizers, but he had used precisely the same language several days earlier to describe Arianism (*Incomprehens.* 1.6; 48.707–8). Several weeks later, after the Jewish festivals have passed, and John has returned to the Arians, he returns to the same image. Their "sickness" he says, is a "festering wound which cannot bear to be touched," but which the physician (the preacher) washes with a soft sponge (*Incomprehens.* 2.7; 48.718). In another sermon on Arianism, he speaks of restoring diseased members to health, "cutting off the putrid members which are incurable," and "bringing complete health to the multitude of the Church" (*Hom. in Melet.* 1; 50.516).

The metaphor of disease and sickness leads easily to the companion metaphor of the preacher as physician, as the passage just cited illustrates. In the final homily on the Judaizers, John says: "This is what physicians do. They give instructions to healthy people about maintaining their health and warding off any illness. But they do not ignore those who disregarded their instructions and become sick; indeed they give special attention to these so that they might deliver them from their illness" (*Jud.* 8.3; 48.931). In other sermons, John expands on the comparison between the preacher and the physician, and, as often happened with the rhetors he becomes so taken up with the comparison that he seems momentarily to lose sight of his point. "When you see the doctor now cauterizing, now fomenting the diseased parts, now employing the knife, now using medicine, now withholding food and drink, and then, bidding [the patient] to partake liberally of the same, then wrapping him up tightly, and again, when he is thoroughly warm, ordering him to drink a whole tumbler of cold water—you do not in such cases criticize the constant change of method" (*Laud. Paul* 5; 50.499). In a wholly different context, Gregory Nazianzus uses almost the same language. The physician "will prescribe medicines and diet and guard against injurious things, that the desires of the sick may not be a hindrance to his art. Sometimes . . . he will make use of the cautery or the knife or more severe remedies" (*Or.* 2.18). What these few illustrations indicate is that the rhetors worked with an arsenal of traditional material learned in the schools, which was often applied with little regard for the specific situation.

In sermons or speeches dealing with the foes of the Church, another favorite ploy was to describe its opponents as ravenous wolves surrounding the helpless flock of Christ.

> Again those sorry Jews, most miserable of all men, are about to hold a fast and it is necessary to protect the flock of Christ. As long as a wild beast is not causing trouble, shepherds lie down under an oak tree or a pine to play the flute, allowing the sheep to graze wherever they want. But when they realize wolves are about to attack, they immediately throw down their flute, grab their sling, lay aside the shepherd's pipe, arm themselves with clubs and stones, and stand before the flock shouting with a loud and booming voice, often driving away the wild beast without casting a stone. So also we, in the days just passed, were frolicking about in the exegesis of the Scriptures as in a meadow not touching on anything contentious because no one was troubling us. But since today the Jews, more troublesome than any wolves, are about to encircle our sheep, it is necessary to arm ourselves for battle so that none of our sheep become prey to wild beasts. [*Jud.* 4.1; 48.871]

Taken at face value, this opening passage from the fourth homily on the Judaizers suggests that the Jews were actively seeking out Christians so as to snatch them from the Church and bring them to the synagogue. Yet, as we saw in the previous chapter, it is not likely that the Jews were pursuing the Christians; indeed it was the Christians who were willingly seeking out the Jews. If the passage is read as a description of the situation in Antioch, it gives a false and misleading impression. In fact, the comparison of the Jews with ravenous wolves is not intended to provide a description of Jewish behavior; it is intended to picture the Jews in the worst possible light to frighten Christians so that they will not attend the synagogue.

The same comparison occurs in other homilies of John's as well as in other writers. In the sermons against the Arians, John says, "When the shepherd [bishop] is present, even if the wolf attacks the flock, the wolf is easily driven away from the sheep; when he is not present, the sheep necessarily find themselves in great peril since no one is there to protect them" (*Incomprehens.* 1.1; 48.701). Already in the second century, Ignatius the bishop of Antioch had described his opponents as "wolves who by evil pleasure take captive" the helpless sheep (*Philad.* 2.1). In the fourth century, Gregory Nazianzus compares the Nicene Christians in Cappadocia to a tiny flock, "harassed by lions, dispersed by tempest . . . scattered upon every mountain and hill, without a shepherd . . . where fearful beasts assail them (*Or.* 42.2). Even Julian called Christians "wild beasts" who gathered around Constantine and "cast their baleful eyes on all men" (*Ep.* 13 [Bidez 33]).

Just how adaptable the stock metaphors and comparisons could be in the hands of a trained rhetor can be seen in the use made of drunkenness. The eighth homily on the Judaizers begins with an extended comparison of Jewish impiety to drunkenness:

> The fast of the Jews—or should I say the drunkenness of the Jews—is past. It is possible to be drunk without wine. Were it not possible to be drunk without wine the prophet would not have said, "Woe to those who are drunk but not with wine" [Isa. 29:9]. . . . It is certainly possible to get drunk with anger, with unnatural lust, with avarice and vanity, and with innumerable other passions. Drunkenness is nothing else than displacement of right reasoning, derangement, the loss of spiritual health.
>
> Not only then is one who drinks large quantities of wine said to be drunk, but also someone who nurtures any kind of passion in his soul—this person is most assuredly drunk. A man who loves someone other than his wife, who spends his leisure time with prostitutes, is drunk. Just as a man who has lost his senses by drinking much strong wine begins to jabber like a coarse slave . . . so also someone who is filled with unbridled lust . . . can only mutter vulgarities. Everything he says is shameful, corrupt, coarse, and ridiculous; his perception goes

haywire, and he is blind to the very things which are before his eyes. For the woman he desires to defile lives always in his imagination. . . . He reminds one of the kind of person seen at assemblies and banquets, who . . . seems oblivious to everything around him even though numerous people speak to him about many things. His thoughts are only on that woman and his dreams are filled with sin. Like a trapped animal he is suspicious and fearful of everything.

Likewise, a person overcome with anger is also drunk. His face becomes swollen, his voice harsh, his eyes bloodshot and his mind is darkened. His reason disappears as though thrown into the sea; his tongue trembles, his eyes are out of focus and his ears deceive him. When anger afflicts the mind it is much worse than any strong wine, creating a storm whose violence is as uncontrollable as the surging sea.

If someone seized by desire or anger is drunk, how much more is an irreligious man who blasphemes God . . . drunk and insane? Drunkenness is even more pitiful than other illnesses because the drunken man does not realize he is drunk, just as the mad do not realize they are insane. . . . Similarly, the Jews who are now drunk do not realize they are drunk. [*Jud.* 8.1; 48.927–28]

Once John has made his point, he passes on quickly to the next section of the sermon. The extended comparison between Jewish impiety and drunkenness is simply a conventional beginning to a polemical homily. No doubt it pleased his audience immensely, though the comparison of one's opponents to drunken men as commonplace as the comparison of one's enemies to wolves. What interested the hearers was not the comparison as such, but John's dexterity in presenting it, elaborating it by the use of several further comparisons, and the sonorous phrases in which it was presented.

Drunkenness was a favorite comparison among the rhetors of the fourth century. It is used by Libanius in his polemics against soldiers (*Or.* 2.38), Christians (*Or.* 1.75), and Christian monks (*Or.* 2.32; 30.8). Indeed drunkenness was so common as a topic in the orations of this period that it is one of the stock descriptions in the handbooks. Young rhetors learned to write well-crafted descriptions of drunkenness as part of their training (Libanius *Opera* 8.477–79). No doubt John's hearers had often heard individuals and groups compared to drunken men. In fact, they heard almost the same description from John himself, applied not to the Jews but to moral laxity:

Avoid the drunkenness which comes without drinking wine. For this kind is more dangerous. Be not astonished at what I say, for it is possible to be drunk without wine. That you may know this is possible, listen to the prophet who said, "Woe to those who are drunk not from wine." But what is this drunkenness which does not come from wine? It takes many and varied forms. For anger makes us drunk; so, too, vainglory, haughty madness, and all the deadly passions which spring up in us produce a kind of drunkenness and satiety which darkens our reason. For drunkenness is nothing more than the distraction of our minds from their natural ways, the straying of reason, and the loss of our understanding. [*Catech. bapt.* 5.4; ed. Wenger, pp. 202–3]

This homily, preached to men and women about to be baptized, continues along the same lines as the eighth homily on the Judaizers. Precisely the same points are made about drunkenness, in the same order, and in the same language. The same comparison occurs in a similar form in several other homilies and in Chrysostom's speeches *On the Statues* delivered in the spring of the year in which he delivered the eighth homily on the Jews (*Stat.* 1.5; 49.22).[6] His hearers must have grown weary of the comparison, but John no doubt thought it a vivid and dramatic way to begin a sermon, at once catching the attention of his audience, yet presenting a familiar theme that they could readily grasp and digest.

Familiarity was, I suspect, a key to the success of the rhetors. A comparison such as drunkenness could be adapted to different situations and different foes, and all who were trained in the techniques of the rhetorical tradition were adept at calling forth the same language and vocabulary of vilification and calumny in different settings. Much of what they say is repetitious and conventional. Julian calls Christians "wretched men" (*Gal.* 201e), and the bishop Eusebius "despicable" (*Gal.* 222a). In turn, John says that Julian was a "wretched and miserable man" (*Pan. Bab.* 1.1; 50.530) and speaks of "the feasts of the wretched and miserable Jews" (*Jud.* 1.1; 844). Julian is said to be a "deceiver," who attracts "dishonorable men and fugitives" who "had been condemned to prison or to work in the mines." He draws to his company "degraded men, women from a brothel . . . panderers and female pimps and a crowd of degenerates" (*Pan. Bab.* 2.14; 50.554). Similarly, the synagogue is portrayed as a gathering place for "whores, thieves, and the crowd of dancers." In the synagogue, the Jews attract "rabble, effeminate men and prostitutes, the crowd from the theater." People claim to go to the synagogue to fast, but what draws them is a "drunken party" (*Jud.* 1.2; 846–47). Everything and anything shame-

6. See also *Res. Chr.* 2 (*PG* 50. 434–35).

ful is associated with the synagogue. "What more can I say? Rapacity, greed, betrayal of the poor, thefts, keeping of taverns. The whole day would not suffice to tell of these things" (*Jud.* 1.7; 853).

This list of epithets can be extended almost indefinitely. Julian says that Christian teaching is "a fiction of men composed by wickedness," a "monstrous tale," "childish and foolish" (*Gal.* 39a). The Jewish religion is said to be "wholly fabulous" and the Jewish Scriptures are filled with "many blasphemous sayings about God." These are the words of the man who aspired to rebuild the temple and restore Jewish sacrificial worship in Jerusalem. In turn Christians called heretics "enemies of the truth" (*Pan. Melet.* 1; 50.516) and Jews "enemies of God whose dances are directed by the devil" (*Jud.* 4.7; 881). Marcionites are "sons of the devil" (*Hom.* 43.2 *in Matt.* 12:38; 57.458). Pagan philosophers are "more abject in disposition than the dogs under the table," men who "do everything for the sake of the belly" (*Stat.* 17.2; 49.173). Jews are said to have "degenerated to the level of dogs" who are "gluttonous" and "live only for their bellies" (*Jud.* 1.2; 845–46). Just so, the Manichees also were "dogs, dumb and raging mad, who are externally modest but within dangerous mad dogs" (*Sermo* 7.4 *in Gen.* 2:9; 54.613). Likewise, Julian "raised his hand to the God who made him and howled as do mad dogs who bark at those who feed them as well as those who do not. His madness was more savage than theirs. . . . He wagged his tail at demons and worshipped them with every kind of ritual" (*Pan. Bab.* 1.1; 50.530).

There is little need to multiply examples. Many of John's sermons and speeches, including the homilies on the Jews, are available in English translation, as are the writings of other ancient rhetors such as Julian and Libanius. Yet even when one has set forth many illustrations of the rhetoric of abuse and placed the speeches in the context of relations between religious groups in the fourth century, it is still difficult for moderns to appreciate the virulence of these ancient religious polemics.[7] Only in the language of international politics do we find anything comparable in our own time, and even there the more fulsome and flamboyant politicans strike us as crude and tasteless. Civility and tact are the rule.

The ancients, however, were not embarrassed by name-calling and obloquy. They seem to have thrived on it, and by providing new occasions for rhetorical display, the religious conflicts of this period revived the art of rhetoric and breathed new life into stale and musty

---

7. On the topic of hostility between religious groups in antiquity, a new study has appeared: Ruggini, *Pagani, ebrei e cristiani: Odio sociologico e odio teologico nel mondo antico* (1980). I have not, however, been able to obtain a copy.

language. The rhetors now had real, not imagined, foes. Yet the asperity, the hostility and enmity, the capacity to hate still give us pause. For surely something of this charged and emotive language must have passed over into the attitudes of people toward one another and their relations with each other. One would think that such language would incite passions and lead an angry crowd to storm the homes of one's enemies. There are some indications that this did happen, as, for example, in the case of the synagogue in Callinicum discussed in Chapter 2, yet this seems to be the exception rather than the rule, at least in the fourth century. In the specific case before us, John's sermons on the Judaizers, there is no indication that his homilies prompted violent actions on the part of Christians toward the Jews in Antioch (Ritter, pp. 87–88). Nor did he envision any. What he desired was that Christians be able to win back friends and family who had deserted the Church by persuasion. But here he was unsuccessful.

The Rhetoric of Abuse and Christian Theology

Alongside these stereotyped insults in the rhetorical tradition, John's sermons on the Judaizers also employ a distinctly Christian invective, drawn from earlier Christian writings and from the Christian and Jewish Scriptures. In John's sermons this language is so completely interwoven with the language of the sophistic tradition that the distinctions between the two blur. Furthermore, by the late fourth century, the Christian vocabulary had become as stereotyped as that of the rhetorical schools. Nevertheless, there is one important difference. This Christian language, used with particular reference to the Jews, reflects a theological interpretation of Judaism (Simon 1964, pp. 239–63). At times, its themes merge with those of the rhetorical tradition—for example, in charging the Jews with immorality. In other places, however, Christian critics of the Jews and Judaizers speak of apostasy, faithlessness, rejection of God, and hardheartedness.

"Do not be surprised if I have called the Jews wretched. They are truly wretched and miserable for they have received many good things from God yet they have spurned them and violently cast them away" (*Jud.* 1.2; 845). This passage from the first homily begins with familiar terms from sophistic invective, but it takes a distinctly Christian turn with the addition of an explanation for presumed Jewish inferiority. The Jews are "wretched and miserable" because they have rejected God's grace. "The sun of righteousness rose on them first, but they turned their back on its beams and sat in darkness. But we, who were nurtured in darkness, welcomed the light and we were freed from the yoke of error. The Jews were branches of the holy root, but they were lopped off. . . . They read the prophets from ancient times, yet they crucified the one spoken of by the prophets" (*Jud.* 1.2; 845).

In the same passage, several lines later, he magnifies this point by citing the Book of Acts. "Nothing is more miserable than those who kick against their salvation. When it was required to keep the law, they trampled it under foot; now when the law has been abrogated, they obstinately observe it. What could be more pitiful than people who provoke God's anger not only by transgressing the law but also by observing the law? This is why the Scripture says, "You stiffnecked and uncircumcised in heart; you always fight against the Holy Spirit" (Acts 7:51; *Jud.* 1.2; 48.845–46). A few lines later, he reinforces the point by citing the Jewish Scriptures. "Ages ago you broke your yoke and snapped your traces" (Jer. 2:20). It was not Paul who said these things, continues John, "but the prophet, using 'yoke' and 'traces' as symbols of dominion because the Jews rejected the Lordship of Christ" (*Jud.* 1.2; 846).

This passage is characteristic of the homilies on the Judaizers. John will cite a text from the New Testament to make his polemical point; then, acknowledging that Jews do not accept the authority of the New Testament, he immediately cites a passage from the Jewish prophets, ostensibly making a similar point. In passages such as these, the technique of sophistic invective merges with scriptural language, the one complementing the other. The technique is, however, the same— exaggeration, insinuation, guilt by association. Chance phrases in the Bible are singled out because they merge easily with the rhetorical language. Jeremiah's phrase "harlot's brow" (Jer. 3:3) becomes a reference to the immorality of the synagogue, and "your house has become a hyena's den" is made to refer to the synagogue as a "den of wild animals" and an "unclean animal at that" (Jer. 7:11). "I have forsaken my house" (Jer. 12:7) becomes "when God forsakes a place, it becomes a dwelling place for demons" (*Jud.* 1.3; 847).

Whether John is quoting the Bible or drawing on the techniques of invective learned in school, his purpose is the same: to present the Judaizers and the Jews in the worst possible light. His hearers knew the synagogues of the Jews were neither dens of immorality, nor gathering places for thieves, nor the dwellings of demons. Indeed, as we saw in the previous chapter, it was because of the sanctity of the synagogue, the spiritual power of the Jewish books, and the efficacy of Jewish rites that Christians went to the synagogue. Yet if John was to try to win back some of the backsliders and to restore some semblance of unity to the Church, the most effective means was to vilify the Jews in the hope of intimidating his hearers and frightening them with the consequences of attending the synagogue. "Can you hide from God who is present everywhere and sees your shameless transgression? Do you not fear God?" (*Jud.* 8.8; 941).

On the other hand, there is more to the sermons on the Judaizers than rhetoric. In several of the passages cited above, as well as similar passages in the homilies, Christian theological convictions color the choice of words and images. This is particularly evident in John's use of the phrase "Christ-killers," which occurs in several places in the homilies. This term had come into the Christian vocabulary in the fourth century, originally to refer to the Jews who lived in Jesus' time.[8] The *Apostolic Constitutions*, a work that, as we have seen, was produced in a community where there was rivalry between Jews and Christians, urges Christians to avoid the "house of demons or the synagogue of 'Christ Killers,' or the assembly of evil doers" (*Const. app.* 2.61.1). Here the historical reference is transmuted to refer to the author's contemporaries, and in John the same transmutation has taken place:

> We must return again to the sick. Do you realize that those
> who are fasting have dealings with those who shouted, "Cru-
> cify him! Crucify him!" [Luke 23:21]; and with those who
> said, "His blood be on us and on our children" [Matt. 27:25]?
> If a band of would-be revolutionaries were apprehended and
> then condemned, would you dare to go to them and talk with
> them? I certainly don't think so! Is it not absurd to be zealous
> about avoiding someone who had sinned against mankind, but
> to have dealings with those who affronted God? Is it not folly
> for those who worship the crucified to celebrate festivals with
> those who crucified him? This is not only stupid—it is sheer
> madness. [*Jud.* 1.5; 850]

Here the phrase "those who crucified him" is taken out of its historical context and applied to the Jews living in John's own day. Clearly the term is emotionally charged and it is for that reason that it appears in the homilies on the Judaizers. Its emotive overtones would excite the congregation to rescue their friends and families and to deter them from participating in Jewish rites. Later in the same passage John makes just such an appeal:

> I beg you to shun them and avoid their gatherings. The harm
> to our weaker brothers is not a small matter, nor is the oppor-
> tunity for them to flaunt their arrogance a minor matter. For

8. For the term "Christ-killers," see *Apoc. Pauli* 49; *Const. App.* 6.25.1; Ps.-Athanasius (*PG* 26. 1224b); Proclus *Or.* 12.2 (*PG* 65. 789a); Basil *Hom.* 20.2 (*PG* 31.529); Asterius of Amasea *Hom. in Ps.* 5 (*PG* 40.424). For the place of the Jews in John's theology of the cross, see Stockmeier, pp. 131–34.

when they see you [judaizing Christians], who worship the
Christ who was crucified by them, observing Jewish customs
and reverencing Jewish ways, how can they not think that everything done by them is the best? How can they not think that
our ways are not worth anything when you, who confess to be
a Christian and to follow the Christian way, run to those who
degrade these same practices? [*Jud.* 1.5; 851]

In other places, however, the charge that the Jews killed Christ
takes on more specific theological overtones. "You did slay Christ, you
did lift violent hands against the Master, you did spill his precious
blood. This is why you have no chance for atonement, excuse, or defense" (*Jud.* 6.2; 907). And in the fifth homily: "You Jews did crucify
him. But after he died on the cross, he then destroyed your city; it was
then that he dispersed your people; it was then that he scattered your
nation over the face of the earth. In doing this, he teaches us that he is
risen, alive, and in heaven" (*Jud.* 5.1; 884). In passages such as these,
John is as much concerned to make a theological point as he is about
the rhetorical effect of his language.[9]

Embedded in these passages is to be found a theological argument
about the status of the Jews after the death of Christ and the destruction of the temple at Jerusalem. Since Christians claimed to be the inheritors of the ancient Jewish tradition, the destruction of the temple
was taken to be a sign that Jewish law had lost its legitimacy. Yet, three
hundred years after the destruction of the temple and the loss of Jerusalem, the Jews were still observing the ancient laws. By also observing
Jewish law, the Judaizers announced to other Christians that the Jewish rites were still holy, still efficacious, still legitimate. Indeed, it appeared that the Jewish rites were more holy than the Christian rites.
As important as it was for John to attempt to frighten and alarm the
Judaizers with lurid accounts of the iniquity of the Jews and to entertain his congregation, in the fashion of the ancient rhetors, by vilifying
Jewish life and practices, it was also necessary that he respond to the

---

9. It would be misleading to suggest that all of John's comments on the Jews are as
hostile as those in the homilies on the Judaizers. In his other writings, he speaks on
occasion with respect for the Jews (*Hom* 5.1 *in Heb.* 2:16; 63.47); in one passage he
calls them allies who supported him against Christian opponents who conspired to have
him deposed from the patriarchate in Constantinople (*p. Redit.* 1.1; 52.439); and
in some places he speaks of the unique relation of Jews to God (*Laud. Paul.* 3.1;
50.483–84). Elsewhere he expresses admiration at the Jewish attitude toward marriage.
"They revere marriage and appreciate God's creation" (*Virg.* 8.2; *PG* 48.538). For a
useful discussion of John's comments on the Jews in his other writings, see Ritter,
pp. 81–90.

theological challenge they presented. If we are to understand John's sermons on the Judaizers and the fervor of his attack on the Jews, it is not sufficient to discuss the rhetorical character of the sermons. We must also discuss the theological problem raised by the Judaizers in Antioch.

· V ·

The Temple in Jerusalem
and Christian Apologetics

To the men and women of the Middle Ages, the figure of Constantine the Great loomed large over the fourth century. Born a pagan, he converted to Christianity and became the first Christian emperor, the convener of councils, the builder of churches, the herald of a new age, the founder of Christian Europe. But to the men and women of John Chrysostom's generation, it was not Constantine, but Julian, raised a Christian only to forsake his "hereditary piety," Julian, the pagan emperor, Julian the Apostate, whose deeds lived in memory. The age of Constantine was part of past history, but Julian's actions, abortive as they may have appeared to later generations, were still remembered not only by the old, says John Chrysostom, but also by the "young people" of his day (*Jud.* 5.11; 48, 900).[1]

A myth was created about Constantine to explain the conversion of the Roman world to Christianity and the establishment of Christian Europe (Linder 1975). To men and women looking back, events in the

---

1. For Julian as part of "our generation," see also *Hom.* 43.3 *in Matt.* 12:38–39 (*PG* 57.460). Constantine, however, was not forgotten. By the end of the fourth century, a cult honoring Constantine had emerged and many legends had begun to circulate (Vogt 1957, cols. 370–72).

fourth century seem to have been moving inexorably toward the for-
mation of a Christian civilization. But the contemporaries of John
Chrysostom did not know they were opening the Christian period.[2]
The march of emperors between Constantine and Theodosius I—
Constantius II, the militant pagan Julian, the non-committal Valentinian, the ardently Arian Valens—gave no one cause to think Constantine stood at the beginning of a new age. Eusebius's dreams of one
God, one emperor, one empire, one Church and his celebration of
Constantine as a "mighty victor beloved of God" had been replaced by
the memory of orthodox bishops languishing in exile, of an emperor
offering sacrifices in cities throughout the east, of laws prohibiting
Christians from teaching literature in the schools, of resourceful and
aggressive Arian leaders attacking the Nicene decrees.

Though Julian reigned for only nineteen months (361–63 C.E.),
what he did and wrote during this brief span was to haunt the memory
of a whole generation of Christians. Even though the Roman Empire
was proclaimed officially Christian in 380 C.E., less than two decades
after his death, the memory of Julian reminded Christians that a
Christian emperor was not inevitable and that the Christian tradition
had but a fragile hold on the minds and hearts of many people. As late
as the fourth decade of the fifth century, Cyril, bishop of Alexandria,
composed a massive rebuttal to Julian's *Against the Galilaeans* because, according to Cyril, many Christians, some of whom were "firm
in faith," were "disturbed by his writings." Julian, unlike other critics,
had been raised a Christian and educated in the Christian Scriptures.
Greeks turned to Julian's writings for arguments against the Christians. Armed with this information, said Cyril, they cast his writings
before us with the taunt that "none of our teachers is capable of rebut-
ting or refuting his works" (*Contra Julianum, Preface*; *PG* 76.508c).

Important as Julian's book *Against the Galilaeans* was in the generations after his death, however, it was not his writings but his deeds
as emperor that made the deepest impression on Christians. Among
these actions, the most noteworthy were Julian's practice of publicly
offering sacrifices in the temples, his so-called school laws prohibiting
Christians from teaching in the schools, his gathering of pagan sympathizers about the throne, his efforts to reorganize the pagan priesthood, and his confiscation of money and land from Christian churches;
but the one thing that set Julian apart and stood out in Christian memory was his endeavor to rebuild the temple in Jerusalem and return the
city to the Jews. In the generation after his death, and for generations

2. Bickerman, p. 82. It is significant that the sixth-century writer Cyril of Scy-
thopolis used the phrase "after the persecution" to refer to the late fourth century, i.e.,
after the time of the Arian emperors and Julian (*V. Euthym.* 1).

afterward, this undertaking was told and retold by an impressive list of Christian writers: Gregory Nazianzus, Ephraem Syrus, Ambrose, Pseudo-Cyril of Jerusalem, Rufinus Socrates, Sozomen, Theodoret of Cyrus, Philostorgius, and John Chrysostom, who refers to the event no less than eight times in his sermons and speeches.[3] Except for one or two passages, all of John's references to Julian's effort to restore the temple occur in essays or homilies preached in Antioch during the years when he was preoccupied with judaizing Christians. The fifth homily on the Judaizers, the longest of the eight homilies, is devoted to the religious problems raised by the rebuilding of the temple at Jerusalem.

Even Porphyry, whose works against Christianity were the most feared by Christians earlier in the fourth century, did not merit the attention Julian did in Christian tradition. For Porphyry and other Greek critics met the Christians with philosophical and religious arguments against Christian beliefs; Julian, however, backed his philosophical and religious arguments with political action. He met them not simply with another treatise, not simply with harsh words or repressive laws, but with a bold historical stroke filled with symbolic overtones for Christians, pagans, and Jews. In the Christian mind, the attempt to rebuild the temple in Jerusalem was a profound attack on the truth of Christianity.

John Chrysostom as an Apologist

In standard accounts of the history of Christian apologetics, John Chrysostom plays a minor role. His fame rests on his preaching, not his apologetic tracts. Yet, as we saw in the first chapter of this book, as a young man John was troubled by the continuing influence of Hellenism in the city of Antioch. Prior to his ordination to the presbyterate, John's primary intellectual preoccupation was the defense of Christianity against paganism, not in the philosophical style of earlier apologists, but in the light of the social conventions of the city of Antioch and the emerging monastic movement.

During this period, John also wrote two essays explicitly designed to defend the truth of Christianity against Hellenism: *That Christ is God* and *On St. Babylas against Julian and the Gentiles*.[4] In these two

---

3. For a thorough discussion of the stories surrounding Julian's effort to rebuild the temple in Jerusalem, see Levenson, pp. 21–23. The references are *Pan. Bab.* 2.22; *Iud.* 5.11 and 6.2; *Jud. et gent.* 16; *Hom.* 4.1 *in Matt.* 1:17; *Exp.* in Ps. 110.4; *Laud. Pauli* 4 (50.489); *Hom.* 41.3 *in Act.* 19:8.

4. Text of *That Christ Is God* (*Jud. et gent.*) in PG 48.813–38; critical edition by

works, he approaches his task somewhat differently than in the essays on monasticism. Here he presents the strife between Christianity and Hellenism as a conflict over the role of divine power in history. Whose power is greatest—that of the gods of the Greeks and Romans, reflected in the fortunes of the empire, or that of Christ, reflected in the fortunes of the Church? In John's lifetime, Christians had undergone persecution at the hands of the Roman emperor, yet the Church continued to flourish. This was seen as proof of the divinity of Christ, for, says John, "It is not the mark of a mere man to bring so much under his sway in so short a time" (*Jud. et gent.* 1; 48.813–14). Both treatises echo a common theme: the power of Christ is the source of the Church's success in the face of hostile rulers (*Jud. et gent.* 15; 48.833; *Pan. Bab.* 2.2; 50.536–37).

This general argument about the power of Christ, which for John means Christ's divinity, is, however, supported by a complementary argument concerning the temple at Jerusalem. Initially, it appears as though this theme is simply an extension of the argument about Christ's power. During the time of Christ, the Jewish temple was the most magnificent in the world, says John, but Christ prophesied of it: "Truly I say to you, there will not be left here one stone upon another that will not be thrown down" (Matt. 24:2). This temple no longer stands; the visitor to Jerusalem, writes John, now sees only "destruction, utter ruin, desolation, devastation" (*Jud. et gent.* 16; 48.834). The Jews belonged to a great nation that had triumphed over many peoples and kings, and had even won battles, by God's help, but this same people, though numerous and wealthy, was unable to rebuild the temple even with the aid of the emperor. All this power could not stand up to the power of Christ, for "one word of Christ destroyed and demolished all these things." Three hundred years had passed and there was no hope that it would be rebuilt. Why were the efforts of the Jewish patriarch, who had money at his disposal, and the many Jews in Palestine, Phoenicia, and elsewhere unsuccessful? Why had Julian's attempt been a failure? The answer, says John, is that "Christ built the Church and no one is able to destroy it; he destroyed the temple and no one is able to rebuild it" (*Jud. et gent.* 16; 48.835; cf. *Pan. Bab.* 2.22; 50.567–68).[5]

Within the framework of these two treatises, the argument about

---

McKendrick. Text of *On St. Babylas* (*Pan. Bab.* 2) in *PG* 50.533–72; critical edition by Schatkin. For an analysis of *Jud. et gent.*, see Harkins, 1970. Some scholars have doubted the authenticity of *Pan. Bab.* 2; for a discussion of the arguments against authenticity and a defense of John's authorship, see Schatkin, 1970.

5. For the relation of the homilies on the Jews to *Jud. et gent.*, see Levenson, pp. 26–27.

the destruction of the temple is part of an argument against *Hellenism*. If the Church survives under persecution, if it grows and flourishes, if churches are to be found in the cities and in the villages, this is proof of the power of Christ. If fire destroys a Greek temple in Daphne, as it did during Julian's visit there, if the oracles do not speak at Julian's beckoning, if temples are falling into disuse and disrepair, if the effort to rebuild the Jewish temple failed, all of these events expose the weakness of paganism and its gods (*Exp. in Ps.* 110.5; 55.285). Arguments such as these were commonplace among religious thinkers during this period.

In the midst of John's historical-political claims about the power of Christ, however, is to be found another type of argument, which is similar to those found in his homilies on the Judaizers and seems, on first reading, to be directed at the Jews. Without the temple in Jerusalem "Jewish worship is hindered, the customs, sacrifices and offerings abolished and the other things of their law have ceased. One cannot set up an altar, offer a sacrifice, make libations, offer a lamb or incense, read the law, celebrate a festival, nor do any other things of this sort outside its gates" (*Jud. et gent.* 16; 48.835). In this passage, John is concerned less about Julian's failure to rebuild the temple than he is about the symbolic importance of the temple as a legitimation of Jewish religion.

The status of the city of Jerusalem and the temple is the most persistent theme in John's sermons on the Judaizers. That this theme should appear in an apologetic treatise against paganism is, at first glance, curious. At the very end of the treatise *That Christ is God*, John mentions that he will return to this theme when he speaks directly to the Jews (*Jud. et gent.* 17; 48.836), but in the text the topic is presented as an argument against paganism. This suggests that the status of the temple was not simply a matter that concerned Christianity and Judaism, but that it also entered into disputes with pagans. In what way are John's sermons on the Judaizers related to his apologetic effort against Hellenism? To answer this question, we must look at Julian's efforts to reconstruct the temple in Jerusalem and at the significance of the temple in early Christian tradition.

Jerusalem in Christian Tradition

In the ancient world, appeal to historical events to legitimate religious claims was common. Victory in war or a long and peaceful reign were taken as signs of divine favor; defeat as a sign of divine displeasure. In Polybius's grand account of the rise of ancient Rome, one of his themes was the role of fortune in guiding the affairs of the city and eventually bringing it to prominence among the peoples of the ancient world. Rome was raised up because of its merit. In John's day, Symmachus, the prefect of Rome, argued that the removal of the statue of the goddess Victoria from the senate house in Rome could only bring harm to the empire. Why, says Symmachus, should we remove a statue that has so long been "advantageous to the state? . . . Who is so friendly with the barbarians as not to require an Altar of Victory?" Rome's misfortunes can be traced to a decline in piety and devotion. Famine is "not the fault of the earth. . . . Mildew did not injure the crops, nor wild oats destroy the wheat." Our misfortunes are due to "sacrilege," for it was necessary that "what was refused to religion should be denied to all" (*Relatio* 3.3; 16).

Similarly, the historical books of the Jews attributed the successes and failures of ancient Israel to the God of Israel and the people's devotion to the one God. When Jerusalem was threatened by the Moabites and Ammonites, King Jehoshaphat stood before the assembly of the people and prayed:

> O Lord, God of our fathers, are you not God in heaven? Do you not rule over all the kingdoms of the nations? In your hand are power and might, so that none is able to withstand you. Did you not, O our God, drive out the inhabitants of this land before your people Israel, and give it forever to the descendants of Abraham your friend. . . . If evil comes upon us, the sword, judgment, or pestilence, or famine, we will stand before this house, and before you . . . and cry to you in our affliction, and you will hear and save. . . . For we are powerless against this great multitude that is coming against us. [2 Chron. 20:5−12]

Jehoshaphat's armies won the battle and the story ends with his men returning to Jerusalem with joy "for the Lord had made them rejoice over their enemies. . . . And the fear of God came on all the kingdoms of the countries when they heard that the Lord had fought against the enemies of Israel" (2 Chron. 20:27−29).

Conversely, when the people were disobedient and did not worship the Lord, as happened under King Ahaz, the people suffered defeat at the hands of their enemies. The kings of Assyria invaded Samaria and carried off the Israelites to captivity. "And this was so because the people of Israel had sinned against the Lord their God, who had brought them out of the land of Egypt from the hand of Pharaoh king of Egypt" (2 Kings 17:7). At the end of the Books of Chronicles, the exile to Babylonia is set in the same historical-theological framework. Because the priests and the people were "exceedingly unfaithful," the

Lord "brought up against them the king of the Chaldeans who slew their young men with the sword . . . brought the vessels of the house of the Lord to Babylon . . . burned the house of God and broke down Jerusalem, and burned all its palaces with fire and destroyed its precious vessels" (2 Chron. 36:14–19).

As inheritors of a religious tradition that saw historical events as signs of God's favor or disfavor, both Jews and Christians in the Roman period drew on this tradition to interpret the events that were happening in their own time. Another factor, however, was the appeal to prophecy. People believed they could correlate events of recent history with ancient prophecies spoken centuries earlier. Among the prophets cited most frequently in this period was Daniel. He was thought not only to foretell future events, as had other prophets, says the Jewish historian Josephus, but had also "fixed the time at which they would come to pass" (Josephus *Ant.* 10.267–68). Christians were to make a great deal out of Daniel's presumed foreknowledge, because on the basis of his prophecies they thought they were able to date the coming of the Messiah, whose advent was thought to conform precisely to the time of Jesus (Tertullian *Adv. Iud.* 8). Perhaps for this very reason, many Jews denied that Daniel should be classed among the prophets, and to this day the book of Daniel is not included among the prophets in the Jewish Bible.[6]

The one event that called for interpretation above all in the first centuries of the Roman period was the destruction of the second temple in 70 C.E. Inevitably, Jews and Christians came into conflict with each other as they attempted to apply ancient prophecies to this event and to discern its meaning within the larger historical and religious tradition. How this dispute took shape can be seen in the appeal to the famous prophecy in Genesis 49:10 to the effect that the "scepter shall not depart from Judah . . . *until* Shiloh comes," or until "he comes to whom it belongs" (Simonetti 1968, pp. 12ff.). Christians took the prophecy to mean that, after the coming of Jesus, there were "no longer any who were called kings of the Jews, and that all those Jewish customs on which they prided themselves, I mean those connected with the temple and the altar and the performance of worship and the garments of the high priests, have been destroyed" (Origen *De princ.* 4.1.3; cf. Justin *Dial.* 52). Christians saw the prophecy fulfilled in the termination of Jewish institutions after the destruction of the temple. This alteration in Jewish life, moreover, corresponded precisely to the

6. On Jews who disputed that Daniel was a prophet, see Theodoret of Cyrus, *Dan. pref.* (*PG* 81.1257–60). On the general question, see Ginzberg, *Legends of the Jews*, 6:413. Interestingly, the Qumran pesher 4Q *Florilegium* (4Q[174]) used the term "prophet" for Daniel; also Josephus *AJ* 10.266–68.

time when Jesus lived. The Jews, while agreeing that the prophecy did have a historical referent, argued on the other hand that the rule in Israel had passed from kings to the patriarchs in Galilee and the exilarchs in Babylonia (*b. Sanhedrin* 5a). This rule was to continue until the coming of the Messiah (Origen *De princ.* 4.1.3). Since the Jews did not believe the Messiah had come, they sought to discover evidence in the historical events of their time that the "scepter" had not departed from Judah.[7] The patriarchs provided such evidence.

That the destruction of the temple raised questions for Jews as well as Christians can be seen in a passage from the tractate *Shabbath* (119b) in the Babylonian Talmud (Schoeps 1950b). A number of rabbis give different explanations as to why Jerusalem has been destroyed: Rabbi Abaye said that it was because the Sabbath was desecrated in the city; Rabbi Abbahu because the reading of the Shema was neglected; Rabbi Hamnuna because the people of Jerusalem neglected schoolchildren; Rabbi Judah because scholars were despised in Jerusalem. Eight different explanations were offered. In another tractate in the Talmud, the destruction of the second temple is attributed to three sins: idolatry, fornication, and shedding of blood (*b. Yoma* 9b). As these texts make clear, the Jews were quite prepared to see the destruction of the temple as a chastening of God's people. What they were not ready to say, however, was that the loss of the temple had altered God's relations with Israel. The Jewish texts repeatedly emphasize that God has not rejected his people or severed his relations with them (*Exodus Rabbah* 31.10). Origen noted that the destruction of the city of Jerusalem occurred "less than one whole generation after the death of Jesus." Never before had there been a period when the Jews were "ejected for so long a time from their ritual and worship." As a consequence of the loss of the city, "new laws" were required, said Origen, that were appropriate for a "way of life established in every place," for the laws given previously "were intended for a single nation ruled by men of the same nationality and customs, with the result that it is impossible for everyone to observe them now" (*Contra Celsum* 4.22). According to Origen's reasoning, the loss of Jerusalem and the dispersal of the Jews invalidated ancient Jewish law, because the legitimacy of the Law was bound to the city of Jerusalem.

For Christians, the decisive point was that the destruction of the temple and the dispersal of the Jews from Jerusalem had occurred

---

7. See also the interesting text in *Lamentations Rabbah* 1.51 linking the coming of the Messiah with the fall of Jerusalem. The Jews, in response to such an interpretation, argued that the Messiah was taken up in a whirlwind to return another time. This sounds like a dispute between Christians and Jews over the meaning of the temple's destruction. I owe this reference to William R. Schoedel.

within a generation of the life and death of Jesus (Origen *Hom.* 14.13 *in Jer.*). In the passage cited above from the *Contra Celsum*, Origen argues that "one of the facts" that showed "Jesus is divine" was the loss of Jerusalem to the Jews and the calamities that Jews had experienced since that time. Without the temple, there were no longer an altar, priests, worship, or sacrifices (*Hom.* 17.1 *in Joshua*). The emergence of the Church coincided with a profound transformation of the condition of the Jewish people and the practice of Jewish religion. "The word of God had abandoned the assembly of the Jews and there is now another assembly, the Church, which is drawn from the nations" (*Hom.* 14.15 *in Jerem.*). In the minds of the early Christians, arguments such as these were not primarily theological arguments, as a modern critic would be inclined to view them, but appeals to the working of the divine in historical events, supported by the words of the prophets.

By the fourth century, such ideas had become widespread in Christian writings. The "fate of the Jews" after the time of Jesus is one of the major themes in Eusebius's *Church History* (Grant 1980, pp. 97–113). In another work, the *Demonstratio evangelica* (17a–c), Eusebius argued that the legislation of Moses had become superfluous with the loss of Jerusalem, because the Law of Moses was "confined to one place." Hence Jewish observance of the Law after the temple's destruction was illegitimate, because the Jews were not allowed to observe the law "in a foreign country." Eusebius's contemporary Athanasius reflected the same tradition when he argued, appealing both to the prophecy in Daniel and the prophecy in Genesis 49:10, that with the coming of Christ there is "no longer king, nor prophet, nor Jerusalem, nor sacrifice, nor vision" among the Jews (*De incarn.* 39–40). And Aphrahat, a Syriac Christian writer, made a similar point in an essay on the paschal sacrifice. After describing the institution of the Passover in Exodus 12, Aphrahat cites Deuteronomy (16:5–6), which says that the paschal sacrifice cannot be offered in any city "but only in the place which the Lord your God will choose for himself." Aphrahat comments: "Great and wonderful are these mysteries, my beloved. When Israel was in its own land, it was lawful for them to make the paschal sacrifice only in Jerusalem. In our day they are scattered among all people and languages, among the unclean and the uncircumcised, and eat their bread in uncleanness among the people" (*Demonstr.* 12.2–3; Neusner, p. 32).

Even Gregory of Nyssa, who had doubts about the persuasiveness of such theological appeals to historical events, repeated the conventional Christian wisdom about Jesus and the temple: "Up to the time that God appeared in Jesus Christ [the Jews] could see in Jerusalem the splendor of royal palaces, the famous temple, and the customary sacrifices through the year. . . . Today not a trace of their temple remains. The splendor of their city is left in ruins" (*Or. catech.* 18). Gregory added, however, that "neither Hellenists nor the leaders of Judaism are willing to regard these things as proof of God's presence." Another type of argument was required to show that the divine nature had been joined to humankind in Jesus Christ. But most Christian writers did not see the difficulty in appealing directly to history to validate one's religious claims.

Christians knew that the first temple, the temple of Solomon, had been destroyed but that at a later time it was rebuilt. The destruction of the second temple, the one standing during the lifetime of Jesus was, however, thought to be different. It would never be rebuilt; its destruction was permanent. In support of this view, they cited the enigmatic passage in Daniel that spoke of the "weeks of years" and the "abomination of desolation" (Dan. 9:27). According to the Septuagint, Daniel says that the "sacrifice and offering will be destroyed." In his commentary on the book of Daniel, Jerome, following earlier Christian tradition (Eusebius *Demon. evang.* 403b–c), interpreted this passage to refer to the destruction of Jerusalem by the Romans. The text means that the cessation of sacrifices and offerings will continue "until the consummation of the world and the end" (*Comm. in Daniel* 9:24). Not all Christians agreed on the precise interpretation of the details, as can be seen in Jerome's commentary, but most agreed that Daniel 9 prophesied a permanent cessation of sacrificial worship in Jerusalem. Jerome, however, adds that the Jews were "not greatly impressed" with this interpretation (*Comm. in Daniel* 9:27).

The interpretation of the prophecy in Daniel was confirmed by the words of Jesus in Matthew 24:1–2.[8] "Jesus left the temple and was going away, when his disciples came to point out to him the buildings of the temple. But he answered them, You see all these, do you not? Truly, I say to you, there will not be left here one stone upon another, that will not be thrown down." This warning of Jesus was taken to be a prophecy that the temple would never be rebuilt (Socrates *Hist. eccl.* 3.20). Cyril, bishop of Jerusalem, cited these words of Jesus' in one of his catechetical lectures on the phrase of the creed "shall come in glory to judge the living and the dead" to show that at the end of time, on the day of judgment, the temple will still be in ruins (*Catech.* 15.15).

By the time that Julian became emperor in 361 C.E., this interpreta-

---

8. Schoedel observes that the fathers of the Church referred as least as often to Luke 19 as to Matthew 24 in discussing Christ's prediction of the destruction of the temple. See, in this connection, Fascher.

tion of the temple in Jerusalem was firmly fixed in the Christian consciousness and handed on to new converts through the catechetical tradition, as the passage from Cyril of Jerusalem shows. The passage of time, by then almost three centuries, the ancient word of Daniel, the prophecy of Jesus, and the spread of Christianity supported the view that Jerusalem would never again belong to the Jews and that the temple would never be rebuilt. The significance of the temple for Christian piety was accentuated by Constantine's lavish building program in Jerusalem and environs early in the fourth century and the swelling tide of pilgrims visiting the holy places (Wilkinson 1971, pp. 10–26). As if to corroborate their convictions, Christians were beginning to transform the city of Jerusalem into a Christian city. The church of the Anastasis was built during this period, as well as other churches, and the first accounts of pilgrims, the *Pilgrim from Bordeaux* and the *Pilgrimmage of Etheria*, foreshadowed a new form of piety centered on the holy places. Significantly, the new Christian buildings, and the goal of Christian pilgrims, were geographically distinct from the older Jewish city centered on the temple mount, as Christian writers were swift to recognize (Eusebius *VC* 3.33).[9]

The Emperor Julian and Jerusalem

The emperor Julian well understood the significance of the city of Jerusalem for Christian piety and the temple ruins for Christian apologetics.[10] Raised a Christian, he had heard Christians speak about the temple in Jerusalem and the prophecies in the Scriptures that the temple would never be rebuilt. In his book *Contra Galilaeos*, preserved in fragments cited by Cyril of Alexandria in his *Contra Julianum*,[11] Julian offered a full-scale refutation of Christianity. What is noteworthy about his book against the Christians is that Julian, a zealous adherent of the traditional religion of the Greek cities, argued that Christianity was not simply an apostasy from Hellenism, but also from Judaism. Indeed a close reading of the fragments of this book shows that his case against Christianity is intimately linked to the legitimacy of Judaism.

Julian was not the first pagan to assail Christianity as an apostasy

9. Linder, 1976; Strumsa; Wilkinson, 1976, pp. 80–81, 88–94; also Levenson, pp. 272–74.

10. For an understanding of Julian's *Against the Galileans* and his program to rebuild the temple, the fundamental study is Lewy. See also J. Vogt, 1939, and, more recently, Levenson, pp. 129–43. For Julian's life, see Bowersock, 1978.

11. Reconstruction of the text of the *Contra Galilaeos* by Neuman.

from Judaism. Already in the second century, Celsus had introduced a Jewish interlocutor into his *True Word* for just that purpose (Origen *Contra Celsum* 2.1–4), and Porphyry offered similar arguments in his book on Christianity (Fragment 1). But Julian made the temple in Jerusalem and the apostasy from Jewish law central. He realized that the very existence of Jewish communities that observed the laws of Moses called into question the claims of Christianity.

According to Libanius, Julian's *Against the Galilaeans*, composed by the pious emperor "during the long winter nights, when other people are usually more interested in matters of sex," was designed to attack the books "in which that fellow from Palestine is claimed to be a god and a son of god" (*Or.* 18.178). In one of his letters, Julian states his intention to write a work, *Against Christianity*, in which he will "strip Jesus of his divinity" (*Ep.* 90 [55] Bidez). In the fragments of his book that are preserved, the same theme appears, although the section dealing explicitly with Christ appears to have been lost. But he does say that the Christians have foolishly allowed themselves to fall into the error of worshipping not the one God, but a "man" (*Gal.* 201e); indeed, they worship the "corpse of a Jew" (*Gal.* 197c), even adoring the "wood of the cross" (*Gal.* 194d). Julian traces this error of ascribing divinity to Jesus to the first disciples; Jesus did not teach that he was a god; he knew nothing of such an idea. The notion that he was the "firstborn son of God or God," is one of the "fictions invented by [Christians] later" (*Gal.* 290e). "Neither Paul nor Matthew nor Luke nor Mark dared to call Jesus God," says Julian (*Gal.* 327a); only John calls him God, but he did not do so "clearly and distinctly" (*Gal.* 213b).

The claim that Christians made Jesus into a god by making him an object of worship is an ancient charge against Christianity, among the earliest that we know (Wilken 1980). In the second century, Celsus said that Christians had established a religious society devoted not to the worship of the one high God, but to a lesser being, on the pretence that he is a great god (Origen *Contra Celsum* 8.15). Christians do not worship a "god, nor even a daimon, but a corpse," says Celsus (*Contra Celsum* 7.68). "You make yourselves a laughing-stock in the eyes of everybody when you blasphemously assert that the other gods who are made manifest are phantoms, while you worship a man who is more wretched than even what really are phantoms, and who is not even any longer a phantom, but in fact dead" (Origen *Contra Celsum* 7.36).

Porphyry, too, writing in the third century, lodged a similar complaint against the Christians. Significantly, this aspect of Porphyry's criticism of Christianity appears in his book *Philosophy from Oracles,* a work designed to defend the traditional religion of Greece and Rome as well as to criticize the Christians (Wilken 1979). Porphyry cited Greek oracles to show that Jesus was a "wise man," indeed, one who deserved to be honored as one of the wisest of men and a man of outstanding piety; but he vigorously criticized the Christians for claiming that he was truly God. This was a foolish idea concocted by the disciples: Jesus never claimed he was divine. Indeed, Porphyry says that Jesus taught men to worship the one high God. It was the error of the Christians to elevate Jesus to divine status (*Phil. orac.*, cited by Augustine in *Consensu evang.* 1.7.11).[12]

From Christian sources, it is clear that pagans continued to bring such arguments against Christians in the latter half of the fourth century, and Christian apologists were forced to take them seriously. The career of Apollinaris, bishop of Laodicea, a city on the Syrian coast not too far from Antioch, shows that the best Christian minds were still profoundly troubled by the charge that Christians only worshipped a "wise man" or an "inspired man" (Muhlenberg, pp. 111–29). Even Augustine's work *On the Harmony of the Gospels*, written around 400 C.E., after Augustine had studied the writings of Porphyry, responded directly to the charge that Christians had made the "man Jesus into a god" (*Consensu evang.* 1.7.10–1.9.14). And as late as book 19 of the *City of God*, the topic is still very much on Augustine's mind (*Civ. Dei* 19.23). Pagan critics could not be ignored by Christian bishops and thinkers.

In this context, we can appreciate the opening words of Julian's *Against the Galilaeans*. "It is I think expedient to set forth to all mankind the reasons by which I was convinced that the fabrication of the Galilaeans is a fiction of men composed by wickedness. Though it has in it nothing divine, by making full use of that part of the soul which loves fable and is childish and foolish, it has induced men to believe that the monstrous tale is truth" (*Gal.* 39a). The monstrous tale is, of course, the myth that had been created concerning Jesus of Nazareth, namely the fiction fashioned by Jesus' disciples to make him into a god. In his reply to Julian, Cyril, who had Julian's entire book before him, recognized that criticism of the divinity of Christ was central to Julian's argument and to the dispute between Christians and Hellenism (*Contra Julianum* 203a; *PG* 76, 809c).

If the attack on the divinity of Christ is central to Julian's arguments against Christianity, one might legitimately ask what role the temple of Jerusalem plays in Julian's book, and how it is that the

---

12. See also Augustine *Civ. Dei* 19.23.

charge that Christianity apostasized from Judaism served to prove that Jesus was not divine? At least from the second century, pagan critics of Christianity realized that the continued existence of Judaism as a religion that claimed faithfulness to the laws of Moses was a powerful argument against the claims of Christianity. That Jews would criticize Christianity for deserting Jewish tradition was self-evident (Justin *Dial.* 10), but that such criticism should come from a Hellenistic philosopher was not, especially when one realized that Celsus and other pagans were sharply critical of Judaism (Origen *Contra Celsum* 3.5). Nevertheless, Celsus argued that Christians had "deserted to another name and another life" (*Contra Celsum* 2.1) by following Jesus, not Moses. "Who is wrong? Moses or Jesus? Or when the Father sent Jesus had he forgotten what commands he gave to Moses? Or did he condemn his own laws and change his mind, and send his messenger for quite the opposite purpose?" (Origen *Contra Celsum* 7.18).

What Julian did was to link this line of thinking with the idea that the temple in Jerusalem was a symbol of the legitimacy of Judaism. The restoration of the temple would show that there was no reason for Christians to abandon the observance of the laws of Moses; hence Judaism could still claim to be the legitimate inheritor of the ancient tradition of Israel. Furthermore, a sure sign that Jesus was not God, as the Christians claimed, was that he prophesied falsely. If his prophecy (Matt. 24) about the temple remaining permanently in ruins were proven false, then Jesus was not divine, but a charlatan and an imposter. Hence, for Julian, the temple in Jerusalem served two purposes: its reconstruction would both legitimate the practice of Judaism and prove that Jesus was not divine and should not be worshiped as God.

To show that Christianity was an apostasy from Judaism, with no genuine foundation within Jewish tradition, Julian appealed to the Jewish Scriptures—the Christian Old Testament. "Since the Galilaeans say that, though they are different from the Jews, they are still, precisely speaking, Israelites in accordance with their prophets, and that they obey Moses above all and the prophets who in Judaea succeeded him, let us see in what respect they chiefly agree with those prophets" (*Gal.* 253c). As was to be expected, one line of argument sought to show that specific biblical prophecies cited by Christians had not come true, and that Jewish prophecies could not be referred to Jesus. Julian cited the famous passage from Isaiah 7:14, "Behold a young woman shall conceive and bear a son." This was taken by Christians to refer to the virgin birth of Jesus and was used to support the claim that Jesus was divine. Julian showed that the text makes no reference to Jesus and that it says nothing about a "god being born of the virgin." Why, then, do Christians call Mary the mother of God, when Isaiah nowhere says that the "only-begotten son of God" was born of the virgin? (*Gal.* 262d).

Similarly, he discusses the passage in Genesis 49:10, "the scepter shall not depart from Judah, nor a leader from his loins," another text attributed to Jesus by the Christians. Julian observed that the text certainly does not refer to the son of Mary, but to the "royal house of David" (*Gal.* 253d). In the same passage, he also mentions Deuteronomy 18:18, "I will raise up from them a prophet like you from among their brethren. . . ." These words, said Julian, were not spoken of the son of Mary either. Even if "one should concede that they were said of him, Moses says that the prophet will be like him and not like God, a prophet like himself and born of men, not of a god" (*Gal.* 253c). Here the argument that Jesus is not divine and the charge that Christianity is an apostasy from Judaism (since its religious claims have no firm basis within the Jewish scriptures) merge into one.

Julian was not, however, satisfied simply to appeal to Jewish prophecy. He also argued from Jewish practice, specifically the continuing observance of the ancient laws of Moses by the Jews, which was evident both to pagans and Christians. "Why is it that you do not abide even by the traditions of the Hebrews or accept the Law which God has given to them" (*Gal.* 238b)? The Jews have "precise laws concerning religious worship," observed Julian, and nowhere do the Scriptures say that God instituted a "second law" to replace the one given to Moses. According to the Scriptures (for example, Deut. 4:2; 27; 26), the laws given by Moses were to be observed forever, without adding to them or taking away from them (*Gal.* 320b). The Scriptures clearly teach "that the Law of Moses was to last for all time" (*Gal.* 320a).

For example, asked Julian, why do you not practice circumcision? (*Gal.* 351a). Julian was, of course, aware that Christians would answer the question by citing St. Paul, "Circumcision is of the heart not of the flesh" (Rom. 4:11–12), and he countered the objection by quoting Jesus: "I have not come to abolish the law and the prophets but to fulfill them" (Matt. 5:17) and "whoever relaxes one of the least of these commandments and teaches men so, shall be called least in the kingdom of heaven" (Matt. 5:19).[13] Note that Julian enlisted Jesus on his side, attributing the change of attitude toward the Law not to the teaching of Jesus, but to his disciples. Jesus kept the Law of Moses. The disciples, not Jesus, introduced a new law.

---

13. This text is included in Neumann's edition of the *Contra Galilaeos*, but not in the Wright edition; text can be found in Neumann, p. 229, and in Cyril of Alexandria *Contra Julianum* 351a–b (*PG* 76.1041a–b).

Then Julian returns to the original question: "Why do you not sacrifice?" Once again, his Christian training provided the objection of Christians that "the Jews too do not sacrifice" (*Gal.* 305d). But, replies Julian, the Jews do sacrifice in their homes and eat what is sacrificed, even giving the right shoulder to the priests. This reference to Jewish sacrifices in Julian's time has puzzled scholars, but what Julian seems to have in mind is the ritual butchering of meat and the eating of a lamb at Passover (Alon 1970, 2:313–14). That is not, however, his chief point. The reason the Jews do not sacrifice, he says, is that "they have been deprived of their temple, or as they are accustomed to call it, their holy place." Since they do not have the temple, "they are prevented from offering the first fruits of the sacrifice to God" (*Gal.* 306a).

Julian's contention, then, was that Christians "do not observe any one of the other customs observed by Jews" (*Gal.* 306a) and by rejecting the observance of the Law proved they were apostates. The temple was the symbol of the legitimacy of *any* observance of Jewish law. That the temple was not standing in Julian's day was a powerful argument for the legitimacy of Christianity. If there were no sacrifices in Jerusalem, Judaism was bereft of its most important symbol.

It is clear then, that one of the reasons Julian wished to rebuild the temple and restore Jerusalem to the Jews was to refute the Christians and prove that Jesus was not divine. Julian was not an ancient Zionist who wished to return the Jews to their homeland. What he did, he did, in the words of the Jewish proverb "because of hate for Haman, not for the love of Mordecai." By restoring the Jewish temple, he hoped to legitimate Jewish law, but he also sought to prove false the prophecy of Daniel and the word of Jesus about the temple. The restoration of the temple would also put a stop to the Christianization of Jerusalem, which had gone on apace since the time of Constantine. Indeed, to some Christians, it appeared that if Julian's plan had been successful, the Jews would eventually have expelled the Christians as the Romans had expelled the Jews (Socrates *Hist. eccl.* 3.20).

At this juncture, it is important to note that Julian's argument about the temple was a distinctly pagan argument against Christianity. It was not derived from Judaism. Indeed, it was probably learned from Christians like Eusebius, who had insisted on the importance of the ancient prophecies concerning the temple and had linked the temple to the legitimacy of Jewish law (*Demon. evang.* 17d; 403b–c). Julian took the Christian idea that the legitimacy of Jewish law was dependent on the temple and turned it against Christianity. For if appeal to historical events could validate religious claims, new events could invalidate those same claims. By rebuilding the temple in Jerusalem,

Julian saw a way to undermine all the appeals to history used by Christians to validate Christian beliefs (Lewy, p. 5). Thus, as much as Julian's interpretation of the temple sounds as though it derived from Jewish arguments, it actually emerged out of the conflict between Hellenism and Christianity. That is not to say that such a claim was unrelated to Judaism, for it depended on the continuing existence of observant Jewish communities to give it credibility. But it was not an argument used by Jews.

Julian's interest in the temple in Jerusalem was also intimately related to his own religious views and his program to restore ancient customs. Sacrifice of animals was for Julian the quintessential religious act. Wherever he traveled in the empire, he offered sacrifices, sometimes to the embarrassment of intellectuals who had abandoned sacrifices in favor of a spiritual form of religion. During Julian's short reign, however, the figure of the emperor, a knife in his hands, his fingers dripping with blood, became familiar to the citizens of the empire. It was said that if Julian returned victorious from Persia, there would be a shortage of cattle throughout the Roman world.

Julian had learned of the importance of animal sacrifices from his Neoplatonist teachers, notably Iamblichus, one of Julian's intellectual heroes, who was a student of Porphyry. In his work *On the Mysteries*, Iamblichus defended theurgy, the doctrine that the divine could be persuaded to do or refrain from doing something through rituals, the use of material means (for example, salves, ointments, herbs and roots), and the sacrifice of animals (Iamblichus *De Mysteriis* 5.23). Union with the divine was best achieved not by contemplation, nor by intellectual effort but by the performance of ritual acts. A close friend of Julian's, Sallustius, expressed the theory in this way: since we have received everything from the gods, we offer a part back in "votive offerings, gifts of hair and adornment, and sacrifices." "Prayers without sacrifices are only words: with sacrifices they are living words. The word gives meaning to the life, while the life [of the animal] animates the word" (Sallustius *Concerning the Gods* 16).[14]

In antiquity all the peoples of the Mediterranean basin practiced animal sacrifice, including the Jews. The Jews, however, had abandoned sacrifices several hundred years earlier when the temple was destroyed. Why not, thought Julian, enlist the Jews as allies in the effort to restore traditional worship to the cities of the Roman Empire? Although the Jews did not agree with the theology of the traditional religion of the cities, they did believe in the efficacy of sacrifices. If the temple and the city were restored to the Jews, Julian reasoned, they

14. See also Iamblichus *De mysteriis* 6.3.

too would be able to join with the other citizens of the empire in "offering prayers on behalf of the imperial office" (Julian *Ep.* 204 [25] Bidez). Although the Jews would not agree with Julian's religious views, he hoped they could be enlisted as allies, further isolating Christians from the rest of the citizens of the empire.

Julian's program to restore the temple thus had three purposes: (1) to prove that Christ's prophecy about the destruction of the temple was false, thereby showing that he was a mere man, not the son of God; (2) to prove that Christianity was illegitimate and apostate, by legitimating the observance of Jewish law; and (3) to enlist the Jews as allies in his religious reform by restoring sacrificial worship in Jerusalem as he intended to do throughout the empire.

The Rebuilding of the Temple as a Challenge to Christianity

Work on the reconstruction of the temple in Jerusalem began in the spring of 363 C.E., but the building was cut short by a fire or some other catastrophe at the site (Ammianus Marcellinus *Hist.* 23.1.2–3). When Julian died unexpectedly several weeks later in a battle on the Persian frontier, the project was abandoned. Some scholars think that the plan to rebuild the temple generated a wave of excitement and expectation among Jewish communities in the empire and beyond (Avi-Yonah, pp. 193–98), but there are no contemporary Jewish sources informing us of the response of the Jews.[15] Only Christian authors say that the news was welcomed by many Jews. Ephraem, a Syriac writer, reports that "the Jews were seized by a frenzied enthusiasm and sounded trumpets" (*Contra Julianum* 1.16; 2.7). Gregory Nazianzus claims, no doubt with rhetorical exaggerations, that Jews donated money and jewelry to assist in rebuilding the temple (*Or.* 5.5). From other Christian writers, it appears that the possibility of a return of Jews to Jerusalem and the rebuilding of the temple strengthened Jewish self-confidence. Rufinus says the Jews thought that "one of the prophets had returned" and that they began to "taunt us and, as though the time of the rule (*regnum*) had returned, to threaten us sharply and to treat us with great insolence, carrying on in boastful and haughty fashion" (*Hist. eccl.* 10.38).

What is remarkable, however, is that even though Julian's plan was

15. Evidence from Jewish sources comes from a later period. Levenson, pp. 164–68.

a failure and there is no evidence that any further attempt was made to rebuild in the generation after Julian's death, the memory of the temple lived on in the minds of Christians.[16] As we saw in Chapter 3, a generation later the Jews of Antioch were still going about the city "boasting that they will get back their city again" (*Jud.* 7.1; 915). The prominence of the temple in John's homilies on the Judaizers in Antioch shows that Julian's plan had a significant impact on Christians in the later fourth century. Its rebuilding would legitimate the practice of Judaism. Gregory Nazianzus says that Julian prophesied that now was the time for the Jews to return to the land and rebuild the temple and "restore the authority of the ancient tradition" (*Or.* 5.3). John echoes the same point in his long homily on the temple. If the city is returned to the Jews, they will be able to return to their "former way of life" (*Jud.* 5.1; 884).[17]

As observed in Chapter 3, too, the expectation of a restoration of Jerusalem also generated a wave of eschatological fervor among judaizing Christians toward the end of the fourth century. The importance of the city and the temple for judaizing Christians during this period can be seen in the interpretation of prophetic texts that speak of the return of the Jews to Jerusalem. Commenting on Isaiah 35:10, "the ransomed of the Lord shall return and come to Zion with singing," Jerome says that the "Jews and our Judaizers" interpret this text to refer not to the "advent of the Savior" but to the second coming, when the Jews will enter Zion with gladness. Similarly, commenting on Zachariah 14:10–12, "Jerusalem shall be inhabited for there shall be no more curse," he observes that the Jews and judaizing Christians say that this refers to the building of the city and a time when "circumcision will again be practiced, sacrifices offered, all the precepts of the Law observed, so that Jews will no longer become Christians but Christians will become Jews" (*Comm. in Zach.* 14:10).

These passages suggest that a return to Jerusalem was thought to be imminent. This interpretation is strengthened by comparing Jerome's exegesis, written at the beginning of the fifth century, with Eusebius's

16. It is somewhat puzzling that Jewish Christians would welcome the rebuilding of the temple. It would of course confirm their claim that Jewish law was still valid and that Jesus had not come to abolish the Law. But it would also discredit the prophecy of Jesus in Matt. 24 that the temple would never be rebuilt. As Christians, and especially as Christians who appealed to the authority of Jesus to legitimate their practices, it is unlikely that they would wish to see Jesus' authority subverted by having his prophecy proven false. Yet that is certainly how the reestablishment of the temple would be viewed by Jews and pagans. I suspect that at the psychological and emotive level Jewish Christians favored the rebuilding of the temple without reflecting on the theological consequences of this development for the authority of Jesus or the truth of Christianity.

17. Cf. also *Jud.* 4.6 (880–81); *Jud.* 6.3 (907–8); *Pan. Bab.* 2.22 (PG. 50.568).

interpretation of some of the same texts in his commentary on Isaiah, also written in Palestine, but earlier, in the fourth century. In Eusebius's commentary, there is no sense of urgency about these passages from the prophets, even though he does mention Jewish interpreters of the texts. The issue centers not on the return to Jerusalem, but on whether the texts refer to the earthly or heavenly Jerusalem. Thus the passage from Isaiah 35 refers not to Zion (i.e., the city of Jerusalem) says Eusebius, but to the heavenly Jerusalem, citing Hebrews 12:22 (*Comm. in Isa.* 35:9–10).[18] Furthermore, there is neither mention of judaizing Christians nor any hint that Jews had any imminent expectations about a return to Jerusalem.

Both the resurgence of judaizing Christianity in the late fourth century and the plan of Julian to restore the city of Jerusalem to the Jews were intimately linked to the existence of vital and visible Jewish communities in the cities of the eastern Mediterranean. Julian's plan to rebuild the temple is unintelligible unless there were Jewish communities who read the Jewish Scriptures and observed the laws of Moses. Julian's arguments about the legitimacy of the Law of Moses, as set forth in the *Contra Galilaeos*, and his claim that Christians had apostasized from the Law of Moses, replacing it with a second law, would have had no force if there were no Jewish communities that *did* observe the Law of Moses. Unless there was a legitimate inheritor of the patrimony of ancient Israel, it made no sense to argue that Christianity was an illegitimate offshoot, an apostate sect.

In an environment, then, in which Judaism was still very much present, Julian issued his challenge to Christianity. By highlighting the relationship of Christianity to Judaism, Julian attacked Christians at an extremely vulnerable point. His argument was not new. Earlier critics had made a similar point, but what was new was that Julian made it central and supported his religious arguments with the announcement that he would return Jerusalem to the Jews and restore the ancient temple and its sacrifices. And though his efforts were unsuccessful, that such an idea could come so close to realization, that the money, men, and materials to carry out the task were available, and that the work had actually been begun on the site of the temple ruins, alarmed Christians. How futile confident appeals to history would appear if the project were successful; what perils lay ahead if the prophecy of Jesus could be refuted by the efforts of a Roman emperor, a mere man?

In his attempt to execute this plan, Julian, in the words of John, had "put the power of Christ on trial" (*Pan. Bab.* 2.22; 50.568). The bravado and boasting of Christian writers about Julian's failure only be-

18. See also *Comm. in Isa.* 25:6–8.

trayed how profoundly he had scandalized the Church. This is why John and other Christian writers emphasized the importance of actually seeing the ruins in Jerusalem (*Jud. et gent.* 16., 48.834; *Jud.* 5.11., 901). As late as the middle of the fifth century, Theodoret, bishop of Cyrus north of Antioch and a native of Antioch, traveled to Jerusalem and when he saw the desolation "with his own eyes," rejoiced in the truth of the prophecies (*Affect.* 11.71).

This new emphasis on the temple renewed the conflict between Christians and Jews over the legitimacy of Jewish law. And even though the ruins of Jerusalem seemed to confirm the Christian view that the Law of Moses had been replaced by a second law, Julian had planted doubts in the minds of Christians. Was there a continuing legitimacy to Jewish observance of the Law? Did the judaizing Christians have a point after all? Was it true that Jesus himself had observed the Law and urged his followers not to abandon one jot or tittle of it? Julian understood the inextricable link between Judaism and Christianity, but drew a different conclusion from the majority of Christians, arguing that if observance of the Law were legitimate, then Christianity was illegitimate. In short, he made the truth of one religion dependent on the invalidity of the other. Julian did this as a pagan critic, but the impact of his work was felt where there were strong groups of judaizing Christians. For judaizing Christians, by celebrating the Jewish festivals, and observing the law, proclaimed by their very actions that the Jewish rites were legitimate. Here arguments became pointless; if one participated in a rite, the very act of participation testified to a belief in its truth. Julian's challenge took on new urgency when large numbers of Christians in Antioch forsook the churches to attend the synagogues. When this upsurge of Judaizing in the Christian communities was supported by rumors that the city of Jerusalem would be returned to the Jews, the situation in Antioch became acute.

Homilies on the Judaizers
and the City of Jerusalem

John's sermons on the Judaizers were occasional pieces, prepared for delivery before a congregation and prompted by the upcoming Jewish festivals, which promised to draw large numbers of Christians. They do not deal systematically with the range of issues generated by the conflict between Christians and Jews during the first four centuries. Designed to stir up the emotions of his hearers, to urge them to seek out erring brothers and sisters, to brand the Judaizers as renegades, they sought to stop the flow of Christians to the synagogue by rhetorical display, intimidation, and social pressure. "Each of you," says John, "bring me one of those who are sick with this disease [Judaism]. . . . Women should go after women, men after men, slaves after slaves, freedmen after freedmen, children after children. In a word—let everyone join with diligence in the hunt for those afflicted with this disease and then return to our next service to receive our praise" (*Jud.* 1.8; 856).

Nevertheless, the sermons are not simply rhetorical showpieces to entice or bully recalcitrant members of John's flock to return. By observing aspects of Jewish law and celebrating festivals with Jews, the Judaizers offered a theological challenge, for if the Jewish rites are observed as divine ordinances, what was the legitimacy of Christian rites? Further, the Judaizers not only "observe Jewish rites," says John; "They also make every effort to defend them." This is why "they deserve a stronger condemnation than the Jews" (*Jud.* 4.3; 875). The central issue raised by the Judaizers, then, is the legitimacy of Jewish law, and, in John's mind, the symbol for the legitimacy of Jewish law was the temple and city of Jerusalem. "It is illegitimate to keep their former [i.e., according to the Law] way of life outside of Jerusalem" (*Jud.* 8.5; 935), for the city of Jerusalem is the "keystone that supports the Jewish rite" (*Jud.* 4.6; 881). In various forms, this argument occurs in all of the homilies on the Judaizers, but it is most fully developed in homilies three, four, five, six, and seven.

In the third homily, John discusses the Jewish Passover, which was celebrated by the Antiochene Jews in John's time. How, asks John, can the Jews celebrate the Passover today when the Scriptures expressly teach that the Passover cannot be celebrated outside of Jerusalem? To support his argument, he cites Deuteronomy 16: "You may not keep the Passover in any of your cities, which the Lord your God is giving you but only in the place in which my name is called on." Moses, says John, is "speaking here about Jerusalem." According to John, this text shows that the Passover is to be confined only to Jerusalem, and if it is not celebrated in Jerusalem it is not legitimate. Further, says John, if the Passover is to be celebrated only in Jerusalem, and God destroys Jerusalem, "is it not clear that he intended to abolish the feast?" (*Jud.* 3.3; 865–66). If the city of Jerusalem is still in ruins, this can only mean that God does not wish the laws about the Passover to be observed any longer.

A similar argument is applied to the blowing of trumpets in the synagogue, a practice that attracted Christians in Antioch (*Jud.* 1.5; 851). In ancient times, says John, when the Jews offered sacrifices they "sounded trumpets." Moses commanded the Israelites to make "trumpets of beaten silver" (Numbers 10), and they were instructed "to sound them over burnt offerings and sacrifices" (*Jud.* 4.7; 881). But, says John, God no longer permits the Jews to sound the trumpets because there is no altar, no ark, no tabernacle, no holy of holies, no priests, no cherubim, no altar of incense, nor any of the other things necessary for sacrifice. In short, if there is no temple, the command to sound trumpets is invalid.

In the seventh homily, John mentions several laws of Moses that cannot be carried out without the temple and priesthood. A law in Exodus 23 says that all males shall come to the temple three times a year to make an offering. However, says John, "Since the temple has been destroyed, they cannot do this." Further, the law commanded that sacrifices be offered by a man with gonorrhea, by a leper, by a menstruating woman, and by a woman who has given birth. These laws cannot be fulfilled either, says John, "because there is no place nor altar" (*Jud.* 7.1; 916). Next John discusses at length the law from Numbers about women suspected of adultery. This law is the basis for the Mishnaic tract *Sotah*, as well as for the commentary in the Gemara in the Palestinian and Babylonian Talmuds. Here, too, John argues that the biblical injunction requires that the adulterous wife be brought before a priest, who will require that she take an oath and offer a grain offering. But, since the Jews were deprived of their "temple, their altar, the tabernacle, and the sacrifices," they "were not able to fulfil these commands" (*Jud.* 7.1; 917). From these examples, John concludes that the Jewish law was not intended to be a law for all time and for use in every place; it was restricted to the city of Jerusalem, for the "Law receives its force from the place" (*Jud.* 7.2; 917). Just as there cannot be an emperor without armies, a crown, or purple robes, so there cannot be "priesthood without a temple."

As further proof, John appeals to the exile of the Jews in ancient times. In contrast to the Jews of today, who continue to observe the Law in exile, he says, the Jews of old refused to keep the Law when they were taken from Jerusalem. When asked by their captors to sing and play musical instruments, the Jews said, "How shall we sing the song of the Lord in a strange Land," for they knew that the Law commanded them not to do so. There was much room in Babylon, says John, for a place of sacrifice, but "since the temple was not there, they steadfastly refrained from offering sacrifice." Nor did they keep the feasts or the Passover while in captivity. Indeed they even broke the Law, as the example of Daniel shows (*Dan.* 10:1–3). He fasted during the days of the Passover when it was expressly forbidden to fast. The Jews of antiquity kept the law strictly, which is to say that they obeyed the Law that said that "they must not observe those rituals outside Jerusalem" (*Jud.* 4.5; 878).

Though many of John's illustrations do concern the temple and the offering of sacrifices, it is clear that the main point of the argument was not that the temple rites could no longer be observed (e.g., ritual acts requiring priests or sacrifices), but that any observance of the Law was now illegitimate. The temple was significant not only because of what once happened there, but as a symbol of the observance of the Law even in those matters that had no relation to the temple cult. Even the reading of the Law, says John, was prohibited outside of Jerusalem (*Jud.* 7.1; 916).

To the Jews arguments of this sort must have appeared fantastic. Judaism did not need the city of Jerusalem or the temple to legitimate the observance of the Law. Long before the temple was destroyed, for example, Jews had been celebrating the Passover outside of the city of Jerusalem and in cities throughout the Mediterranean world. This is not to say that the loss of the temple and the city did not generate a spiritual crisis within Judaism. In Jewish tradition there is evidence of discussions concerning the legitimacy of certain ritual acts traditionally associated with the temple. In *Rosh Hashannah*, a tractate in the *Mishnah*, it is said that "if a festival of Rosh Hashannah fell on a Sabbath, the shofar might be sounded in the holy city but not in the provinces." After the temple was destroyed, the question was raised as to what should be done. Some said that Rabbi Jochanan ben Zakkai said that it could be blown wherever there was a Jewish court; others claimed that Rabbi Jochanan said it could only be blown in Jabneh (*M. Rosh Hashannah* 4.1). Similarly, the Lulav was carried seven days in the temple, but only one day in the provinces. Here, too, a question arose after the destruction of the temple. In this case, Rabbi Jochanan ben Zakkai ruled that in the provinces the Lulav should be carried seven days in memory of the temple (*M. Rosh Hashannah* 4.3).

Instances such as these indicate that Jews had discussed the problems raised by the destruction of the temple. However, within Judaism the destruction of the temple never assumed the theological importance it did in Christianity, and the religious crisis provoked by the loss of Jerusalem was resolved long before the fourth century. There is no trace in Jewish sources that Jews thought the loss of the temple invalidated the observance of the Law. When Israel's enemies chided the Jews because God had apparently deserted them, Jewish teachers comforted their people with promises from the Scriptures that the covenant was eternal and that one day they would return to Jerusalem (Marmorstein 1935, pp. 238–39). As for the specific problems of the cessation of sacrifices, other Jewish teachers, drawing on resources from Jewish tradition, showed that animal sacrifices were not necessary for reconciliation with God:

Once as Rabbi Jochanan ben Zakkai was coming forth from Jerusalem, Rabbi Joshua followed after him and beheld the temple in ruins. "Woe unto us," Rabbi Joshua cried, "that this, the place where the iniquities of Israel were atoned for, is laid waste!" "My son," Rabbi Jochanan said to him, "Be not grieved. We have another atonement as effective as this. And what is it? It is acts of loving kindness, as it is said, 'For I desire mercy and not sacrifice'." [*Avot de Rabbi Nathan* 4.5][19]

In light of Jewish tradition, John's arguments about the legitimacy of the law and the temple in Jerusalem were unpersuasive. This is only further evidence that the homilies on the Judaizers must be seen in the larger social and religious context of ancient Antioch and not simply in the light of relations between Jews and Christians. The arguments of the homilies on the Judaizers respond more directly to Greek critics of Christianity and to Judaizers nurtured in the Christian tradition than to the Jews. The significance of the Jews lay less in what they said than in their very existence as a people who claimed the inheritance of ancient Israel and continued to observe the ancient laws of Moses.

In the homilies, John occasionally mentions actual disputes with Jews. In Homily 6, for example, he says that in response to the Christian claim that the temple was destroyed because God had rejected His people, the Jews say that they lost the temple and their homeland "because of their sins." "This is the reason," say the Jews, "that we are not recovering our homeland" (*Jud.* 6.2; 906). In the same homily, he mentions that Jews attribute the loss of the city not to the will of God, but to the deeds of evil men—that is, the Romans who had waged war on them (*Jud.* 6.4; 909–10). As we saw earlier in this chapter, Jewish sources roughly contemporary with John discuss this same subject (Schoeps 1950b, pp. 150–53), and it is likely that explanations for the temple's destruction arose not simply within Jewish circles but also in disputes with pagans or Christians. Similarly, in Homily 7, John discusses the text from Genesis 1:16, "Let us make mankind in our image and likeness," a passage that had long been a matter of dispute between Christians and Jews because Christians used the text to support the divinity of Jesus (*Jud.* 7.3; 919).

But topics such as these that may have arisen in disputes between Jews and Christians are not central to the homilies on the Judaizers. And it is noteworthy that in the few instances in the homilies where John purports to be introducing Jewish responses he sometimes uses the optative; "Jews would say" (*Jud.* 6.2; 906, line 2).[20] In light of ev-

---

19. See also *b. Berakoth* 32b.
20. In other places he uses the indicative: *Jud.* 6.3, 908; 6.4, 909.

erything we know about the situation in Antioch, it is possible that John engaged in actual disputes with the Jews, but in the homilies on the Judaizers, he is preoccupied with the Christians in his congregation who had adopted Jewish practices.

The Destruction of Jerusalem
and the Divinity of Jesus

The longest homily among the eight, and the one offering the most extensive theological and historical discussion of the temple and the city of Jerusalem, is the fifth. In the fourth, John had discussed the legitimacy of Jewish law. However, since some people still thought the Jews were going to "regain their own city" and "return to their former way of life and have their temple rebuilt" (*Jud.* 5.1; 883), he decided to discuss the city and the temple. In the fifth homily, as in the others, the argument appears that observance of Jewish law depends on possession of the city. In the past, says John, even though the Jews had a definite promise from God that the city would be returned, they did not observe the Law in the intervening years before it was restored to them. If, he says to the Christians in his congregation, you ask the Jew today why he observes the Law, and he replies, "Because I expect to recover my city," you should say to him: "Stop fasting, then, until you recover it. Certainly, until the holy ones of old returned to their own fatherland, they practiced none of the rites which you now practice. From this it is clear that you are violating the law, even if you are going to recover your city, as you say" (*Jud.* 5.1; 883).

From John's opening remarks, it appears that this sermon is concerned chiefly with the Jews and the legitimacy of Jewish law. In his opening remarks, however, he says that he is preaching not simply "to stitch up the mouths of the Jews," but also to present the "proper teachings" of the Church. These teachings can be found in the Scriptures, where Jesus prophesied what would happen in the future. Since these prophecies have come true, they show that Jesus prophesied truly and is therefore divine. He said, "Jerusalem will be trod upon by many nations until the times of the nations are fulfilled" (Luke 21:24). This means that the temple will be trod on "until the consummation of the world." Jesus also prophesied that "no stone will remain upon a stone in that place" (Matt. 24:2; *Jud.* 5.1; 884). The Jews, however, reject Jesus' testimony because they see him as a "man among men," not "God and master of the world."

Already in the first sermon, John had charged that the Jews were similar to the Arians because both criticized Jesus for claiming to be

God (*Jud.* 1.1; 845). The fifth sermon was preached to challenge the contention that Jesus was not truly divine. Here John argues, as he had argued in his apologetic tracts, that "it was not the mark of a mere man" to have power over historical events (*Jud. et gent.* 1; 48.813–14). The theme was central to John's apologetic writings and reappears in the homilies on the Judaizers, most explicitly in the one dealing extensively with the destruction of the temple. In most of the homilies the polemic is directed against the legitimacy of the Law, but here the discussion of the Law and the temple are linked explicitly to the larger claim that Jesus is truly divine.

Before turning directly to the discussion of the temple, John discusses a number of Christ's other prophecies. His first illustration is somewhat strange, but it reveals how people in the fourth century thought divine action could be legitimated in historical events. When the woman in the gospels anointed Jesus with oil, Jesus said "wherever this gospel is preached in the whole world, what she had done will be told in memory of her" (Matt. 25:13). This prophecy has come true, says John, because "in all the churches we hear this woman being spoken of [when the passage in Matthew is read]" and the story is heard by all kinds of people, "those who stand in the highest place, generals, famous men and women, the illustrious, brilliant people in all the cities" (*Jud.* 5.2; 885). Though the woman who anointed Jesus was humble, her dress and appearance that of a lowly peasant, her deed not memorable and witnessed by only a few, yet it is told and retold and heard by countless numbers of people to this day.

A curious argument indeed, but it would not have struck someone in the fourth century as implausible. For the words of Jesus took the form of a prophecy ("what she has done will be told in memory of her"), and it was assumed that the prophecy was to be judged true or false by an appeal to history. Such arguments were commonplace. The prophecy of Jesus that "this gospel will be preached throughout the whole world (Matt. 24:14)" has come true, argued Theodoret of Cyrus, a bishop in Syria, because "the churches are built surpassingly great and beautiful, in the middle of cities, villages, fields and most remote places and are more illustrious than the highest mountains [referring to Micah 4]. . . . The Greek temples, however, are completely destroyed and removed from the foundations, but the churches of God, both in multitude and beauty, surpass the stars of heaven" (*Interp. in Mic.* 4:1–3; PG 81.1760a–1761b). Theodoret adds, however, that the Jews do not see things this way, preferring to see the text of Micah as referring to return of Jews from Babylon.

John gives another illustration in Homily 5, this one directly linked to the fortunes of the Church. Christ said: "On this rock I shall build my church; and the gates of hell will not prevail against her" (Matt. 16:18). Had the Church been a strong and powerful institution, aligned with earthly powers, its success would be understandable, says John, but it began as a tiny plant and grew even though it received no support from the rulers, becoming strong "not from the peace granted by the rulers but from the power of God" (*Jud.* 5.2; 886). As further evidence, John cites the reputed words of Gamaliel, who according to the book of Acts said of the Christian movement, "If this plan or this undertaking is of men, it will fail; but it it is of God you will not be able to destroy it. You might even be found opposing God." (Acts 5:35−39). No man, not even the great men of the Greeks—Zeno, Plato, Socrates, Diagoras, Pythagoras, Apollonius of Tyana—could bring about such success, yet the Jews only see Jesus as a "mere man who violated their law" (*Jud.* 5.3; 887). But what lawbreaker and deceiver, asks John, has "gotten for himself so many churches all over the world, what rogue extended his worship to the ends of the earth, what imposter has every man bowing down before him, and this in the face of ten thousand obstacles?" (*Jud.* 5.3; 887−88).

Finally, John comes to the chief topic of the sermon. The greatest proof that Christ is truly God is that he "predicted the temple would be destroyed, that Jerusalem would be captured, and that the city would no longer be the city of the Jews as it had been in the past." If only ten, twenty, or fifty years had passed since the destruction of the temple, one might understand doubts about Jesus' prophecy, but over three centuries have passed and there is not "a shadow of the change for which you are waiting" (*Jud.* 5.3; 888). With this introduction, John turns to a comparison of the previous captivities of the Jews with the present "captivity."

The first captivity was in Egypt as prophesied in Genesis 15:13− 14. The length of the exile, 400 years, was specified "with complete accuracy." The second captivity was in Babylonia, and was prophesied in Jeremiah 29:10−14. Here, too, the time and place are mentioned (*Jud.* 5.5; 891). The third "captivity" took place under Antiochus Epiphanes. This was not a captivity in the sense that the Babylonian exile or the sojourn in Egypt were, but Antiochus desecrated the temple in Jerusalem and subjugated the Jews, "putting an end to the Jewish way of life" (*Jud.* 5.6; 893). These events, too, were foretold by the prophet Daniel long before they happened and with perfect accuracy. John takes some liberties with the prophecy in Daniel, since this book was open to many different interpretations, as Jerome shows in his commentary (*Comm. in Dan.* 9:24−27). Porphyry had argued (correctly) that the book was not a prophecy but a record of past events (Jerome, *Comm. in Dan.*, *Preface*), a point vigorously disputed by Christian commentators. Jews, though not sharing Porphyry's views, denied that Daniel belonged among the prophets (Theodoret of Cyrus, *Comm. in Dan., Preface*; PG 81.1257–60). If he was not a prophet, he could not be used to support Christian views about the fulfillment of ancient prophecies.

John was, no doubt, aware of the Jewish view that Daniel was not a prophet. Hence he appeals to Josephus, "an authority highly respected in the eyes of the Jews," who placed the Book of Daniel in the sixth century B.C.E. and interpreted Daniel's words as a prophecy of the events that took place in the second century B.C.E. under Antiochus Epiphanes. Josephus also saw other passages from Daniel (notably Dan. 9:24) as prophecies of the war with the Romans. "Daniel predicted in the same way," says John, citing Josephus, "the domination of the Romans, the taking of Jerusalem and the destruction of the temple." Note well, says John, that it is a Jew who speaks these words and that he does not say that the temple "will be restored again," nor does he specify a time "when the restoration will take place" (*Jud.* 5.9; 897). As did the prophets of old, Josephus says that Jerusalem will be destroyed, but he does not say that the captivity will end. If the present "captivity" were to come to an end, the prophets would have foretold it, but no prophet "specified the time" (*Jud.* 6.2; 905).

John then turns to the passage in Daniel, "seventy weeks are decreed over your people and over the holy city" (Dan. 9:24). The Jews argue that with these words Daniel specifies a time, says John. But the text does not say that; it simply gives the length of time before the captivity was to begin (*Jud.* 5.9; 898). Then follows a discussion of the chronology of Daniel, ending in the argument that the key to the text is to be found in the phrase in 9:27, "when the consummation will be given up to desolation." This will take place, says John, after the cessation of sacrifices, as Jesus said in Matthew 24:15: You will see the "abomination of desolation" spoken of by the prophet Daniel in the holy place (*Jud.* 5.10; 899). These events happened at the time of the Roman siege of the city, as Josephus had already shown. "When the prophets predicted the other captivities they spoke not only of the captivity but also the length of time appointed for each bondage to last; for this present captivity however, they set no time, but on the contrary said that the desolation would endure until the end" (*Jud.* 5.10; 899).

According to John, the history of events since the time of the temple's destruction proves that the prophecy was trustworthy. If the Jews had never attempted to rebuild the temple during this time, one might say that they could do so only if they made the effort. But the course of events shows the reverse, for the Jews have attempted to rebuild the temple, not once, but three times and were unsuccessful in every effort.

John first mentions the Bar Kochba revolt (132–35 C.E.) in the time of the emperor Hadrian, who put down the rebellion, and gave the city a new name, Aelia Capitolina, to seal its destruction. Parenthetically, it may be noted that though John says the name Aelia Capitolina was used to his day, he always refers to the city as Jerusalem. If the city really went by the name Aelia Capitolina, it is doubtful that it would have played such a role in Christian polemics.

The next attempt to rebuild the temple took place under Constantine, but again the emperor put down the revolt. There is no historical record of this event. Possibly John refers to the revolt under Gallus later in the fourth century, but the text as it now stands cannot be corroborated by other sources. His point, however, is clear: the second attempt also failed.

Some of his hearers have said that what happened under Constantine and Hadrian is "old and outdated," part of ancient history, John observes. He will now speak, therefore, of what happened "in our own age" under the emperor Julian. Julian, in an effort to gain support from the Jews for his religious reforms, asked them to restore their ancient cult. But the Jews said that "it would not be right to sacrifice outside of the city of Jerusalem." "If you wish to see us sacrificing give us back the city, restore the temple, open up the holy of holies for us, fix the altar, and we will sacrifice at that time" (*Jud.* 5.11; 900).[21] The Jews, however, did not realize they were asking the impossible, because it was God who had overturned their city and only God could restore it. Julian provided the money and sent builders and overseers, because he hoped to persuade them, after they began their own sacrifices, to offer sacrifices to the Roman gods and "to frustrate the statement of Christ which did not allow for the rebuilding of the temple."

The failure of Julian's effort to rebuild the temple in Jerusalem, then, is proof that Christ was not an ordinary man among men, but the divine son of God. His word was more powerful than the feeble efforts of men, for by his word alone he defeated the emperor Julian and the "whole Jewish people." If one visits Jerusalem today, says John, "you will see only the bare foundation." Of this we are all "witnesses for it happened not long ago but in our own time" (*Jud.* 5.11; 901). Furthermore, these things did not happen under a Christian emperor, but under an impious emperor, during a time when "Hellenism flourished" and Christians were persecuted. The prophecy of Christ is proven true by the historical "facts."

21. This dialogue between the Jews and Julian is probably John's invention for the rhetorical purposes of the sermon (Levenson, pp. 153–55).

Finally, John returns to the general theme that dominates the entire sermon, namely, that the fulfillment of the ancient prophecies and the continued existence of the Church is evidence of the power and divinity of Christ. The prophet Malachi foretold what would happen when he wrote, "From furthest east to furthest west my name is great among the nations" (Mal. 1:10–11). These things are now happening says John, because Malachi did not say "in one city, as under the laws of the Jews, but 'from the rising of the sun until its setting.'" He did not say "in Israel," but "in the nations." He is speaking of a "rite" that would be celebrated from the rising of the sun until its setting, as Zephaniah also prophesied (Zeph. 2:11). Moses had commanded the Jews to "worship in one place," but Jesus taught mankind that God will be worshipped not in Jerusalem, but "in spirit and in truth" (John 4:24).[22] When Christ said this, he "removed the obligation to observe one place of worship and introduced a more lofty and spiritual way of worship" (*Jud.* 5.12; 902–03). The proof that this is so is that the temple in Jerusalem was destroyed.

At the end of the sermon, John returns to the concrete situation in Antioch and the reason for his sermon. Let the words of my sermon encourage you to seek out those who have fallen into the errors of the Judaizers, he says:

> I ask you to rescue your brothers, to set them free from this error, and to bring them back to the truth. There is no benefit in listening to me unless the example of your deeds match my words. What I said was not for your sakes but for the sake of those who are sick. I want them to learn these facts from you and to free themselves from their wicked association with the Jews. [*Jud.* 5.12; 903]

Jews, Judaizers, and Greeks

John's homilies on the Judaizers in Antioch, though preached to dissuade Christians from participating in Jewish festivals and attending the Jewish synagogue, were not simply concerned with the Judaizers and the Jews. For a third partner in the controversy was Julian, who had threatened the Christians by attempting to rebuild the temple and return the city of Jerusalem to the Jews. As a Christian leader, John Chrysostom felt himself besieged from two sides. The Judaizers were deserting the rites of the Church to observe Jewish laws and tra-

---

22. John 4:24 was an important text in forming Christian attitudes towards Judaism (Wilken 1971, pp. 69–92).

dition, and the Greeks charged that Christianity was an apostate religion without legitimation in the very tradition it claimed as its own. What was at issue in the dispute with the Judaizers, as John makes clear throughout the homilies, was neither simply the defection of Christians to Judaism nor the unity and cohesion of the Church, but the truth of Christianity.

His homilies on the Judaizers were an attempt to argue for the truth of the Christian religion. At a later time, when Christianity had become the dominant religion in the Roman world, and there were no rival communities to contest Christian beliefs, Christian teachings would appear self-evident, supported by the Church's Scriptures, by the apparent victory of the Church over its foes, and the testimony of Christian lives. In the fourth century, however, Christians lived in a pluralistic world and it could not be assumed without argument that Christian beliefs were true or that the Christian way of relating scriptural prophecies to historical events was manifest. It was not enough simply to assert one's beliefs. The Christian point of view had to be argued against sagacious critics and defended in the face of rival claims.

Though Greeks and Jews presented a common front against Christianity, it was the Jews alone who had the capability to prove Christianity false. This was the great historical fact that gave Julian's program its power and prompted John's vehement attack on the Judaizers in Antioch. For if Jewish communities in the cities of the Roman Empire threatened the religious claims of Christians merely by keeping the Law, how much more would the restoration of the temple and the return of the city of Jerusalem sanction and legitimate the practice of Judaism? And what could intimidate Christian leaders more than members of the Church adopting Jewish ways and even claiming that, in observing Jewish rites, they were following the example of Jesus? Even though Julian's program was unsuccessful, he had planted an idea in the minds of his contemporaries and shown that the restoration of the temple in Jerusalem was a distinct possibility. Julian would not easily be forgotten. In the generations after his death, the idea that Jerusalem would be returned to the Jews came back again and again to haunt Christian leaders and raise doubts in the minds of the faithful. Twenty-five years after Julian's death, rumors that the temple would be restored still alarmed Christian leaders.

Since the Christian movement had first emerged into public view early in the second century, its opponents had brought many arguments against Christian practice, against Christian belief, against the Christian reading of history. But all of these arguments were words, appeals to philosophical ideas or religious principles. Of all the arguments brought against the truth of Christianity, Julian's effort to rebuild the temple, restore sacrifices, and return the Jews to Jerusalem was the most threatening. For his attack was not simply verbal; it was a conspicuous historical gesture. And the symbolic importance of his act was drawn neither from the Hellenic tradition nor from Judaism, but from the Christian tradition itself. Julian's plan stirred Christians deeply because the restoration of the temple would puncture the historical appeals Christians had been making for centuries and deflate the confident claim that ancient prophecies were now being fulfilled in the life of the Christian Church.

Nevertheless, the homilies on the Judaizers in Antioch would never have been preached had John been faced simply with Greek critics or Jews. The catalyst in Antioch was neither Julian nor the powerful Jewish community, but the judaizing Christians. For, by keeping the Law, by celebrating Jewish festivals, by seeking out Jewish magicians, the Judaizers proclaimed that Judaism was spiritually more potent than Christianity. What greater proof of the truth of Judaism than for the followers of Christ to observe Jewish law?

The Judaizers confronted the young presbyter in Antioch, beset by captious pagans and truculent heretics, with his most formidable challenge. For the Judaizers were not outsiders, but Christians, men and women who had been baptized and instructed in the Christian faith, who participated in the Eucharist, and who by their actions gave the lie to Christianity: "If the Jewish rites are holy and venerable, our way of life must be false" (*Jud.* 1.6; 852).

Epilogue

Many religious works from antiquity have double lives, a life in the time in which they were first composed and a second life as they were read, studied, and used by later generations. Because of John's popularity as a preacher, the purity of his Greek style, and his exemplary life and martyrdom, his writings have exerted a powerful influence on later Christians. In the generation immediately after his death, some of his works began to circulate through the Church, and it was not long before translations into Latin and Syriac and other languages began to appear. This process has continued over the centuries and today hundreds of manuscripts of his writing are to be found in the libraries of Western Europe, the Soviet Union, Greece, the Middle East, and the United States.

The homilies on the Judaizers appear frequently in the manuscripts of John's works. A cursory glance at the manuscript tradition (Aubineau; Carter) will show that these writings were often copied and, along with some of his other well-known works, regularly included in collections of his writings. Chrysostomus Baur, John's biographer, who devoted his life to the study of John's writings, knew of approximately 120 manuscripts when he died almost two decades ago, but a recent estimate, based on information from the Institut de Recherche et d'Histoire des Textes in Paris, suggests that the figure may be closer to two hundred (Krawczynski and Riedinger, p. 8).

Given the popularity of these homilies among the writings of John Chrysostom, it is apparent that the sermons on the Jews have been a factor in forming Christian attitudes in times and places far removed from ancient Antioch. Sections from the homilies were excerpted in Byzantine times and incorporated in the Byzantine liturgy for Holy Week. Already in the sixth century, little more than a hundred years after John's death, a Greek writer in the time of Justinian, (Pseudo) Caesarius, composed a series of works in which he drew freely on John's homilies on the Jews, lifting whole passages verbatim (Riedinger, pp. 373–82). The eight homilies were translated into Russian in the eleventh century at a time when Jewish homes were being plundered and the first pogrom in Russian history was taking place in the grand duchy of Kiev under Prince Vladimir (Hauptmann, p. 642).

John's homilies on the Jews took on quite a different meaning when they were read in medieval Europe, in Byzantium, or in Russia. For when Christianity had become the dominant religion and the Jews were subject to repressive laws and excluded from the life of society, the homilies on the Judaizers served to support and encourage the anti-Jewish attitudes that had become characteristic of the Christian tradition and to foster hatred, hostility, and persecution. Any full consideration of the historical significance of John's homilies on the Judaizers must take into consideration their later use and influence on Christian thinking and action. The meaning of religious texts is not exhausted by their original setting; what happens to them later is often more significant than their first life.

The impact of the homilies on the Judaizers on later Christian attitudes and on relations between Jews and Christians in Europe is, however, a topic for another book. Here I have restricted myself to the setting in which they were first delivered. This is not all there is to be said about these writings, but it is a necessary part of understanding them, especially since much modern discussion of these homilies has read them not in light of this original context but from the perspective of later Christian attitudes.

The Roman Empire in the fourth century was not the world of Byzantium or medieval Europe. The institutions of traditional Hellenic culture and society were still very much alive in John Chrysostom's day. The Jews were a vital and visible presence in Antioch and elsewhere in the Roman Empire and they continued to be a formidable rival to the Christians. Judaizing Christians were widespread. Christianity was still in the process of establishing its place within the society and was undermined by internal strife and apathetic adherents. Without an appreciation of this setting, we cannot understand why John preached the homilies and why he responds to the Judaizers with such passion and fervor. The medieval image of the Jew should not be imposed on antiquity.

Every act of historical understanding is an act of empathy. When

I began to study John Chrysostom's writings on the Jews, I was inclined to judge what he said in light of the unhappy history of Jewish-
Christian relations and the sad events in Jewish history in modern
times. As much as I feel a deep sense of moral responsibility for the
attitudes and actions of Christians toward the Jews, I am no longer
ready to project these later attitudes onto the events of the fourth century. No matter how outraged Christians feel over the Christian record
of dealings with the Jews, we have no license to judge the distant past
on the basis of our present perceptions of events of more recent times.

Yet, having said this, a further word is necessary. For John's homilies are part of a Christian interpretation of Judaism that must be sub-
jected to theological criticism. Like many early Christian thinkers,
John assumed that the rise of Christianity and the destruction of the
city of Jerusalem, events that seemed coterminous, meant that Judaism
had lost its theological legitimacy. This judgment was based on a reading of the Scriptures as well as on an interpretation of the course of
events since the first century. Such confidence about the theological
meaning of the fall of Jerusalem, though self-evident to many Christians in John's day, is no longer possible. The fall of Jerusalem did not,
as early Christians thought, mean the demise of Judaism. The Jewish
people, and the practice of Judaism, have persisted, indeed prevailed,
and the Jews are today as much a part of our world, and in some ways
as much a part of Christian consciousness, as they were in the ancient
world. Indeed, whatever the religious meaning of the fall of Jerusalem,
its significance today can only be measured by the equally important
events of the survival of the Jewish people after the Holocaust and the
establishment of the modern state of Israel. If the appeal to historical
events in antiquity was thought to yield religious meaning to Christians, why should not events in our own time be equally pregnant with
meaning?

The theological meaning of events in history is always filled with
ambiguity, whether their significance is supported by centuries of tradition or is fresh in the minds of contemporaries. John, however, saw
no such ambiguity. To him the meaning of the destruction of the temple was patent, demonstrable, indubitable. Yet his interpretation ignored one significant fact—the continuing existence of Jewish communities that, by their very way of life, demonstrated that their loss of
the temple and the city of Jerusalem had not severed the covenant with
the God of Abraham, Isaac, and Jacob. And within his own congregation there were Christians who lived as though the Law of Moses were
still in force. Though these Judaizers were a minority, they were living
testimony that the Jewish way of life had not lost its legitimacy. For
reasons discussed in this book, John could take seriously neither the

way of life of the Jews nor the claims of the Judaizers among the Christians. He saw no way to acknowledge the ongoing reality of Israel without calling into question the truth of the Christian faith. That John's view won out is significant for the later history of Christianity for it has shaped all Christian thought about Judaism since his time; but that is no reason why it should be our own view.

Selected Bibliography

Only those classical and Hebraic sources not readily available in the standard collections are listed.

Ackermann, L.
    1889.   *Die Beredsamkeit des heiligen Johannes Chrysostomus.* Würzburg.
Alon, Gedalia.
    1967.   *History of the Jews in the Land of Israel in the Period of the Mishnah and the Talmud.* 2 vols. (In Hebrew) Tel Aviv.
    1970.   *Studies in the History of Israel.* 2 vols. (In Hebrew) Tel Aviv.
    1977.   *Jews, Judaism and the Classical World.* Jerusalem.
Ameringer, T. E.
    1920.   *The Stylistic Influence of the Second Sophistic on the Panegyrical Sermons of St. John Chrysostom.* Washington, D.C.
Antioch-on-the-Orontes.
    1934–72.   Publications of the Committee for the Excavation of Antioch and Its Vicinity, vols. 1–5. Princeton, N.J.
Applebaum, S.
    1958.   "The Province of Syria-Palestine as a Province of the Severan Empire." *Zion* 23:35–45.
    1961.   "The Jewish Community of Hellenistic and Roman Teucheira in Cyrenaica." *Scripta Hierosolymitana* 7:27–53.
    1974.   "The Organization of the Jewish Communities in the Diaspora." In *The Jewish People in the First Century*, edited by S. Safrai and M. Stern, pp. 464–503. Assen, Holland.
    1976.   "The Social and Economic Status of the Jews in the Diaspora." In *The Jewish People in the First Century*, edited by S. Safrai and M. Stern, pp. 701–27. Assen, Holland.

Asmus, R.
1904. *Julians Galiläerschrift im Zusammenhang mit übrigen Werken.* Freiburg im Breisgau.

Aubineau, Michel.
1966. *Grégoire de Nysse: Traité de la virginité.* Sources chrétiennes, 119. Paris.
1968. *Codices Chrysostomi Graeci.* Vol. 1. Paris.

Auf der Mauer, P. Ivo.
1959. *Mönchtum und Glaubensverkündigung in den Schriften des heiligen Johannes Chrysostomus.* In Paradosis, vol. 14. Freiburg im Breisgau.

Avigad, N.
1955. "Excavations at Beth She'arim, 1954, Preliminary Report." *Israel Exploration Journal* 5:205–39.

Avi-Yonah, M.
1970. *In the Days of Rome and Byzantium.* Jerusalem (In Hebrew)
1976. *The Jews of Palestine: A Political History from the Bar Kokhba War to the Arab Conquest.* New York.

Aziza, Claude.
1978. "Julien et le Judaisme." In *L'empereur Julien: De l'histoire à la légende* (331–1715), edited by René Braun and Jean Richer. Paris.

Baer, I.
1956. "Israel, the Christian Church, and the Roman Empire from the Days of Septimius Severus to the Edict of the Toleration of 313 C.E." *Zion* 21:1–49. (In Hebrew)

Bamberger, B. J.
1968. *Proselytism in the Talmudic Period.* 2nd ed. New York.

Barb, A. A.
1963. "The Survival of Magic Arts." In *The Conflict between Paganism and Christianity in the Fourth Century*, edited by A. Momigliano, pp. 100–25. Oxford.

Bardenhewer, Otto.
1879. *Polychronius: Bruder Theodors von Mopsuestia.* Freiburg im Breisgau.

Baur, C.
1907. *S. Jean Chrysostom et ses oeuvres dans l'histoire littéraire.* Louvain, Belgium.
1960. *John Chrysostom and His Time.* London. 2 vols.

Baynes, Norman H.
1955. *Byzantine Studies and Other Essays.* London.

Ben-Sasson, Haim Hillel.
1966. "Jewish-Christian Disputation in the Setting of Humanism and Reformation in the German Empire." *Harvard Theological Review* 59:369–90.

Bernardi, J.
1969. *La prédication des pères cappadociens.* Paris.

Bickerman, E.

1951. "Les Maccabées de Malalas." *Byzantion* 21:63–82.

Blanchetiere, F.
1980. "Julien philhellène, philosémite, antichrétien." *Journal of Jewish Studies* 31:61–81.

Blau, Ludwig.
1914. *Das altjüdische Zauberwesen*. Berlin.

Bloch, Herbert.
1945. "A New Document of the Last Pagan Revival in the West." *Harvard Theological Review* 38:199–244.
1963. "The Pagan Revival in the West at the End of the Fourth Century." In *The Conflict between Paganism and Christianity in the Fourth Century*, edited by A. Momigliano, pp. 193–218. Oxford.

Blumenkranz, B.
1961. "Die christlich-jüdische Missionskonkurrenz (3 bis 6 Jahrhundert)." *Klio* 39:227–33.

Bowersock, G. W.
1973. "Syria under Vespasian." *Journal of Roman Studies* 63:133–40.
1974. *Approaches to the Second Sophistic*. University Park, Pa.
1978. *Julian the Apostate*. Cambridge, Mass.

Bowman, Steven Barrie.
1974. "The Jews in Byzantium, 1261–1453." Ph.D. diss., Ohio State University.

Braude, W. G.
1940. *Jewish Proselytizing in the First Five Centuries*. Providence, R.I.

Brinkerhoff, D. M.
1970. *A Collection of Sculpture in Classical and Early Christian Antioch*. New York.

Brock, S. P.
1976. "The Rebuilding of the Temple under Julian: A New Source." *Palestine Exploration Quarterly* 108:103–7.
1977. "A Letter Attributed to Cyril of Jerusalem on the Rebuilding of the Temple." *Bulletin of the School of Oriental and African Studies* 40:267–86.

Brown, Peter R. L.
1971. "The Rise and Function of the Holy Man in Late Antiquity." *Journal of Roman Studies* 61:80–101.

Browne, Laurence E.
1933. *Eclipse of Christianity in Asia*. Cambridge, England.

Browning, R.
1952. "The Riot of A.D. 387 in Antioch. The Role of the Theatrical Claques in the Later Empire." *Journal of Roman Studies* 42:13–20.
1970. "Himerius." *The Oxford Classical Dictionary*. Oxford.
1976. *The Emperor Julian*. London.

Burns, M. A.
1930. *Saint John Chrysostom's Homilies on the Statues: A Study of their Rhetorical Qualities and Forms*. Washington, D.C.

Cameron, Alan.
>   1977.   "Paganism and Literature in Late Fourth Century Rome." In
>   *Christianisme et formes littéraires de l'antiquité tardive en occi-*
>   *dent.* Fondation Hardt pour l'étude de l'antiquité classique. En-
>   tretiens 23:1–40. Geneva.

Canet, Louis.
>   1914.   "Pour l'édition de S. Jean Chrysostome *Logoi Kata Ioudaiōn* et de
>   Theodoret *Hypomēna eis ton Daniel.*" *Mélanges d'archeologie et*
>   *d'histoire* 34:7–200.

Canivet, Pierre.
>   1977.   *Le Monachisme Syrien selon Théodoret de Cyr.* Theologie Histo-
>   rique, 42. Paris.

Carter, Robert.
>   1962.   "The Chronology of St. John Chrysostom's Early Life." *Traditio*
>   18:357–64.
>   1969–70.   *Codices Chrysostomici Graeci.* Vols. 2 and 3. Paris.
>   1970.   "The Future of *Chrysostom* Studies." In Texte und Untersuch-
>   ungen, vol. 107, pp. 14–21.

Cavafy, C. P.
>   1975.   *Collected Poems.* Translated by Edmund Keeley and Philip Sher-
>   rard. Edited by George Savidis. Princeton.

Cavallera, F.
>   1905.   *Le schisme d'Antioche.* Paris.

Charlesworth, J. H.
>   1975.   "Early Syriac Inscriptions in and around Antioch." Seminar pa-
>   pers, Society of Biblical Literature, vol. 1, pp. 81–91. Missoula,
>   Mont.

John Chrysostom.
>   1955.   *Les Cohabitations suspectes.* Edited by J. Dumortier. Paris.
>   1957.   *Huit catéchèses baptismales inédites.* Edited by A. Wenger.
>   Sources chrétiennes, 50. Paris.
>   1963.   *Baptismal Instructions.* Edited by P. Harkins. Ancient Christian
>   Writers, 31. Philadelphia.
>   1966.   *A Théodore.* Edited by J. Dumortier. Sources chrétiennes, 117.
>   Paris.
>   1966.   "Chrysostom's Homilies Against the Jews: An English Transla-
>   tion." Maxwell, C. M. Ph.D. diss., University of Chicago. Univer-
>   sity Microfilms: Ann Arbor, Mich., 1967.
>   1966.   *La Virginité.* Edited by H. Musurillo and B. Grillet. Sources chré-
>   tiennes, 125. Paris.
>   1966.   "Quod Christus sit Deus." Edited by N. McKendrick. Ph.D. diss.,
>   Fordham University, N.Y.
>   1967.   "De sancto Babyla, Contra Iulianum et Gentiles." Edited by M. A.
>   Schatkin. Ph.D. diss., Fordham University. University Microfilms:
>   Ann Arbor, Mich., 1968.
>   1968.   *A une jeune veuve sur le mariage unique.* Edited by B. Grillet and
>   G. Ettlinger. Sources chrétiennes, 138. Paris.

1970. *Sur l'incomprehensibilité de Dieu.* Edited by A-M. Malingrey and R. Flaceliere. Sources chrétiennes, 282. Paris.

1972. *Sur la vaine gloire et l'éducation des enfants.* Edited by A-M. Malingrey. Sources chrétiennes, 188. Paris.

1973. "St. John Chrysostom's Homily on the Protopaschites." Edited by M. Schatkin. *Orientalia Christiana Analecta* 195:167–86.

1979. *Discourses Against Judaizing Christians.* Edited by Paul Harkins. The Fathers of the Church, 68. Washington, D.C.

1979. *Jerome, Chrysostom and Friends: Essays and Translations.* Edited by Elizabeth A. Clark. New York. Includes translation of John Chrysostom's *Adversus eos qui apud se habent subintroductas virgines* and *Quod regulares feminae viris cohabitare non debeant.*

1980. *Sur le sacerdoce (dialogue et homélie).* Edited by A-M. Malingrey. Sources chrétiennes, 272. Paris.

Clark, Elizabeth.

1971. "John Chrysostom and the Subintroductae." *Church History* 46:171–85.

Cohen, J.

1976. "Roman Imperial Policy Toward the Jews from Constantine until the End of the Palestinian Patriarchate," *Byzantine Studies* 3: 1–29.

Coleman-Norton, P. R.

1930. "St. Chrysostom and the Greek Philosophers." *Classical Philology* 25:305–17.

1931. "St. John Chrysostom's Use of Josephus." *Classical Philology* 26:85–89.

Corpus Inscriptionum Iudaicarum.

1936–52. Edited by J. B. Frey. 3 vols. Rome. Revised edition of vol. 1 by B. Lifshitz, New York, 1975.

Coser, Lewis.

1956. *The Functions of Social Conflict.* Glencoe, Ill.

Curzon, Robert.

1955. *Visits to Monasteries in the Levant.* 2nd ed. London.

Degen, P. Heinrich.

1921. *Die Tropen der Vergleichung bei Johannes Chrysostomus.* Olten, Switzerland.

DeLange, N. R. M.

1976. *Origen and the Jews.* University of Cambridge Oriental Publications, 25. Cambridge.

Devreesse, Robert.

1945. *Le patriarcat d'Antioch depuis la paix de l'Église jusqu'à la conquête Arabe.* Paris.

Didascalia Apostolorum in Syriac, The.

1979. Edited and translated by Arthur Vööbus. *Corpus Scriptorum Christianorum Orientalium.* Scriptores Syri, vols. 176, 177, 178, 179. Louvain, Belgium.

Didascalia et Constitutiones Apostolorum.
    1905.   Edited by F. X. Funk. Paderborn, Germany.
Downey, Glanville.
    1938–39.   "The Gate of the Cherubim at Antioch." *Jewish Quarterly Review, n.s.* 29:67–77.
    1961.   *A History of Antioch in Syria from Seleucus to the Arab Conquests.* Princeton, N.J.
    1962.   *Antioch in the Age of Theodosius the Great.* Norman, Okla.
Dumortier, Jean.
    1951.   "La valeur historique du dialogue de Palladius et la chronologie de saint Jean Chrysostome." *Mélanges de science religieuse* 8: 51–56.
    1953.   "La culture profane de S. Jean Chrysostome." *Mélanges de science religieuse* 10:53–62.
Eckstein, F., and Waszink, J. H.
    1950.   "Amulett." *Reallexikon für Antike und Christentum*, vol. 1, cols. 407–10. Stuttgart.
Elderkin, George.
    1934.   "The Figure Mosaics." *Antioch on-the-Orontes* 1:42–48.
Eltester, Walther.
    1937.   "Die Kirchen Antiochias im IV Jh." *Zeitschrift für die neutestamentliche Wissenschaft und die Kunde der älteren Kirche* 36: 251–86.
Fabricius, Cajus.
    1962.   *Zu den Jugendschriften des Johannes Chrysostomus: Untersuchungen zum Klassizismus des vierten Jahrhunderts.* Lund, Sweden.
Fascher, Erich.
    1964.   "Jerusalems Untergang in der urchristlichen und altkirchlichen Überlieferung." *Theologische Literaturzeitung* 89:81–98.
Festugière, A. J.
    1959.   *Antioche païenne et chrétienne.* Paris.
Fischel, Henry A.
    1971.   "Greek and Latin Language, Rabbinical Knowledge of." *Encyclopaedia Judaica*, vol. 7, cols. 885–87.
Floëri, F., and Nautin, P.
    1957.   *Homélies Pascales.* Source chrétiennes, 48. Paris.
Frend, W. H. C.
    1967.   *Martyrdom and Persecution in the Early Church: A Study of Conflict from the Maccabees to Donatus.* New York.
Fustel de Coulanges, Numa Denis.
    1873.   *The Ancient City.* Translated by William Small, New York, 1955.
Gager, John.
    1971.   *Moses in Greco-Roman Paganism.* Nashville, Tenn.
Gager, John G.
    1973.   "The Dialogue of Paganism with Judaism: Bar Kochba to Julian." *Hebrew Union College Annual* 44:89–118.

Garnsey, Peter.
    1970. *Social Status and Legal Privilege in the Roman Empire*. Oxford.
Geyer, Paul, ed.
    1898. *Itinera Hierosolymitana*. In *Corpus Scriptorum Ecclesiasticorum Latinorum*, Vol. 39. Vienna.
Ginzberg, Louis.
    1946–64. *The Legends of the Jews*. 7 vols. Philadelphia.
    1976. *An Unknown Jewish Sect*. New York.
Glatzer, Nahum N.
    1962. "The Attitude Toward Rome in Third-Century Judaism." In *Politische Ordnung und menschliche Existenz*, edited by Alois Dempf et al., pp. 243–57. Munich.
Goldin, Judah.
    1976. "The Magic of Magic and Superstition." In *Aspects of Religious Propaganda in Judaism and Early Christianity*, edited by Elisabeth Schüssler-Fiorenza, pp. 115–48. Notre Dame, Ind.
Goodall, Blake.
    1979. *The Homilies of St. John Chrysostom on the Letters of Paul to Titus and Philemon*. Berkeley, Calif.
Goodenough, Erwin.
    1953–68. *Jewish Symbols in the Greco-Roman Period*. 13 vols. New York.
Grant, R. M.
    1972. "Jewish-Christianity in Antioch in the Second Century." *Recherches de science religieuse* 60:97–108.
    1977. *Early Christianity and Society: Seven Studies*. San Francisco.
    1980. *Eusebius as Church Historian*. Oxford.
Grego, Igino.
    1973. *La reazione ai giudeo-christiani del IV secolo*. Jerusalem.
Gregory, Timothy.
    1979. *Vox Populi: Violence and Popular Involvement in the Religious Controversies of the Fifth Century A.D.* Columbus, Ohio.
Grissom, Fred A.
    1978. "Chrysostom and the Jews: Studies in Jewish Christian Relations in Fourth Century Antioch." Ph.D. diss., Southern Baptist Theological Seminary. Louisville, Ky.
Groh, Dennis.
    1977. "Galilee and the Eastern Roman Empire in Late Antiquity." *Explor* 3:78–93.
Guerard, O., and Nautin, P.
    1979. *Origène: Sur la Pâque*. Christianisme antique, 2. Paris.
Guignebert, L.
    1923. "Les demi-chrétiens et leur place dans l'Église antique." *Revue de l'histoire des religions* 88:65–102.
Haddad, G.
    1949. *Aspects of Social Life in Antioch in the Hellenistic-Roman Period*. New York.

Hak, Mordecai.
    1940. "Was Julian's Declaration Forged?" *Javneh* 2:119–39. (In Hebrew)
    1940–41. "Notes to the Article 'Julian the Emperor and the Building of the Temple.'" *Zion* 6:158–59. (In Hebrew)
Hardy, B. Cameron.
    1968. "The Emperor Julian and his School Law." *Church History* 38:131–43.
Harkins, Paul W.
    1970. "Chrysostom the Apologist on the Divinity of Christ." *Kyriakon: Festschrift Johannes Quasten*, vol. 1, pp. 440–51. Münster, Germany.
    1979. See Chrysostom.
Harmand, Louis.
    1955. *Libanius: Discours sur les patronages.* Paris.
Harnack, Adolf von.
    1908. *The Mission and Expansion of Christianity.* 2 vols. London.
Harris, R.
    1926. "Hadrian's Decree of Expulsion of the Jews from Jerusalem." *Harvard Theological Review* 19:199–206.
Hauptmann, Peter.
    1970. "Russische Christenheit und Ostjudentum." In *Kirche und Synagoge*, edited by K. H. Rengotorff and S. von Kortzfleisch, vol. 2, pp. 639–67. Stuttgart.
Hefele, Charles Joseph.
    1907–8. *Histoire des conciles d'àpres les documents originaux.* Vols. 1 and 2. Paris.
Heinemann, I.
    1931. "Antisemitismus." *Paulys Realencyclopädie der klassischen Altertumswissenschaft*, supplementary vol. 5, cols. 3–43. Stuttgart.
    1974. "The Jews in the Eyes of the Ancient World." In *Jews and Judaism in the Eyes of the Hellenistic World*, edited by M. Stern, pp. 7–31. Jerusalem. (In Hebrew)
Hinck, Hugo.
    1873. *Polemonis Declamationes.* Leipzig.
Horowitz, H. S., ed.
    1917. *Sifre Numbers.* Leipzig.
Hubbell, Harry M.
    1924. "Chrysostom and Rhetoric." *Classical Philology* 19:261–76.
Huber, Wolfgang.
    1969. *Passa und Ostern: Untersuchungen zur Osterfeier der alten Kirche.* Berlin.
Iamblichus.
    1966. *Des mystères d'Égypte.* Edited by E. des Places. Paris.
Inscriptions grecques et latines de la Syrie.
    1929–70. Edited by L. Jalabert and R. Monterde. Paris.
Jones, A. H. M.
    1953. "St. John Chrysostom's Parentage and Education." *Harvard Theological Review* 46:171–73.

1964*a*.   *The Later Roman Empire: A Social, Economic and Administrative Survey.* Oxford.

1964*b*.   "The Social Background of the Struggle between Paganism and Christianity." In *The Conflict between Paganism and Christianity in the Fourth Century,* edited by A. Momigliano, pp. 17–39. Oxford.

Judant, D.
    1969.   *Judaisme et christianisme: Dossier patristique.* Paris.

Julian.
    1880.   *Juliani imperatoris librorum contra Christianos quae supersunt.* Edited by C. J. Neumann. Leipzig.

    1922.   *Imperatoris Caesaris Flavii Claudii Iuliani epistulae, leges, poemata, fragmenta varia.* Edited by J. Bidez and F. Cumont. Paris.

    1949–54.   *The Works of the Emperor Julian.* Edited by W. C. Wright. 3 vols. Loeb Classical Library. Cambridge, Mass.

    1932–72.   *L'Empereur Julien: Oeuvres complètes.* Edited J. Bidez. Paris.

Juster, J.
    1914.   *Les Juifs dans l'empire romain.* 2 vols. Paris.

Kazan, S.
    1961–65.   "Isaac of Antioch's Homily Against the Jews." *Oriens Christianus* 45:30–53; 46:87–98; 47:89–97; 49:57–78.

Kelly, J. N. D.
    1972.   *Early Christian Creeds.* 3rd ed. New York.

    1976.   *Jerome: His Life, Writings, and Controversies.* New York.

Kennedy, George A.
    1974.   "The Sophists As Declaimers." In *Approaches to the Second Sophistic,* edited by G. W. Bowerstock, pp. 17–22. University Park, Pa.

    1980.   *Classical Rhetoric and Its Christian and Secular Tradition.* Chapel Hill, N.C.

King, N. Q.
    1960.   *The Emperor Theodosius and the Establishment of Christianity.* Philadelphia.

    1961.   "The Pagan Resurgence of 393: Some Contemporary Sources." *Studia Patristica* 4. Texte und Untersuchungen, vol. 79, pp. 472–77. Berlin.

Klijn, A. F. J.
    1974.   "The Study of Jewish Christianity." *New Testament Studies* 20: 419–31.

Klijn, A. F. J. and Reinink, G. J.
    1973.   *Patristic Evidence for Jewish Christian Sects.* Leiden.

Koch, Glenn Alan.
    1976.   "A Critical Investigation of Epiphanius' Knowledge of the Ebionites." Ph.D. diss., University of Pennsylvania.

Koetting, Bernhard.
    1968.   "Die Entwicklung im Osten bis Justinian." In *Kirche und Synagoge,* edited by K. H. Rengstorff and S. von Kortzfleisch, vol. 1, pp. 136–74. Stuttgart.

Kohut, A.

 1892. "Lakes of the Holy Land." *Jewish Quarterly Review* 4:692–96.

Kollwitz, J.

 1950. "Antiochia am Orontes." *Reallexikon für Antike und Christentum*, vol. 1, cols. 461–69. Stuttgart.

Kopecek, Thomas A.

 1973. "The Social Class of the Cappadocian Fathers." *Church History* 42:453–66.

 1974. "Curial Displacements and Flights in Later Fourth Century Cappadocia." *Historia* 23:319–42.

 1979. *A History of Neo-Arianism.* 2 vols. Patristic Monograph Series, 8. Philadelphia.

Kraabel, A. T.

 1968. "Judaism in Western Asia Minor." Ph.D. diss., Harvard University.

 1980. "The Diaspora Synagogue: Archaeological and Epigraphical Evidence since Sukenik." In *Aufsteig und Niedergang der romischen Welt*, edited by W. Haase, part 2, vol. 19, pp. 497–510. Berlin.

Kraeling, C. H.

 1932. "The Jewish Community at Antioch." *Journal of Biblical Literature* 51:130–60.

Krauss, S.

 1893–94. "The Jews in the Works of the Church Fathers." *Jewish Quarterly Review* 5:122–157; 6:82–99, 225–261.

 1902. "Antioche." *Revue des études juives* 45:27–49.

Krawczynski, S., and Riedinger, U.

 1964. "Zur Überlieferungsgeschichte des Flavius Josephus und Klemens von Alexandreia im 4-6 Jahrhundert." *Byzantinisches Zeitschrift* 57:6–25.

Laistner, M. L. W.

 1951. *Christianity and Pagan Culture in the Later Roman Empire.* Ithaca, N.Y.

Langmuir, Gavin I.

 1966. "Majority History and Post-Biblical Jews." *Journal of the History of Ideas* 27:343–64.

Lassus, J.

 1934. "La Mosaique de Yakto." *Antioch-on-the-Orontes* 1:114–56.

 1938. "L'Église cruciforme de Kaoussie." *Antioch-on-the-Orontes* 2: 5–44.

Leclercq, H.

 1907. "Antioche." *Dictionnaire d'archeologie chrétienne et de liturgie*, vol. 1, pp. 2359–439. Paris.

Leipoldt, J.

 1954. "Buch." *Reallexikon für Antike und Christentum*, vol. 2, cols. 688–717. Stuttgart.

Levenson, David B.

 1979. "A Source and Tradition Critical Study of the Stories of Julian's Attempt to Rebuild the Jerusalem Temple." Ph.D. diss. Harvard University.

Levi, Doro.
>   1941. "The Evil Eye and the Lucky Hunchback." *Antioch-on-the-Orontes* 3:220–32.
>   1947. *Antioch Mosaic Pavements.* 2 vols. Princeton, N.J.

Levine, Lee I.
>   1975. *Caesarea under Roman Rule.* Leiden.

Lewy, H.
>   1940–41. "Emperor Julian and the Building of the Temple," *Zion* 6:1–32. (In Hebrew). Reprinted in H. Lewy, *'Olamot Nipgashim*, Jerusalem, 1960.

Libanius.
>   1903–27. *Libanii Opera.* Edited by R. Förster. Leipzig.
>   1959. "Antiochikos (Oration 11)." Edited by G. Downey. In *Proceedings of the American Philosophical Society* 103:652–86.
>   1965. *Autobiography (Oration 1): The Greek Text.* Edited by A. F. Norman. London.
>   1969–77. *Selected Works.* Edited by A. F. Norman. 2 vols. Loeb Classical Library. Cambridge, Mass.

Lieberman, Saul.
>   1942. *Greek in Jewish Palestine.* New York.
>   1962. *Hellenism in Jewish Palestine.* New York.
>   1974. *Texts and Studies.* New York.

Liebeschuetz, J. H. W. G.
>   1972. *Antioch: City and Imperial Administration in the Later Roman Empire.* Oxford.
>   1979. *Continuity and Change in Roman Religion.* Leiden.

Lifshitz, Baruch.
>   1967. *Donateurs et fondateurs dans les synagogues juives.* Cahiers de la Revue Biblique, 7. Paris.

Lifshitz, Baruch and Schwabe, M.
>   1973–74. *Beth She'arim.* 2 vols. Rutgers, N.J.

Linder, Amnon.
>   1974. "The Roman Imperial Government and the Jews under Constantine." *Tarbiz* 44:95–143. (In Hebrew)
>   1975. "The Myth of Constantine the Great in the West: Sources and Hagiographic Commemoration." *Studi Medievali* 16:48–95.
>   1976. "Ecclesia and Synagoga in the Medieval Myth of Constantine the Great." *Revue Belge de philologie et d'histoire* 54:1019–60.
>   1979. "Jerusalem Between Judaism and Christianity in the Byzantine Period." *Cathedra* 11:109–19. (In Hebrew)

Lurie, B.
>   1957. *The Jews in Syria.* Jerusalem. (In Hebrew)

Maas, P.
>   1900. "Die Maccabäer als christliche Heiligen." *Monatschrift für Geschichte und Wissenschaft des Judentums* 44:145–56.

Maat, W. A.
>   1944. *A Rhetorical Study of St. John Chrysostom's De Sacerdotio.* Washington, D.C.

McCollough, C. Thomas.
    "Judaism in the Later Roman Empire and Christian Exegesis of the Hebrew Scriptures." Ph.D. diss. University of Notre Dame, Ind. (forthcoming)

McKendrick, N.
    1966.   See Chrysostom.

MacMullen, Ramsay.
    1966.   "Provincial Languages in the Roman Empire." *American Journal of Philology* 87:1–17.
    1974.   *Roman Social Relations*. New Haven, Conn.

Malalas, John.
    1926.   *Ioannis Malalae Chronographia*. Edited by L. Dindorf. Bonn.

Malina, A.
    1976.   "Jewish Christianity or Christian Judaism." *Journal for the Study of Judaism* 7:46–57.

Malkowski, John.
    1975.   "The Element of Akairos in Chrysostom's Anti-Jewish Polemic." In Texte und Untersuchungen, vol. 115, pp. 222–32. Berlin.

Malley, William J.
    1978.   *Hellenism and Christianity*. Analecta Gregoriana, 210. Rome.

Mancini, I.
    1977.   *L'Archéologie judeo-chrétienne*. Jerusalem.

Manns, F.
    1979.   *Bibliographie du judeo-christianisme*. Preface by P. B. Bagatti. Studium Biblicum Franciscanum Analecta, 13. Jerusalem.

Margalioth, M.
    1966.   *Sepher Ha-Razim: A Newly Recovered Book of Magic From the Talmudic Period*. Jerusalem. (In Hebrew)

Markus, R. A.
    1970.   *Saeculum: History and Society in the Theology of St. Augustine*. Cambridge.

Marmorstein, A.
    1935.   "Judaism and Christianity in the Middle of the Third Century." *Hebrew Union College Annual* 10:223–64.
    1950.   *Studies in Jewish Theology*. London.

Marrou, Henri-Irenée.
    1938.   *Mousikos Anēr. Étude sur les scenes de la vie intellectuelle figurant sur les monuments funéraires romains*. Grenoble.
    1956.   *A History of Education in Antiquity*. London.
    1958.   *Saint Augustine et la fin de la culture antique*. 4th ed. Paris.

Matthews, J. F.
    1975.   *Western Aristocracies and the Imperial Court*. Oxford.

Maxwell, C. M.
    1966.   See Chrysostom.

Meeks, Wayne A. and Wilken, Robert L.
    1978.   *Jews and Christians in Antioch*. Society of Biblical Literature Sources for Biblical Study, 13. Missoula, Mont.

Méridier, L.
    1906. *L'influence de la seconde sophistique sur l'oeuvre de Grégoire de Nysse*. Rennes.
Meyers, Eric, and Strange, James F.
    1977. "Survey in Galilee." *Explor* 3:7–17.
Meyers, Eric M.; Kraabel, A. Thomas; and Strange, James F.
    1976. *Synagogue Excavations at Khirbet Shema, Upper Galilee, Israel, 1970–72*. Annual of the American Schools of Oriental Research, 42. Durham, N.C.
Morgan, Michael.
    Sefer Ha-Razim. Unpublished translation. University of Alberta, Edmonton.
Mühlenberg, Ekkehard.
    1969. *Apollinaris von Laodicea*. Göttingen.
Musurillo, H.
    1954. *The Acts of the Pagan Martyrs: Acta Alexandrinorum*. Oxford.
Natali, Alain.
    1975. "Christianisme et cité à Antioche a la fin de IVe siècle d'après Jean Chrysostome." In *Jean Chrysostome et Augustin*, edited by Charles Kannengiesser, pp. 41–60. Paris.
Neusner, Jacob.
    1971. *Aphrahat and Judaism: The Christian-Jewish Argument in Fourth-Century Iran*. Leiden.
Nilsson, Martin P.
    1945. "Pagan Divine Service in Late Antiquity." *Harvard Theological Review* 38:63–69.
Norden, Eduard.
    1923. *Die antike Kunstprosa*. Leipzig.
Obermann, Julius.
    1931. "The Sepulchre of the Maccabean Martyrs." *Journal of Biblical Literature* 50:250–65.
O'Donnell, James.
    "The Demise of Paganism," *Traditio* 35:45–88.
Palladius.
    1928. *Palladii dialogus de vita sancti Johannis Chrysostomi*. Edited by P. R. Coleman Norton. Cambridge.
Papyri graecae magicae.
    1928–31. Edited by K. L. Preisendanz. 2 vols. Leipzig. Revised edition by Albert Henrichs, Stuttgart, 1973–74.
Parkes, James.
    1934. *The Conflict of the Church and the Synagogue*. New York.
    1969. *Prelude to Dialogue*. London.
Pasquato, Ottorio.
    1976. *Gli spettacoli in S. Giovanni Crisostomo: Paganesimo e christianesimo ad Antiochia e Constantinopli nel IV secolo*. Orientalia Christiana Analecta, 201. Rome.

Payr, Theresia.

    1962. "Enkomion." *Reallexikon für Antike und Christentum*, vol. 5, cols. 332–43. Stuttgart.

Petit, Paul.

    1955. *Libanius et la vie municipale à Antioche au IVe siècle après Jean Chrysostome*. Paris.

Pharr, P. Clyde, trans.

    1952. *Codex Theodosianus*. Princeton, N.J.

Phillips, C. Robert.

    1979. "Julian's Rebuilding of the Temple: A Sociological Study of Religious Competition." *Society of Biblical Literature Seminar Papers*, vol. 2, pp. 162–72. Missoula, Mont.

Piganiol, André.

    1947. *L'Empire chrétien*. Paris.

Porphyrius.

    1919 *"Gegen die Christen": 15 Bücher, Zeugnisse, Fragmente und Referate*. Edited by A. von Harnack. Abhandlungen der könig. preuss. Akademie d. Wissenschaft, phil.-hist. Klasse, 1. Berlin.

Puech, Aimé.

    1891. *St. Jean Chrysostome et les moeurs de son temps*. Paris.

Rampolla del Tindaro, Mariano.

    1899. "Martyre et sépulture des Machabées." *Revue de l'art chrétien* 48:290–305, 377–92, 457–65.

Rauschen, Gerhard.

    1897. *Jahrbücher der christlichen Kirche unter dem Kaiser Theodosius dem Grossen*. Freiburg im Breisgau.

Reichardt, Klaus Dieter.

    1978. "Die Judengesetzgebung im Codex Theodosianus." *Kairos* 20: 16–39.

Rengstorf, Karl Heinrich, and von Kortzfleisch, Siegfried.

    1968. *Kirche und Synagoge: Handbuch zur Geschichte von Christen und Juden*. Stuttgart.

Rhetores graeci ex recognitione Leonardi Spengel.

    1854–94. Edited by C. Hammer. 3 vols. Leipzig.

Riedinger, R.

    1969. *Pseudo-Kaisarios: Überlieferungsgeschichte und Verfasserfrage*. Byzantinisches Archiv, 12. Munich.

Riedinger, U.

    1964. See Krawczynski.

Ritter, A. M.

    1973. "Erwägungen zum Antisemitismus in der Alten Kirche: Acht Reden über die Juden." In *Bleibendes im Wandel der Kirchengeschichte*, Festschrift H. von Campenhausen, edited by B. Moeller and G. Ruhbach, pp. 71–91. Tübingen.

Ritzer, Korbinian.

    1970. *Le mariage dans les églises chrétiennes du Ier au XIe siecle*. Paris.

Rokeah, David.

1971. "People of Israel and Torah of Israel in the Pagan-Christian Polemic in the Roman Empire." *Tarbiz* 40:462–71. (In Hebrew)

Rordorf, Willy.

1962. *Der Sonntag: Geschichte des Ruhe- und Gottesdiensttages im ältesten Christentum.* In *Abhandlungen zur Theologie des alten und neuen Testaments*, vol. 43. Zurich.

Ruether, Rosemary R.

1969. *Gregory of Nazianzus, Rhetor and Philosopher.* Oxford.

1974. *Faith and Fratricide.* New York. 1969.

Ruggini, Lellia Cracco.

1980. "Pagani, ebrei e cristiani: Odio sociologico e odio teologico nel mondo antico." In *Gli Ebrei nell'alto medioevo.* Settimane di studio del centro italiano di studi sull'alto medioevo, no. 26. Spoletto.

Safrai, S.

1974. "Relations between the Diaspora and the Land of Israel." In *The Jewish People in the First Century*, edited by S. Safrai and Menachem Stern, vol. 1, pp. 184–216. Assen, Holland.

Safrai, S. and Stern, M., eds.

1974–76. *The Jewish People in the First Century.* 2 vols. Assen, Holland.

Sallust.

1966. *Concerning the Gods and the Universe.* Edited by A. D. Nock. Hildesheim, Germany.

Sauvaget, J.

1941. *Alep: Essai sur le développement d'une grand ville syrienne, des origines au milieu du XIXe siècle.* Bibliothèque archeologique et historique. Paris.

Sawhill, John Alexander.

1928. *The Use of Athletic Metaphors in the Biblical Homilies of St. John Chrysostom.* Princeton.

Schalit, A.

1960. "Jewish Military Colonies in Phrygia and Lydia." *Jewish Quarterly Review* 59:298–318.

Scharf, Andrew.

1971. *Byzantine Jewry from Justinian to the Fourth Crusade.* New York.

Schatkin, Margaret.

1970. "The Authenticity of St. John Chrysostom's *Contra Julianum et Gentiles (de Sancto Babyla)*." *Kyraikon: Festschrift Johannes Quasten*, vol. 1, pp. 474–89. Münster, Germany.

1974. "The Maccabean Martyrs." *Vigiliae Christianae* 28:97–113.

Schoedel, William R.

1978. "Ignatius and the Archives." *Harvard Theological Review* 71: 97–106.

Schoeps, Hans Joachim.

1950a. "Die jüdischen Prophetenmorde." In *Aus frühchristliche Zeit*, pp. 126–43. Tübingen.

1950*b*.   "Die Templezerstörung des Jahres 70 in der jüdischen Religionsgeschichte." In *Aus frühchristliche Zeit*, pp. 144–83. Tübingen.

Schuerer, Emil.

1979.   *The History of the Jewish People in the Age of Jesus Christ (175 B.C.–A.D. 135)*. Vol. 1. Revised and edited by Geza Vermes and Fergus Millar. Edinburgh.

Schultze, Victor.

1930.   *Altchristliche Städte und Landschaften*. Vol. 3. *Antiocheia*. Gütersloh, Germany.

Schwabe, M.

1930*a*.   "Letters of Libanius to the Patriarch of Palestine." *Tarbiz* 1/2: 85–110. (In Hebrew)

1930*b*.   "A New Document on the History of the Jews in the Fourth Century of the Common Era. Libanius ep. 1251 (F)." *Tarbiz* 1/3: 107–21. (In Hebrew)

1949.   "Toward the History of Tiberias: Epigraphic Studies." In *Sefer Yochanan Levi*, edited by M. Schwabe and J. Gutman, pp. 216–221, Jerusalem. (In Hebrew)

Schwabe, M. C., and Lifschitz, Baruch.

1973–74.   See Lifschitz.

Schwartz, Eduard.

1905.   *Christliche und jüdische Ostertafeln*. Abhandlungen der Göttingen Akademie der Wissenschaften, phil.-hist. Klasse, vol. 8, no. 6. Berlin.

Seeck, Otto.

1906.   *Die Briefe des Libanius zeitlich geordnet*. Texte und Untersuchungen, n.s. vol. 15, pts. 1–2. Leipzig.

Segal, Alan.

1977.   *Two Powers in Heaven: Early Rabbinic Reports about Christianity and Gnosticism*. Leiden.

Semahot.

1966.   *The Tractate Mourning*. Edited by Dov Zlotnick. New Haven, Conn.

Sifre Numbers.   See Horowitz.

Simmel, Georg.

1955.   *Conflict*. Glencoe, Ill.

Simon, Marcel.

1936.   "La polémique anti-juive de S. Jean Chrysostome et le mouvement judaisant d'Antioche." *Mélanges Franz Cumont*. In *Annuaire de l'Institut de Philologie et d'Histoire Orientales et Slaves*, vol. 4, pp. 403–21. Brussels.

1962.   *Recherches d'histoire judeo-chrétienne*. Paris.

1964.   *Verus Israel. Étude sur les relations entre chrétiens et juifs dans l'empire romain (135–425)*. Paris.

Simonetti, M.

1953.   "Sulla struttura dei panegyrici di S. Giovanni Crisostomo." *Ren-*

   diconti del R. Istituto Lombardo di Scienze e Lettere, vol. 86, pp.
   159–80. Milan.

 1968. *Rufin d'Aquilée. Les Bénédictions des Patriarches*. Sources chrétiennes, 140. Paris.

Skimina, Stanislaus.

 1927. *De Ioannis Chrysostomo rythmo oratorio*. Krakow.

Smallwood, M.

 1959, 1961. "The Legislation of Hadrian and Antoninus Pius against
   Circumcision." *Latomus* 18:334–37; 20:93–96.

Smith, Morton.

 1973. *Clement of Alexandria and a Secret Gospel of Mark*. Cambridge,
   Mass.

Spengel, L. See *Rhetores Graeci*.

Stead, G. Christopher.

 1976. "Rhetorical Method in Athanasius." *Vigiliae Christianae* 30:
   121–37.

Stern, Menachem.

 1964. "Sympathy for Judaism in Roman Senatorial Circles in the Period
   of the Early Empire." *Zion* 29:155–67. (In Hebrew)

 1974a. "The Jewish Diaspora." In *The Jewish People in the First Century*, edited by S. Safrai and Menachem Stern, vol. 1, pp. 117–
   83. Assen, Holland.

 1974b–80. *Greek and Latin Authors on Jews and Judaism*. Jerusalem.

Stockmeier, Peter.

 1966. *Theologie und Kult des Kreuzes bei Johannes Chrysostomus*. Tri-
   erer Theologischen Studien, 18. Trier.

Strumsa, Gedalia.

 1979. "Which Jerusalem?" In "Jerusalem between Judaism and Christianity in the Byzantine Period," edited by Amnon Linder, *Cathedra*
   11:119–24. (In Hebrew)

Sukenik, E. L.

 1950–51. "The Mosaic Inscriptions in the Synagogue at Apamea on the
   Orontes." *Hebrew Union College Annual* 23:541–51.

Symposion: Studies on John Chrysostom.

 1973. Analecta Vlatadon, 18. Thessaloniki.

Tchalenko, Georges.

 1953. *Villages antiques de la Syrie du nord*. 3 vols. Paris.

Tcherikover, Victor A.

 1963. "The Decline of the Jewish Diaspora in Egypt in the Roman Period." *Journal of Jewish Studies* 14:1–32.

Theodoret of Cyrus. *Histoire des Moines de Syrie*.

 1977–79. Edited by P. Canivet and A. Leroy-Molinghen. Sources chrétiennes, 234 and 257. Paris.

Trachtenberg, Joshua.

 1961. *Jewish Magic and Superstition: A Study in Folk Religion*. Cleveland.

Urbach, E. E.

 1959. "The Rabbinical Laws of Idolatry in the Second and Third Centuries in the Light of Archaeological and Historical Facts." *Israel Exploration Journal* 9:149–65, 229–45.

1964. "The Laws Regarding Slavery as a Source for Social History of the Second Temple, the Mishnah and Talmud." *Papers of the Institute of Jewish Studies*, vol. 1, pp. 1–95. London.

1981. "Self Isolation in the First Three Centuries—Theory and Practice." In *Jewish and Christian Self Definition*, edited by E. P. Sanders, A. I. Baumgarten, and Alan Mendelson, vol. 2, pp. 269–98. Philadelphia.

Van de Paverd, Frans.

1970. *Zur Geschichte der Messliturgie in Antiocheia und Konstantinopel gegen Ende des vierten Jahrhunderts.* Orientalia Christiana Analecta, 187. Rome.

Venables, Edmund.

1880. "Flavianus I of Antioch." In *A Dictionary of Christian Biography*, edited by William Smith and Henry Wace, vol. 2, cols. 527–31. London.

Verosta, Stephen.

1960. *Johannes Chrysostomus: Staatsphilosoph und Geschichtstheolog.* Graz, Austria.

Visser, A. J.

1954. "Johannes Chrysostomus als anti-Joods polemicus." *Nederlandsch Archief voor Kerkgeschiedenis*, n.s. 40:193–206.

Vogler, Chantal.

1979. "Les juifs dans le Code Theodosien." In *Les Chrétiens devant le fait juif*, edited by Jacques le Brun, pp. 35–74. Le point théologique, vol. 33. Paris.

Vogt, Joseph.

1939. "Kaiser Julian und das Judentum." *Morgenland* 30:1–74.

1957. "Constantinus der Grosze." *Reallexikon für Antike und Christentum* vol. 3, cols. 306–79. Stuttgart.

Walzer, Richard.

1949. *Galen on Jews and Christians.* London.

Weitzmann, Kurt.

1941a. "Illustrations of Euripides and Homer in the Mosaics of Antioch." *Antioch-on-the-Orontes* 3:233–47.

1941b. "The Iconography of the Reliefs from the Martyrion." *Antioch-on-the-Orontes* 3:135–49.

Wilamowitz-Moellendorf, U. von.

1912. *Die griechischen Literatur des Altertums.* In *Die Kultur der Gegenwart*, edited by Paul Hinnenberg, vol. 1, pt. 8. Berlin.

Wilken, Robert L.

1971. *Judaism and the Early Christian Mind.* New Haven, Conn.

1976. "Melito, The Jewish Community at Sardis, and the Sacrifice of Isaac." *Theological Studies* 37:53–69.

1979. "Pagan Criticism of Christianity: Greek Religion and Christian Faith." In *Early Christian Literature and the Classical Intellectual*

        Tradition, edited by Robert L. Wilken and William R. Schoedel, pp. 117–34. Théologie historique, 53. Paris.

1980.   "The Christians as the Romans (and Greeks) Saw Them." *Jewish and Christian Self-Definition: The Shaping of Christianity in the Second and Third Centuries*, edited by E. P. Sanders, vol. 1, pp. 100–25. London.

1980.   "The Jews and Christians Apologetics after Theodosius' *Cunctos Populos.*" *Harvard Theological Review.* 73:451–71.

Wilken, Robert L. and Meeks, Wayne A. See Meeks.

Wilkinson, John.

1971.   *Egeria's Travels.* London.

1976.   "Christian Pilgrims in Jerusalem during the Byzantine Period." *Palestine Exploration Quarterly* 108:75–101.

Williams, A. L.

1935.   *Adversus Judaeos: A Bird's Eye View of Christian Apologetics.* Cambridge.

Wytzes, J.

1977.   *Der letzte Kampf des Heidentums in Rom.* Études préliminaires aux religions orientales dans l'empire romain, vol. 56. Leiden.

Index of Modern Authors

Index of Subjects

Designer: Sandy Drooker
Compositor: G&S Typesetters, Inc.
Text: Linotron 202 Sabon
Display: Phototypositor Sabon
Printer: Thomson-Shore, Inc.
Binder: John H. Dekker & Sons